The *Really* Inconvenient Truths

IAIN MURRAY

The *Really* Inconvenient Truths

Seven Environmental Catastrophes Liberals
Don't Want You To Know About—
Because They Helped Cause Them

IAIN MURRAY

Since 1947
**REGNERY
PUBLISHING, INC.**
An Eagle Publishing Company • Washington, DC

Cataloging-in-Publication data on file with the Library of Congress

ISBN 978-1-59698-054-9

Published in the United States by

Regnery Publishing, Inc.
One Massachusetts Avenue, NW
Washington, DC 20001
www.regnery.com

Manufactured in the United States of America

10 9 8 7 6 5 4 3 2 1

Books are available in quantity for promotional or premium use. Write to Director of Special Sales, Regnery Publishing, Inc., One Massachusetts Avenue NW, Washington, DC 20001, for information on discounts and terms or call (202) 216-0600.

For Pat, Jim, Kristen, Helen, and George.
No better inspiration was ever needed.

Contents

Preface

I am writing this in my living room on a balmy winter's day. From my window, I can see a host of different trees and plants. From my back window, I gaze out on woods surrounding a stream, through which deer occasionally wander. Our cat, James, occasionally nuzzles my legs or decides to see what fun he can have by jumping on my keyboard before going to stare longingly at the birds in the woods.

In short, I am surrounded by nature.

I value this nature. Its mere existence gives me pleasure and contributes to my sense of well-being. There are very few people who do not appreciate a cool breeze on a summer's day, the lap of the waves on a beach, or the view from the top of a forested hill. We all marvel at God's creation.

I enjoy a relatively low-carbon lifestyle. My family of four emits less carbon dioxide than the average family of four, according to a host of different calculators. Many of our meals are home-cooked from scratch. We eat leftovers rather than order in. I work from home to minimize travel when I can. My car is a 2000 Saturn that gets twenty-seven miles per gallon.

Yet I am not an environmentalist. I do what I do because I am free to do so, and the virtues of thriftiness and the economic incentive of frugality compel me to use less than I could.

Since I started working on environmental regulation five years ago, I have come to the conclusion that the liberal environmental movement is grounded in the idea that freedom is detrimental to the environment. My experience—as a government regulator, as a student, and as a policy expert—shows me that the exact opposite is the case. The dogmatic ideologies and restrictive policies pushed on us by the environmental Left have harmed nature more than helped it, but the environmentalists have never borne the blame.

That is why this book had to be written. America needs to know that laws and policies that were introduced in the name of saving the environment are hurting it, and that we can expect more of the same if liberal environmentalists continue to have a free run.

In this election year, Republican politicians tell us that conservatives need to adapt and develop an "environmental" policy. In truth, no adaptation is needed. As this book will show, conservative principles of freedom, local democracy, and tradition serve to help the environment whenever they are allowed to work. Growing wealth allows people to bank some of their wealth in the form of environmental quality, as I have done. Wealthier is healthier, and richer is cleaner. As long as certain principles of stewardship are applied, the conservative agenda is an environmental agenda.

By turning the nature that surrounds us into some separate, distinct object called the "environment," liberals have cut us off from nature. Conservatives live within nature, and know they are part of it. It is time to strike back at the idea that humanity is a cancer on the planet and to reveal just how damaging liberal policies have been.

The liberal caricature would suggest that all the trees I see out of my window would have been cut down were it not for liberal rules and regulations. Yet if the liberals truly had their way, I would not be sitting here, even with my low-carbon lifestyle.

Environmentalism deserves to be as discredited as Marxism. Humanity—and the planet—would be better off without either of them.

Woodbridge, Virginia
January 7, 2008

I.

Al Gore Is Bad for the Planet

Al Gore

Savior of the Planet?

Former vice president Albert Gore Jr. may be one of the most powerful people in the world today. Despite the Nobel Laureate's failure to win the presidency of the United States, he leads a movement that transcends borders and commands massive amounts of political power and wealth. He is the undisputed global head of the environmental movement and as such directs much of the modern liberal agenda. Modern "green" environmentalism is up there alongside radical feminism, racial demagoguery, and anti-globalization as one of the driving forces of the liberal coalition.

Indeed, it is probably safe to say that the environment has replaced the working man as the rallying point for the Left on economic issues. With labor unions reduced to insignificance outside the government sector, environmentalists are shaping much of liberal economic thinking.

The goal has not changed: socialist-style central control of the economy. But the justification is no longer the struggle to "free" the working class from the "chains" of capitalism (capitalism, ironically, has ruined that little crusade by empowering the working class to free itself) but by the need to "free" the environment from the oppression of ruthless, unthinking, exploitative markets. Environmentalism validates intrusive regulation, punitive taxes, massive bureaucracy, and even world government.

Global warming, Al Gore's current crusade, shows this most clearly. Global warming, naturally, requires global action. We in the industrial world must make massive sacrifices—particularly in America. Coal (our primary source of electricity today) must be abolished and replaced with "greener" renewable sources such as solar and windmills—but nuclear power is verboten. Americans are "addicted" to cars and oil (a misrepresentation shamefully legitimized by President Bush[1]), so we should all take public transit; if we have to drive, we need to use biofuels to fill our gas tanks.

With this justification (and capitulation by their conservative opponents), liberals demand control over all forms of energy use, and therefore over the entire American economy.

That is why, when gas prices, driven up by global instability and the OPEC cartel, pinch the budgets of their constituents, liberal politicians do not look at ways to bring *down* the price of gas. They can't, because green economic theory wants to see gas prices rise, in turn because using gasoline releases greenhouse gases that are "bad for the planet." Instead, they use the classic stage magician's trick of diverting attention. They rail against "Big Oil," accuse the gasoline manufacturers and retailers of "price gouging," and then hold high-profile hearings where they can lecture oilmen on their impropriety when all they have done is follow the basic laws of supply and demand. They do this every year, despite the Federal Trade Commission's reporting every year that no "price gouging" has occurred. Meanwhile, they continue to pass environmental regulations leading to more and more requirements being placed on the oil companies, which in turn lead to higher and higher prices. If anyone is "gouging" the public, it's liberal politicians—both federal and local.

So global warming forms a perfect case study if we want to examine the lies, hypocrisy, and incompetence that characterize modern environmental liberalism and which have led to environmental disaster. Al Gore's crusade is based on misrepresentation of fact. It exposes his desire for others to do what he is unwilling to do himself. And Al Gore's crusade is already beginning to lead to a massive human and environmental tragedy.

Science Fiction

The scientific case for global warming alarmism is based on a series of truths that, far from being inconvenient, are actually trivial.[2] First is the basic physical principle that certain gases absorb heat, and so, all things being equal, the more of these "greenhouse" gases like carbon dioxide there are in the atmosphere, the warmer it will be. Second, greenhouse gases, particularly carbon dioxide, have steadily increased in the atmosphere since the industrial revolution. Finally, we have indeed seen a small increase in global average temperatures—about one degree Fahrenheit—over the last one hundred years.

Out of this molehill of scientific truth has been built a mountain of catastrophe theory that Al Gore and the green lobby use to advance their case for a complete realignment of the world's economic system.

This mountain-building starts with scientists who use the correlations they have identified between greenhouse gases and temperature rises to build computer models of what might happen to global temperatures if greenhouse gas concentrations accelerate as fast as some other economists and scientists estimate they will. These models find different suggested increases, based primarily on what happens to global development this century.

On top of these models, other scientists develop yet more computer models, trying to determine—if the first models are correct—what might happen to say, pine trees, sea levels, crops, or tropical storms. In turn, economists have developed computer models that assess whether the world will suffer or be better off.

From these computer simulations, Al Gore and his colleagues have advanced the argument that we face catastrophe very soon if we do not drastically curtail our use of the fossil fuels that release greenhouse gases when we burn them. They have suggested national emissions caps, taxes on energy use, and even personal carbon dioxide rations.[3] (Want to drive Junior to his Little League game? Tough luck, you used all your monthly CO_2 rations on your flight to grandpa's funeral last week.)

Yet it doesn't take a genius to realize that all those computer models are guesswork based on guesswork. Let's go back to the very first step, the correlation identified between greenhouse gases and temperature rise. While it looks quite strong, there's uncertainty even there (and other factors seem to correlate better—see Figure One). As the National Academy of Sciences reported in 2001:

> Because of the large and still uncertain level of natural variability inherent in the climate record and the uncertainties in the time histories of the various forcing agents . . . a causal linkage between the buildup of greenhouse gases in the atmosphere and the observed climate changes during the twentieth century cannot be unequivocally established.[4]

Even the United Nations' Intergovernmental Panel on Climate Change still cannot conclusively link greenhouse gases to the observed temperature rises. Its latest report in 2007 says there is a 90 percent chance that the one-degree increase in temperature seen in the twentieth century was caused by man's greenhouse gas emissions. That leaves a 10 percent chance that it was not, which may seem small, but which actually represents a massive uncertainty in scientific terms. For instance, in a medical study trying to find whether a disease was caused by certain bacteria, the study would not be regarded as convincing unless there was less than a 5 percent chance of there being another explanation.

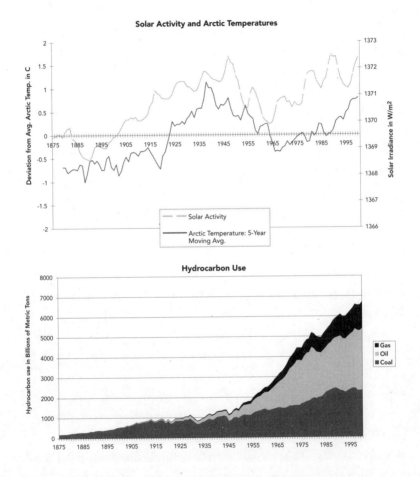

FIG 1: Possible Alternative to Greenhouse Gases as the Cause of Global Warming. Arctic surface air temperature compared with total solar irradiance as measured by sunspot cycle amplitude, sunspot cycle length, solar equatorial rotation rate, fraction of penumbral spots, and decay rate of the 11-year sunspot cycle (8,9). Solar irradiance correlates well with Arctic temperature, while hydrocarbon use does not correlate.[5]

These sorts of uncertainties exist throughout the science. It only takes a moment's thought to realize that heaping uncertainties upon uncertainties results in a much greater uncertainty at the end. Even so, these uncertainties are routinely dismissed by Al Gore and his friends.[6] Uncertainty cannot be an excuse for inaction, they say. It's a line worthy of the Wizard of Oz, even as Toto was pulling his curtain away; even though you don't know if that giant floating head is real, you should still do what it says.

Yet it's not just uncertainty that should make us doubt the hysteria about global warming. It's outright misrepresentation by Al Gore and his colleagues. For instance, my friend and colleague Marlo Lewis spent months fact-checking the claims made by Al Gore in his Oscar-winning film, *An Inconvenient Truth*. You'll note I didn't say "documentary," because Marlo found so many inaccuracies in the vice president's script that it should have qualified under the "Drama" category, not "Documentary."

Marlo identified almost fifty clear examples where *An Inconvenient Truth*, in its presentation of the evidence, was one-sided, misleading, exaggerated, speculative, or just plain wrong.[7] A few examples:

- Gore clearly links global warming to the destruction of New Orleans by Hurricane Katrina. No reputable scientist has linked Katrina directly to global warming. Gore also misrepresents the state of the active scientific debate over the role of global warming in hurricanes generally.[8]
- Gore suggests that global warming might trigger a mini-Ice Age in Europe resulting from the disruption of the Gulf Stream, which brings warm water to Northern Europe. Clearly having been impressed by the laughable global warming disaster film *The Day After Tomorrow*, Gore ignores the strong scientific consensus that such an event is highly unlikely.[9]

- Gore suggests that sea levels might rise twenty feet, drowning Manhattan and other cities. He argues that the Greenland ice sheet might "slip" into the sea, which is impossible as it sits in a bowl-shaped depression caused by its own weight.[10] The Intergovernmental Panel on Climate Change assesses that likely sea level rise this century even with large increases in temperature is in the order of twenty inches, not twenty feet.[11]

Marlo is not the only one to have identified these errors. The British government was so happy that the movie backed its political stance that it sent a copy to every publicly run high school in the country, to be used in geography, science, and citizenship classes. One parent and school governor, a truck driver named Stuart Dimmock, took Her Majesty's Government to court over this. He won.

Dimmock alleged that the use of the movie breached the Education Act of 1996, which forbids the promotion of "partisan" political views. The judge, Justice Burton, interpreted "partisan" as meaning "one-sided" rather than promoting any particular political party, and the Court found for Dimmock. It ruled that there were nine instances in which Vice President Gore went so outside the scientific mainstream that it deemed his presentation "alarmist" and "apocalyptic." Students would have to be informed of the actual state of the science when the film was shown in the classroom, so drawing attention to the fact that the Nobel Laureate was being somewhat economical with the truth.

Here are the nine errors, together with Justice Burton's comments:

1. Sea level rise of up to 20 feet (7 metres) will be caused by melting of either West Antarctica or Greenland in the near future.

In what the judge called "one of the most graphic parts of the film," Gore says as follows:

If Greenland broke up and melted, or if half of Greenland and half of West Antarctica broke up and melted, this is what would happen to the sea level in Florida. This is what would happen in the San Francisco Bay. A lot of people live in these areas. The Netherlands, the Low Countries: absolutely devastation. The area around Beijing is home to tens of millions of people. Even worse, in the area around Shanghai, there are 40 million people. Worse still, Calcutta, and to the east Bangladesh, the area covered includes 50 million people. Think of the impact of a couple of hundred thousand refugees when they are displaced by an environmental event and then imagine the impact of a 100 million or more. Here is Manhattan. This is the World Trade Center memorial site. After the horrible events of 9/11 we said never again. This is what would happen to Manhattan.

They can measure this precisely, just as scientists could predict precisely how much water would breach the levee in New Orleans.

Judge's comments: "This is distinctly alarmist, and part of Mr. Gore's 'wake-up call.' It is common ground that if indeed Greenland melted, it would release this amount of water, but *only* after, and over, millennia, so that the Armageddon scenario he predicts, insofar as it suggests that sea level rises of seven metres might occur in the immediate future, is not in line with the scientific consensus."

2. Low-lying inhabited Pacific atolls are being inundated because of anthropogenic global warming.

Gore states, "that's why the citizens of these Pacific nations have all had to evacuate to New Zealand."

Judge's comments: "There is no evidence of any such evacuation having yet happened." In other words, this is a flat-out fabrication.

3. Shutting down of the "Ocean Conveyor."

Gore says:

> One of the ones they are most worried about where they have spent a lot of time studying the problem is the North Atlantic, where the Gulf Stream comes up and meets the cold wind coming off the Arctic over Greenland and evaporates the heat out of the Gulf Stream and the stream is carried over to western Europe by the prevailing winds and the earth's rotation ... they call it the Ocean Conveyor. .... At the end of the last ice age ... that pump shut off and the heat transfer stopped and Europe went back into an ice age for another 900 or 1000 years. Of course that's not going to happen again, because glaciers of North America are not there. Is there any big chunk of ice anywhere near there? Oh yeah [pointing at Greenland].

Judge's comments: "According to the IPCC, it is very unlikely that the Ocean Conveyor (known technically as the Meridional Overturning Circulation or thermohaline circulation) will shut down in the future, though it is considered likely that thermohaline circulation may slow down."

4. Direct coincidence between the rise in CO_2 in the atmosphere and in temperature, by reference to two graphs.

Gore shows two graphs relating to a period of 650,000 years, one showing rise in CO_2 and one showing rise in temperature, and, as the judge says, "asserts (by ridiculing the opposite view) that they show an exact fit."

Judge's comments: "Although there is general scientific agreement that there is a connection, the two graphs do not establish what Mr. Gore asserts."

5. The snows of Kilimanjaro.

Mr. Gore asserts that the disappearance of snow on Mt Kilimanjaro is expressly attributable to global warming.

Judge's comments: "It is noteworthy that this is a point that specifically impressed Mr. Milliband [the then British environment secretary]. However, it is common ground that the scientific consensus is that it cannot be established that the recession of snows on Mt. Kilimanjaro is mainly attributable to human-induced climate change."

6. Lake Chad, etc.

Judge's comments: "The drying up of Lake Chad is used as a prime example of a catastrophic result of global warming. However, it is generally accepted that the evidence remains insufficient to establish such an attribution. It is apparently considered to be far more likely to result from other factors, such as population increase and over-grazing, and regional climate variability." We'll discuss this in more detail later.

7. Hurricane Katrina

Judge's comments: "Hurricane Katrina and the consequent devastation in New Orleans is [sic] ascribed to global warming. It is common ground that there is insufficient evidence to show that."

8. Death of polar bears

By reference to what the judge calls "a dramatic graphic of a polar bear desperately swimming through the water looking for ice," Mr Gore says:

A new scientific study shows that for the first time they are finding polar bears that have actually drowned swimming long distances up to sixty miles to find the ice. They did not find that before.

Judge's comments: "The only scientific study that either side before me can find is one which indicates that four polar bears have recently been found drowned because of a storm. That is not to say that there may not in the future be drowning-related deaths of polar bears if the trend of regression of pack-ice and/or longer open water continues, but it plainly does not support Mr Gore's description." We'll look at this issue in more detail later as well.

9. Coral reefs

Gore says:

Coral reefs all over the world because of global warming and other factors are bleaching and they end up like this. All the fish species that depend on the coral reef are also in jeopardy as a result. Overall species loss is now occurring at a rate 1,000 times greater than the natural background rate.

Judge's comments: "The actual scientific view, as recorded in the IPCC report, is that, if the temperature were to rise by 1-3 degrees Centigrade, there would be increased coral bleaching and widespread coral mortality, unless corals could adapt or acclimatise, but that separating the impacts of climate change-related stresses from other stresses, such as over-fishing and polluting, is difficult."

Take away these dramatic images and there is very little left in the film beyond the trivial truths we have already noted (and a lot of flannel about Al Gore himself). An analysis by my colleagues at the Competitive Enterprise Institute found that the nine errors accounted for over half of the scientific content of the movie. *An Inconvenient Truth* has been weighed in the balance and found wanting.

I could go on, but this book cannot be about the science of global warming or it will be 40,000 pages long. In fact, the science question is probably responsible for a good proportion of global deforestation, given how much has been written about it. Interested parties would be well served to consult one of the many lengthy treatments of just how badly informed the public has been on the subject. Two good examples are *The Politically Incorrect Guide™ to Global Warming* by my colleague Chris Horner, and *Meltdown: The Predictable Distortion of Global Warming by Scientists, Politicians and the Media* by Pat Michaels of the University of Virginia.

Gore's Destruction

I've found that when you start to poke too many holes like these in the alarmists' case, they resort to a sort of "what the heck?" argument. "Well, even if industrial emissions of greenhouse gases are not going to cause all of these disasters—or even make the planet noticeably warmer," we're often told, "what is lost if we abandon dirty sources of power, reduce our energy consumption, and embrace clean fuels?"

This "no regrets" argument is telling in two ways. First, it shows that the doomsday talk is really a justification for the policies—government control of the energy industry—the environmentalists would want anyway. Second, it shows how liberals can be completely blind to the positive effects of prosperity and the deadly effects of poverty.

Indeed, Gore's policies are more damaging to the world than global warming. That was the conclusion of Yale economist William Nordhaus, who has been developing economic models of climate since the 1970s.[12] Models, of course, are always suspect, but his models should be no more suspect than the ones Al Gore relies on, because they are intrinsically linked. If Gore's right, so is Nordhaus. Professor Nordhaus' results are illuminating.

He finds that unchecked global warming of about 3 degrees Celsius would cost the world about $22 trillion in damages this century. By avoiding emissions and checking growth, Al Gore's package of measures—no new coal power plants, lower household energy use, and so on—would reduce global warming's toll to $10 trillion. Yet precisely because the policies limit economic growth and impede development, they would come at a high cost: $34 trillion, to be exact. So the world would suffer a total of $44 trillion worth of damage from the combination of residual warming and Al Gore's self-inflicted economic wounds. Yes, $44 trillion; twice the cost of unchecked global warming.

How does Gore characterize the cost of his policies? He doesn't really. In *An Inconvenient Truth* he plays it as a moral issue, saying:

> Now it is up to us to use our democracy and our God-given ability to reason with one another about our future and make moral choices to change the policies and behaviors that would, if continued, leave a degraded, diminished, and hostile planet for our children and grandchildren—and for humankind.

Let's ignore the inelegance of that sentence (are our children not part of humankind?) and consider whether it is really the moral choice to adopt policies that are going to leave the world twice as poor as it would be if what they are aimed at preventing actually occurs. More honest environmentalists occasionally admit the conflict here: wealth vs. the environment. Yet, not only do they exaggerate the threat to the environment, they underestimate the positive effects of wealth. It's not about Cadillac

Escalades vs. Lodgepole Pines. It's about access to energy vs. continued poverty.

Access to energy is crucial to development. Gore's preferred policies, by making energy more expensive and less available, will steepen the climb faced by those in the developing world, where billions of people have never turned on an electric light, and women in particular are condemned to back-breaking labor, gathering firewood to carry it for miles to burn in poorly ventilated huts.

As we'll see in more detail later, access to affordable energy would be a godsend in liberating the developing world. Yet Gore would prefer to leave Indians and Africans in the dark unless they use expensive alternative energy. I wonder what Mother Teresa would have thought of that?

Suffice it to say that Al Gore's case for a rapid realignment in our energy system is based on a series of half-truths and exaggerations. Yet that is nothing compared to the hypocrisy he and his friends display when it comes to their personal energy use, or to the damage the policies advanced in *An Inconvenient Truth* will cause the world.

Al Gore's Big Fat Carbon Footprint

At the end of *An Inconvenient Truth*,[13] Al Gore outlines some things the individual can do to "make a difference" about global warming. First and foremost among these is cutting the energy you use at home. For instance:

> Choose energy-efficient lighting.... Choose energy-efficient appliances when making new purchases.... Heat and cool your house efficiently.... Get a home energy audit.[14]

You might therefore suppose that Al Gore himself would practice what he preaches.

Of course not. The Tennessee Center for Policy Research performed a home energy audit on the former vice president and revealed him to be a Class A hypocrite. In Tennessee, utilities bills are public records. The Center was therefore able to discover the following:

The average household in America consumes 10,656 kilowatt-hours (kWh) per year, according to the Department of Energy. In 2006, Gore devoured nearly 221,000 kWh—more than twenty times the national average.

Last August alone, Gore burned through 22,619 kWh—guzzling more than twice the electricity in one month than an average American family uses in an entire year. As a result of his energy consumption, Gore's average *monthly* electric bill topped $1,359. [Emphasis added]

Since the release of *An Inconvenient Truth*, Gore's energy consumption has increased from an average of 16,200 kWh per month in 2005, to 18,400 kWh per month in 2006.

Gore's extravagant energy use does not stop at his electric bill. Natural gas bills for Gore's mansion and guest house averaged $1,080 per month last year.[15]

That's an exceptional amount of energy. For the average household, for instance, running an air conditioner all summer uses about 4,000 kilowatt-hours of electricity, and that represents one of the biggest energy outlays any household has.

The energy use is all the bigger when you consider that, if Al Gore had indeed followed the helpful tips he gave us all in *An Inconvenient Truth*, his energy use would be all the lower.

Al Gore's office was unable to deny the charges. His spokesperson pointed out that, "The bottom line is that every family has a different carbon footprint. And what Vice President Gore has asked is for families to calculate that footprint and take steps to reduce and offset it." Indeed, every family has a different carbon footprint, but you would think that when you calculated that footprint and discovered it was the equivalent of a Sasquatch track, you would follow your own advice and try to reduce your energy use rather than increasing it.

Gore's office still had another way to weasel out of the accusation. The Gores, it transpired, purchased Green Power from Nashville Electric. The energy from Green Power comes from alternative sources such as windmills, which kill birds but at least do not emit too much carbon dioxide. At $4 extra per kilowatt-hour, it only cost the vice president an extra $5,893 a year for the privilege. Tennessee's median household income is $38,945,[16] which means that Gore spent 15 percent of the average household income in his home state for the privilege of being green.

Yet Gore's slipperiness didn't stop there. His office also claimed that he "offset" his greenhouse gas emissions. An offset is when you pay a firm to somehow neutralize your emissions. They do this in various ways. Some firms plant trees, which when grown absorb carbon dioxide from the atmosphere. Others invest in emission-reduction schemes in the developing world, essentially paying Asians and Africans not to emit. Yet others engage in financial deals reminiscent of the Enron scandal. If this reminds you of the medieval idea of indulgences, you've got the right idea.

Even offset companies admit that their products aren't much use in helping the environment. The Carbon Neutral Company, for instance, admits that offsets "will be unable to reduce greenhouse gas emissions...in the short term." Instead, it suggests that people should buy emissions for the following reasons: "(1) demonstrate commitment to taking action on climate change; (2) add an economic component to climate change; (3) help engage and educate the public; and (4) may provide local social and environmental benefits that help to encourage the use of low-carbon technologies." In short, carbon offsets merely help their purchasers feel good about themselves. Unsurprisingly, the main purchasers of offsets are committed environmentalists.[17]

As far as Al Gore is concerned, the story gets stranger. Gore gets his offsets from a company called Generation Investment Management. That company was founded by and is part-owned by none other than Al Gore. So Gore buys his offsets from himself? No, that—unusual as it sounds—is not as strange as what really happens. He gets his offsets as part of his benefits package from the company.[18] Gore therefore doesn't even pay for his offsets. He gets them free because he has persuaded other people they need to buy offsets.

So how did Gore's liberal supporters react when they heard about what can only be described as his hypocrisy? Did they condemn Al Gore and demand he change his ways? No, they bombarded the Tennessee Center with vile, hate-filled e-mails. Some accused the Center of stealing Gore's utility bills, which as already explained are public records. Others issued death threats. Still others, bizarrely for supposedly inclusive liberals, questioned the Tennessee Center staff's sexuality: "You guys are the faggiest fags I've ever come across."[19] (This is surprisingly common. I myself received an e-mail accusing me of being a "limp-wristed neocon" after publishing a letter in the New York Times. For the record, I am neither.)

Yet Gore's hypocrisy doesn't end there. The Nashville mansion is not Al Gore's only residence. He owns a house in the Northern Virginia suburbs and a condo on the San Francisco waterfront, which should tell you something about Gore's own belief in predictions of sea level rise.

Beyond real estate, The Smoking Gun Web site found that he demands First Class airfare whenever he flies places to deliver his lectures on global warming.[20] Sean Hannity of FOX News has broadcast footage of Al Gore traveling on private jets, which is even worse by his professed standards. Yet in *An Inconvenient Truth*, Gore gives the following advice on air travel:

> Flying is another form of transportation that produces large amounts of carbon dioxide. Reducing air travel even by one or two flights per year can significantly reduce emissions.... If your airplane travel is for business, consider whether you can telecommute instead.

Private jets emit about sixteen times more CO_2 per passenger than a Boeing 777.[21] They come in for particular scorn from other environmentalists. Lester Brown of the Earth Policy Institute told the *Wall Street Journal*:[22]

> Carbon offsets and these other things are feel-good solutions... I'm always interested in people who buy a carbon offset for their jet to fly between their four big homes. These kinds of programs postpone more meaningful action.

Yet Gore and his friends have their defenders. Eric Carlson of the Carbon Fund tried to defend the poor dears in the same article:

> Obviously these people have different lifestyles from yours or mine... At the same time, they're not obligated to do anything. We praise those who are doing things. We're trying to get to a market where the superwealthy are leaders in reducing their [carbon dioxide] footprint and playing a major role in changing this market.

So that's all right, then.

Well, of course it isn't. It illustrates the aristocratic attitude of so many of today's liberal environmentalists and their fellow travelers. If the super-rich aren't obligated to reduce their actual carbon emissions on the grounds that their lifestyles require it, why in Heaven's name should the middle class and the poor be obliged to sacrifice more of their small incomes in the name of stopping global warming? One of the reasons these people are so enamored of punitive taxes and useless carbon offsets is because they can afford them. The rest of us can't and that, incredibly, is described as selfishness.

Perhaps Al Gore could take a lesson from one unlikely convert to the cause of global warming alarmism. In his September 2007 rant from the cave, Osama bin Laden repeated what many liberal environmentalists believe:

> [T]he life of all mankind is in danger because of global warming resulting to a large degree from the emissions of the factories of the major corporations; yet despite that, the representative of these corporations in the White House insists on not observing the Kyoto accord, with the knowledge that the statistics speak of the death and displacement of millions of human beings because of global warming, especially in Africa.

Now, unlike Gore, Osama is walking the walk. As my colleague Myron Ebell pointed out, he's cut down on his air travel, telecommutes from home, and it appears he doesn't use a car at all. Myron concludes, "Osama appears to have adopted the ideal radical environmentalist lifestyle down to the very last detail—it really is back to the cave."

Live Earth: A Global Fiasco

One thing Osama certainly wouldn't have watched, even if he has a carbon-consuming TV in his cave, is Gore's Live Earth concerts of July 2007. Not just because of his contempt for western

pop culture (Live Earth London headliner Madonna was called a
prostitute by al Qaeda in Iraq in September 2007), but because
barely anybody watched it anywhere. In fact, the story of the
Live Earth concerts is a perfect case study of the liberal transnational idea accompanied by environmentalist incompetence.

The idea was simple. As he turned from failed politician to
movie star, Al Gore got to know a whole bunch of environmentally
concerned celebrities. He persuaded a group of musicians and
impressarios that it would be a good idea to emulate the 1980s
Live Aid concerts, which had drawn attention to famine in Africa.
The Live Earth concerts would be held all over the world, rather
than just in the UK and U.S., as had been the case with Live Aid.
By grabbing the attention of young people who tuned in to hear
the music, they would spread the word and also raise money for
their cause. They would become the first truly global lobby group.

Logistics experts must have been staggered at the proposed
scale of the endeavor. Concerts were scheduled for nine cities on
six continents for the day of July 7, 2007. Wealthy sponsors like
Microsoft contributed to the publicity. MSN, Microsoft's Internet arm, made arrangements for live video streaming of all the
concerts over the World Wide Web. Artists agreed to appear in
the location nearest where they were touring in order to reduce
the emissions associated with traveling. It was a beautiful ideal,
it seemed.

Yet from the beginning, it was tainted by politics, accusations
of hypocrisy, and incompetence.

Roger Daltrey, lead singer of veteran rockers, The Who, was
annoyed about the hypocrisy he saw involved. He told *The Sun*
newspaper:

> The last thing the planet needs is a rock concert. I can't believe
> it. Let's burn even more fuel. We have problems with global
> warming, but the questions and the answers are so huge I don't
> know what a rock concert's ever going to do to help.

Daltrey also showed that he understood more about the economics of alternative fuels (see below) than Al Gore:

My answer is to burn all the [expletive deleted] oil as quick as possible and then the politicians will have to find a solution.

Daltrey's concerns about hypocrisy were echoed by the front man for award-winning British band Muse. Matt Bellamy told the BBC:

Private jets for climate change, not sure about it, that seems to be a bit on edge really—that's an issue really, so we need to think about it.

Bellamy's peers in the young British supergroup Arctic Monkeys were equally non-plussed. In an interview with French news agency Agence France Presse (AFP), they expressed their bemusement at the concerts:

"It's a bit patronizing for us twenty-one-year-olds to try to start to change the world," said Arctic Monkeys drummer Matt Helders, explaining why the group is not on the bill at any of Al Gore's charity concerts.

"Especially when we're using enough power for ten houses just for (stage) lighting. It'd be a bit hypocritical," he told AFP in an interview before a concert in Paris.

Bass player Nick O'Malley chimes in: "And we're always jetting off on airplanes!"

Nevertheless, artists swarmed to be associated with the event. Yet more than a few were reformed 1980s bands like Crowded House, Duran Duran, or The Police. These bands tended to have new albums out or concert tours scheduled and might be suspected of needing publicity. Madonna, who headlined the London concert, had her first UK hit in 1983, before much of the intended audience was born. While a testament to Madonna's staying power, it was like Doris Day headlining Woodstock.

The concert series had run into some trouble before July 7, but on the big day things didn't get much better. Live Earth kicked off in Sydney, Australia. The Sydney Football Ground saw a capacity crowd of 45,000 assemble to watch, among other artists, the reunion of New Zealand popsters Crowded House. Yet within the first couple of hours, the crowd began to dwindle. It was apparently very difficult to purchase a beer and the lack of Australia's favorite liquid refreshment began to bite. The *Sydney Morning Herald* called the event "Livid Earth," reporting:

> Scores were seen leaving within the first two hours of the nine-hour festival, fed up with the lack of basic services, cutting their losses on a $99 ticket. Gate attendants were heard telling the human tide that they should complain to the promoter. It was "unAustralian," one spectator protested. "This is what happens when you let hippies organise a big event," another said. One woman, asked by Missy Higgins "how you all are back there," earned a wry round of applause from the stands when she shouted: "Sober." [23]

During Crowded House's set at the end of the concert, in a bizarre echo of the likely consequences of Al Gore's policies, the lights went out.

Things were not much better elsewhere in the globe. The Johannesburg, South Africa, concert was very poorly attended, with only 2,000 people in the Coca Cola Dome as the first artists began to sing.[24] Organizers for the global warming concert blamed the low turn-out on, erm, cold weather and resorted to handing out tickets for free.

Attendances at the two main concerts in London and Giants Stadium, New Jersey, were certainly respectable, but a couple of days later, the viewership numbers came out.

The British Broadcasting Corporation had a week before Live Earth broadcast uninterrupted live coverage of the Concert for Diana, organized by her sons Princes William and Harry to commemorate the tenth anniversary of the tragic death of Diana, Princess of Wales. That concert and Live Earth London were relatively equal in star power. The Diana concert proved very popular, drawing 11.4 million viewers. Live Earth was a total flop by comparison, attracting only 3.1 million viewers at its peak.

Not only was this figure about a quarter of its nearest direct competitor in terms of spectacle, it was below average for a normal Saturday in July. Unsurprisingly, the organizers blamed the good summer weather. Given the excuse used in Johannesburg, it seems that the perfect performer for a Live Earth concert would have been a band called Goldilocks and the Three Bears: the weather needed to be not too cold, not too warm, but just right.

It was a similar story in the U.S. The blanket coverage by NBC, Bravo, and other affiliate cable stations drew a peak audience of just 4.5 million. Similar coverage for the Live 8 concerts in 2005 drew a peak audience twice as high, at 9.6 million. The most charitable interpretation of the audience figures is 19 million, which includes anyone who watched the event for six minutes before changing the channel. Anyone watching the event might well have been disposed to switch over quickly. In between the acts, the viewers were given lectures as to how to live "greener" by installing bamboo flooring, for instance. Before the events, the organizers claimed that two billion people worldwide would see them. They fell only about 1.98 billion short.

What about the revenues from the concerts? Given that the money would be raised from all over the world, it would be interesting to see how the proceeds would be allocated and for what purposes. A nonpartisan British group called Intelligent Giving was interested to find out exactly what would be done with the money. According to their Web site they were given quite the runaround in trying to find out.[25]

The story goes like this. Live Earth's UK agent told Intelligent Giving that the proceeds of the concerts would be split between the Alliance for Climate Protection, "an American outfit backed by Al Gore," and other non-governmental organizations. The Alliance did not respond to further inquiries. Another group associated with the concerts, Stop Climate Chaos, contradicted the UK agent and told the web site that all funds would go to the Alliance. However, the group had seen a claim on the BBC news Web site that suggested that proceeds would be split between the Alliance, Stop Climate Chaos, and another organization called The Climate Group. The Climate Group passed the buck to a communications firm that said that, in fact, all money would go to the Alliance. With me so far?

This time, the Alliance responded to a phone call. The spokesman told Intelligent Giving that the proceeds would be sent back to the countries. They reported, "The nice spokesman told us that there was a Plan which detailed how the money was to be split up. But it hasn't been published yet, apparently." Just to be sure, the group consulted the Alliance's web site. The web page declared that all proceeds would be used to "lobby the U.S. government to change the laws on climate change in America."

Intelligent Giving concluded the following on July 6:

There are, we think, two possible conclusions to be drawn from this experience:

1. Live Earth is badly run. We wanted the answer to a basic question. Several representatives *thought* they knew the answer but they all told us different things.

2. Live Earth is primarily a publicity stunt. We could have got an instant answer, we suspect, if we wanted to know what Madonna will be wearing on Saturday. But there was no clear response when it came to the basic question of how Live Earth will use its cash (or concerts) to stop climate change.

We spent a lot of time on this wild-goose chase but we still know as little about Live Earth as we did last week. It doesn't bode well. This is at best, the most confused, and at worst, the most secretive charitable outfit we've come across.

I'd add a third possibility. That Live Earth was a massive wealth-transfer scheme, designed to channel money from concerned citizens across the globe into the pockets of wealthy Washington lobbyists.

The Alliance for Climate Protection is an interesting organization, by the way. In 2005, it had receipts of only $70,000.[26] Yet in January 2008, it awarded a contract to The Martin Agency, a top advertising agency that created the famous GEICO "caveman" ads, for a TV campaign costing about $100 million. That's a pretty fast expansion.

And just how much money was raised by Live Earth? I have been unable to find out. On Monday, July 9, the Associated Press reported that, "figures for the money raised will be available later in the week." [27] Those figures were never released, as far as I can tell from searches of news databases.

Al Gore Is Bad for the Planet

Live Earth revealed Al Gore and the liberal environmental movement to be hypocritical and incompetent, with a tinge of shadiness in the finances. Even if we agreed with Gore's science and his goals, we would have to count the concert series as a failure. Weighing the costs (in terms of greenhouse gases emitted and fuel

consumed) against the benefits (in terms of raising awareness),
Live Earth left the planet worse than it found it.

The same could be said of Al Gore. If he didn't exist—or if he
had taken up his family business of growing tobacco near
Carthage, Tennessee—a lot less fuel would have burnt, and fewer
greenhouse gases emitted.

These environmental costs, while small in a global sense, are
fitting analogies for the impact of Al Gore—and environmentalism and liberalism broadly. Nice ideas combined with arrogance
and hatred of industry yield disasters in terms of environment,
health, and safety.

In the wake of Live Earth, one African academic quickly
pointed out how the philosophy behind the concerts, rather than
staving off humanitarian disaster, actually encouraged one.

Kofi Bentil is a lecturer in economics at Ashesi University in
Ghana. On July 11, he published an opinion piece in Ghana's
Accra Mail newspaper that accurately skewered the environmentalist's pretensions. "Few people in Africa got to see Al Gore and
his troupe of rock-star ecologists strutting their stuff two week-
ends ago," he began, "because most have neither television nor
electricity. That's just as well, because they would have been
aghast at Live Earth's bizarre message. In Africa, we have much
more serious things to worry about than climate change. Indeed,
if they achieve their objective the concerts will have done harm
to the people of Africa."

Bentil targeted not just Live Earth but also the old colonial
master, Britain. In a new form of imperialism, which author Paul
Driessen has styled eco-imperialism,[28] the liberal British government has not only swallowed Gore's argument hook, line, and
sinker, but has moved to impose it on Africans who thought they
were free of over-educated paternalists from Britain forever. Bentil points out that, motivated by Gore's climate change alarmism,
the British Department for International Development has

sought to encourage "Development by Dung" on the grounds that, "As poor countries develop, it is essential that they do not follow the same failed patterns of energy use." He comments, "So it's dung not diesel for Africa—while India and China soar ahead because they are too big, and nuclear-armed, to stop."

Why have Africans relied on dirty fuels like wood and dung for their power? Bentil asks. The answer he gives is simple: not from some desire to save the earth, but because they don't have access to diesel and electricity. Dung—"renewable" but primitive—inflicts massive harm on Africans in terms of respiratory damage. Lung damage as a cause of childhood death is followed by diarrhea, caused by dirty water, which is in turn caused by a lack of affordable energy to pump water. Moreover, underlying most of Africa's health problems is malnutrition. This is caused by inefficient farming and poor food distribution. Efficient farming and better distribution would require more affordable energy and better infrastructure. Better infrastructure would require more affordable energy. Are you beginning to sense a pattern here?

Bentil concludes:

Please, Europe and America, spare us! You can cut your own emissions if you want, but don't tell us what to do. We really have much more serious and urgent threats to deal with. Unfortunately, our beggarly governments are very susceptible to diktats from on high, especially when they are offered aid (which they use to line the coffers of their bank accounts): don't encourage them!

This is the authentic voice of the developing world. Africa needs to develop. To develop, it requires affordable energy. At present, the most affordable by far sources of energy are fossil fuels—predominantly coal and oil. Yet those are exactly what

Live Earth was aimed at curbing. The conclusion is inescapable: while the aim of Live Aid was to help Africa, the aim of Live Earth, if achieved, would harm Africa.

John Christy would agree. Christy is professor of atmospheric science and director of the Earth System Science Center at the University of Alabama in Huntsville. He is also Alabama's state climatologist and has served as a lead author of the UN's Intergovernmental Panel on Climate Change periodic reports (which shows that not everyone involved in that group is an alarmist). A distinguished climatologist, John also served early in his career as a missionary in Africa. Unlike, it seems, many climatologists who talk about the need for fewer emissions, John has seen firsthand the terrible burdens that energy poverty imposes.

In 2003, he told the Committee on Resources of the U.S. House of Representatives about the reality of energy-starved life in Africa:

> I lived upcountry with people who did not have access to useful energy. Put simply, access to energy means life, it means a longer and better life. I watched as women walked in the early morning to the forest edge, often several miles away, to chop wet green wood for fuel. They became beasts of burden as they carried the wood on their backs on the return trip home. Wood and dung are terrible sources of energy, with low useful output while creating high pollution levels. Burning wood and dung inside the homes for cooking and heat created a dangerously polluted indoor atmosphere for the family. I always thought that if each home could be fitted with an electric light bulb and a microwave oven electrified by a coal-fired power plant, several good things would happen. The women would be freed to work on other more productive pursuits, the indoor air would be much cleaner so health would improve, food could be prepared more safely, there would be light for reading and

advancement, information through television or radio would be received, and the forest with its beautiful ecosystem could be saved. Access to inexpensive, efficient energy would enhance the lives of the Africans while at the same time enhance the environment.

If Live Earth was really about helping the poorest of the world, it would be advocating greater use of fossil fuels throughout the world. Thank God nobody watched it.

Liberalism's Wake of Destruction

In Africa, we worry about what improvements might be prevented or delayed by Al Gore's agenda. Around the rest of the world, we can see the destruction reaped by environmentalism and liberalism.

To be precise, environmentalism and liberalism by themselves are not the culprits in the disasters discussed in the following chapters. Love of nature, concern for the quality of air and water, and even worry about man's impact on the planet can all reflect well on a person's character, and even yield beneficial fruit.

The problem is that both the environmental movement and the Far Left remain utterly devoted to discredited, harmful ideas: central-planning and government regulation. These are the open enemies of free enterprise and property rights.

The central planners have long argued that "capitalism"—by which they largely mean enterprise and property—is destroying the planet. In this, they have convinced most of the media, and even some conservatives who flippantly advocate "paving the rainforests," because they buy into the idea that free enterprise and the environment are enemies.

In truth, central planning and big government—just like their champion Al Gore—have proved to be bad for the planet.

Chapter One

Malaria

The Plague of Environmentalists

A headache is the first symptom. Muscle pains set in soon. Then it starts to get really bad.

Fever kicks in, along with shivers. The fever gets severe, and the infected person starts to sweat profusely, sometimes a cold sweat, sometimes feeling as though she is burning up. As the immune system works in overdrive, the millions of plasmodia—the microscopic creatures causing the illness—swim up the bloodstream into the brain.

The brain begins to swell, but the other organs also struggle. As one journalist told it from Zambia:

> This is when the body starts to break down. The parasites have destroyed so many oxygen-carrying red cells that too few are left to sustain vital functions. The lungs fight for breath, and the heart struggles to pump. The blood acidifies. Brain cells die. The child struggles and convulses and finally falls into a coma.[1]

In more than half-a-million cases every year, the child dies.

Malaria is the leading cause of death in Zambia for pregnant women and children under five, but it strikes across age and sex lines. Each year sees an estimated 500 million cases, and one million deaths.

Governments, international health agencies, and charities are desperately trying to fight the disease. We can't fight the real culprit—the blood-borne plasmodia—and so we fight the carrier:[2] the mosquito that carries the plasmodia in her saliva.

Bed nets that stop the insect sucking their blood while people sleep, blood screenings, and public-information campaigns all can help prevent contraction or spur early treatment. There is no vaccine, though, and no cure, per se.

There is, however, one highly effective way of preventing the spread of malaria. Dichloro-Diphenyl-Trichloroethane, or DDT, is proven to be very effective at stopping malaria. It could save hundreds of thousands of lives and spare millions from suffering every year—if only it didn't offend liberal environmentalists and overreaching governments. It has been at the center of environmental campaigns for almost fifty years.

You might think that in retrospect, liberals might regret their war against DDT, or at least look back at it as a well-meaning mistake. On the contrary, the environmental Left persists in its fight against the chemical, and holds up its ban as one of the early crowning achievements of its movement. Indeed, Al Gore regularly cites the war against DDT as one of his inspirations.

The Michael Moore of 1962

Rachel Carson's name is invoked by environmentalists as an early prophet and a hero. Her 1962 book, *Silent Spring*, is one of the founding texts of liberal environmentalism. It also is a shoddy bit of scholarship that may be responsible for millions of deaths, by spurring the ill-considered assault on DDT.

Swiss chemist, Paul Hermann Muller, received the Nobel Prize for Medicine in 1948 for recognizing and unleashing DDT's high efficiency in killing the insects that spread malaria, yellow fever, and other "vector-borne" diseases. The miracle chemical became widely used as an agricultural pesticide over the next decade. In Egypt and Brazil, the insecticide was instrumental in the eradication of malaria. Attempts to repeat the success in other countries, however, suffered setbacks as some insect populations developed resistance to large-scale spraying because of its widespread agricultural use.

Yet DDT use had been a spectacular success in its primary role: killing the insects that bear terrible diseases. Even before Muller won his prize, it saved thousands of soldiers during World War II from the misery of parasitic infestation that was endemic during World War I.[3] Yet there were side effects as a result of its widespread use in agriculture. In particular, large bird life appeared to be affected. This led Carson, a popular naturalist and author, to pen in 1962 a sensationalist account of the impact of pesticides on birds, hinging around an apocalyptic scenario where no birds meant no birdsong, hence her title, *Silent Spring*. She also included in her book a claim that pesticides were increasing cancer incidence among children (something that the data cannot support) and implausible anecdotes of immediate human harm, such as one about a woman who developed leukemia overnight.

In 1992, a leading entomologist, J. Gordon Edwards, professor of entomology at San Jose State University, wrote a comprehensive account of Rachel Carson's distortions of the truth for the magazine *21st Century*.[4] He titled it, provocatively, "The Lies of Rachel Carson,"[5] and anyone who reads the full article will come away under no illusions that Rachel Carson was being anything other than deliberately manipulative.

Professor Edwards was himself a committed environmentalist when he first came across *Silent Spring*, and was eager to read it. He noticed a few inaccuracies in the first few pages, but was happy to ignore them as he was happy with the message. However, as he got further along in the book, he began to be concerned. Edwards writes:

> As I neared the middle of the book, the feeling grew in my mind that Rachel Carson was really playing loose with the facts and was also deliberately wording many sentences in such a way as to make them imply certain things without actually saying them. She was carefully omitting everything that failed to support her thesis that pesticides were *bad,* that industry was *bad,* and that any scientists who did not support her views were *bad.*

The professor then noted that most of Carson's sources were "very unscientific" and that, although there were many footnotes and references, these actually all referred to a small number of such sources. When he looked up the actual scientific sources cited, he was surprised to find out that they did not support Carson's claims about the dangers of pesticides.

Professor Edwards was not alone:

> Finally, I began to join the detractors of *Silent Spring,* and when hearings were held to determine the fate of DDT in various states of this nation, I paid my own way to some of them so that I could testify against the efforts to ban that life-saving insecticide. It was gratifying to find that great numbers of scientists and health officials whom I had always held in high esteem were also testifying at those hearings, in defense of DDT and in opposition to the rising tide of antipesticide propaganda in environmental publications and in the media.

Indeed, Professor Edwards was so certain of the lack of harm that DDT posed to human health that he would regularly consume DDT in his talks, something that former congressman and exterminator Tom DeLay also once did on a dare.

Here are just a few of the lies and misleading statements Professor Edwards enumerated:

- The book's dedication, which contains a quotation from Nobel laureate humanitarian Albert Schweitzer, gives the impression that he was worried about pesticides. Yet Schweitzer himself said in his autobiography, "How much labor and waste of time these wicked insects do cause us...but a ray of hope, in the use of DDT, is now held out to us."[6]

- After referring to untruthful allegations that persons ingesting as little as one tenth of a part per million (ppm) of DDT will then store "about 10 to 15 ppm," Carson states that "such substances are so potent that a minute quantity can bring about vast changes in the body." (She does not consider the metabolism and breakdown of DDT in humans and other vertebrates, and their excretion in urine, and so on, which prevents the alleged "biological magnification" up food chains from actually occurring.) Carson then states: "In animal experiments, 3 parts per million [of DDT] has been found to inhibit an essential enzyme in heart muscle; only 5 parts per million has brought about necrosis or disintegration of liver cells...." This *implies* that considerable harm to one's health might result from traces of DDT in the diet, but there has been *no* medical indication that her statements are true.

- Carson refers to an incident in which a worker spilled a "25 percent solution" of chlordane on herself and died soon afterwards. Carson omitted the sheer size of the incident and the other elements involved—twenty-five pounds of chlordane, thirty-nine pounds of solvent, and ten pounds of emulsifier.

- Carson equates herbicides with radiation, a comparison Edwards finds "despicable, for there is a tremendous difference between their mutagenic potentials."

- Carson argues that weeds are necessary in fields of crops. She also asserts that crabgrass cannot grow in healthy soil. Both of these statements are contrary to generations of experience.

- On the Japanese beetles that caused so much damage in the Eastern United States, Edwards has this to say: "Carson bemoans the efforts to control the Japanese beetles in Detroit in 1959, saying, 'Little need was shown for this drastic and dangerous action.' She then says that a naturalist in Michigan, whom she claimed was very well informed, stated that the Japanese beetle had been present in Detroit for more than thirty years. (No *entomologist* had ever seen one there.) Carson's naturalist also said that the beetles had not increased there during all that time. Perhaps she misquoted the naturalist, or perhaps he was just lying, or maybe he simply did not recognize the local *Strigoderma* beetles that faintly resemble Japanese beetles.

  "Certainly it is impossible that the voracious Japanese beetles were actually present there for thirty years, remaining hidden from all entomologists and home-owners! Everywhere those beetles have invaded they quickly multiplied to a pest status within a few years, causing tremendous damage to flowers, fruits, and (as larvae) destroying the roots of grasses and other plants. Even Rachel Carson should not expect us to believe that in Detroit they displayed entirely different behavior."

- Carson cites an ornithologist named George Wallace, who blamed deaths of robins on DDT. Edwards says, "In many feeding experiments birds, including robins, were forced to ingest great quantities of DDT (and its breakdown product, DDE). Wallace did not provide any evidence that indicated the Michigan State University robins may have been killed by those chemicals. Researcher Joseph Hickey at the University of Wisconsin had testified before the Environmental Protection

Agency hearings on DDT specifically that he could not kill any robins by overdosing them with DDT because the birds simply passed it through their digestive tract and eliminated it in their feces. Many other feeding experiments by the U.S. Fish and Wildlife Service and various university researchers repeatedly showed that DDT and DDE in the diet could not have killed wild birds under field conditions.

If Carson had mentioned these pertinent details it would have devastated her major theme, which continued to be the awful threats posed by DDT to all nonhuman creatures on the face of the Earth. Instead of providing the facts that would clarify such conditions, she spent several more pages on unfounded allegations about DDT and various kinds of birds."

- When Carson lists about 90 species of birds she says were affected by DDT, she fails to note that the Audubon Christmas Bird Counts "continued to reveal that *more* birds were counted, *per observer,* during the greatest 'DDT years,' including those types that Carson had declared to be declining in numbers." Marshes sprayed with DDT showed an explosion in bird numbers as diseases carried by insects declined.

- Carson cites James DeWitt of the U.S. Fish and Wildlife Service in support of her contention that bird reproduction was affected, because in his experiments with quails fed DDT, "few of the eggs hatched." Edwards comments, "Carson gives no indication of *how many* might be considered as 'few eggs hatching.' Perhaps she thought that her readers would never see the rather obscure journal in which DeWitt's results were published in 1956, the *Journal of Agriculture and Food Chemistry.* Otherwise, she surely would not have so badly misrepresented DeWitt's results. The dosage he fed the quail was 100 parts per million in all their food every day, which was roughly 3,000 times the daily DDT intake of humans during the years of the greatest DDT use. The quail did not just hatch 'a few' of their eggs, as DeWitt's data clearly reveal.

"As the published data from DeWitt's experiments show, the 'controls' (those quail with no DDT) hatched 83.9 percent of their eggs, while the DDT-fed quail hatched 75 to 80 percent of theirs. I would not call an 80 percent hatch 'few,' especially when the controls hatched only 83.9 percent of their eggs.... Carson either did not read DeWitt's article, or she deliberately lied about the results of DeWitt's experiments on pheasants, which were published on the same page. The 'controls' hatched only 57.4 percent of their eggs, while the DDT-fed pheasants, (dosed with 50 ppm of DDT in all of their food during the entire year) hatched 80.6 percent of theirs. After two weeks, the DDT chicks had 100 percent survival, while the control chicks only had 94.8 percent survival, and after eight weeks the DDT chicks had 93.3 percent survival while the control chicks only had 89.7 percent survival. *It was false reporting such as this that caused so many leading scientists in the United States to take Rachel Carson to task.* [Emphasis added.]"

- Edwards gave up taking notes after 125 pages, and commented, "The text continues in this vein for another 172 pages, with chapter heads such as 'Rivers of Death,' 'The Human Price,' 'The Rumblings of an Avalanche,' and 'Beyond the Dreams of the Borgias.' I trust that this partial analysis of Carson's deceptions, false statements, horrible innuendoes, and ridiculous allegations in the first 125 pages of *Silent Spring* will indicate why so many scientists expressed opposition, antagonism, and perhaps even a little rage after reading Carson's diatribe. No matter how deceitful her prose, however, the influence of Carson's *Silent Spring* has been very great and it continues thirty years later to shape environmentalist propaganda and fund-raising as well as U.S. policy."

Silent Spring was the 1960s equivalent of a Michael Moore documentary: sensationalized, overwrought, with science seriously misrepresented and conclusions unsustainable.

Yet it worked at an emotional level. Local groups across America and Europe began agitating for local bans on DDT use and when scientists seemingly proved a link between DDT presence and the thinning of eggs of major avian predators such as the osprey and the iconic Bald Eagle, pressure for national bans became intense. The EPA's own scientists agreed with experts like Professor Edwards and concluded that, "DDT is not a carcinogenic hazard to man.... DDT is not a mutagenic or teratogenic hazard to man.... The use of DDT under the regulations involved here [does] not have a deleterious effect on freshwater fish, estuarine organisms, wild birds or other wildlife." The EPA Administrator, however, ignored his scientists[7] and banned almost all uses of the chemical in 1972, with a small exemption for public health that has never been invoked.

Africa's Silent Spring

Perhaps if this had been the extent of the ban, it might have been tolerable; DDT had done the work it needed to do in the U.S. and other agricultural pesticides were just as convenient to use. This wasn't enough for liberal activists. They mounted a campaign to outlaw DDT even where it was still being used to combat malaria and, more importantly, in areas where it had not yet been tried such as sub-Saharan Africa.

In countries like Uganda, there is a striking correlation between incidence of malaria and GDP levels. Elimination of malaria, in short, is essential to the elimination of poverty. DDT is an important (but not the only) weapon in the fight against malaria, because it is affordable, effective, persistent, and relatively harmless to the human population. When used sparingly—as a weapon against mosquitoes not an agricultural pesticide—it is highly effective in controlling malaria and thereby lifting millions out of poverty.

Those benefits seem immaterial to the liberal establishment. The banning of DDT forms the founding myth of the modern liberal environmental movement. It cannot afford to see its first great achievement questioned—which is the only reasonable explanation for its sustained campaign against allowing any use of the chemical anywhere. In 2001, they launched a major effort against the proposed exemption under the Stockholm Convention to allow use of DDT for the protection of human health. Organizations like Greenpeace, the World Wildlife Fund, Physicians for Social Responsibility, and over two hundred other groups lobbied for a complete ban. Thankfully, they failed, at least partly because of the opposition of developing nations. But they have other arrows in their quiver.

Most African countries that need to use DDT are highly dependent upon foreign aid, and so rather than trying to persuade African nations to curtail their use of something that keeps their citizens alive, they lobby the donor organizations to attach conditions. Mozambique, for instance, is dependent for over 80

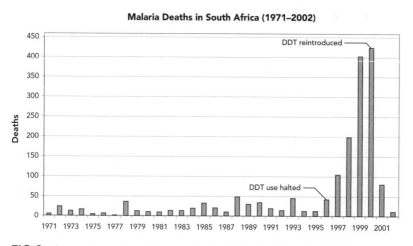

FIG 2: The consequences of abandoning DDT use in South Africa[8]

percent of its health funding from foreign aid, and it stopped use of DDT decades ago because the donors despicably refused to fund DDT use. Similarly, the European Union has told African nations their agricultural exports might not be allowed into European markets if DDT use was "widespread."

It is clear, however, that DDT use can be extremely effective. South Africa, rich enough that it does not have to pander to the liberal tastes of foreign aid organizations, has learned its lesson. It stopped use of DDT in KwaZulu Natal province in 1996, but saw malaria incidence increase from twenty deaths that year to 340 in 2000. It reintroduced DDT and has now got the number of deaths back down to under fifty. In between the DDT programs, it tried newer and more expensive alternatives, but their relative ineffectiveness was revealed.

Dr. Sam Zaramba, who is the director general of health services for the Republic of Uganda, is quite clear on the efficacy of DDT. He wrote in the *Wall Street Journal* on June 12, 2007:

In 2006, Uganda worked with President George Bush's Malaria Initiative to train 350 spray operators, supervisors, and health officials. In August 2006 and again in February 2007, we covered 100,000 households in the southern Kabale district with the insecticide Icon. Nearly everyone welcomed this protection. The prevalence of the malaria parasite dropped. Today, just 3 percent of the local population carries the disease, down from 30 percent.

This exercise pays for itself. With 90 percent fewer people requiring anti-malarial medication and other public-health resources, more healthy adults work and more children attend school. When we repeated the test program in Kabale and neighboring Kanungu district this year, our spray teams required little new training and were rapidly mobilized. Our health officials at every level were able to educate our communities, implement spraying programs and evaluate operations. With each passing year, it will now be easier and less expensive to run the programs. But DDT lasts longer, costs less and is more effective against malaria-carrying mosquitoes than Icon. It functions as spatial repellent to keep mosquitoes out of homes, as an irritant to prevent them from biting, and as a toxic agent to kill those that land. The repellency effect works without physical contact. And because we will never use the chemical in agriculture, DDT also makes mosquitoes less likely to develop resistance.

Dr. Zaramba does not mince words, bluntly calling the developed world's restrictions on DDT "contemporary colonialism."

The liberal campaigns against DDT are therefore clearly contributing to continuing suffering in Africa. One prominent African physician uses a striking analogy to bring home the extent of the tragedy:

> Dr Wenceslaus Kilama, chairperson of Malaria Foundation International, has said, the malaria epidemic "is like loading up seven Boeing 747 airliners each day, then deliberately crashing them into Mt Kilimanjaro."[9]

Uganda's Council on Racial Equality publishes heart-rending pictures of children lost to malaria at the Kampala orphanage. In a school of five hundred orphans, fifty children (10 percent of the entire school) were lost to malaria in 2005 alone. Across Uganda, 50,000 children died from malaria that year. The same is true year after year. Their happy voices will never fill an April playground with laughter again. That is the true *Silent Spring*.

Dead Children Don't Matter

Yet liberals routinely deny their policies have led to this death and devastation. They say there is no DDT ban, ignoring their efforts to secure an outright ban and their manipulation of aid agencies to produce a de facto ban in the poorest nations. Liberals say mosquitoes develop resistance to DDT, making it useless—a claim that is only relevant to wide-spread agriculture use, which no one is advocating any more. They say there is evidence that DDT harms human health, when all the legitimate studies are inconclusive at worst. Tying Rachel Carson's work to thousands of deaths is offensive, liberals say, missing the point that her legacy, not her words, seems to be what drives those who are truly responsible. Of course Rachel Carson did not kill millions herself; the very suggestion is preposterous. Yet it is truly preposterous to argue that her legacy played no part in the DDT ban. Liberals even suggest sinister motives for those advocating DDT use, alleging they are in the pay of DDT makers, a bizarre argument when you consider that DDT's patent expired long ago and could be made affordably by local chemical companies all over the world.

You can see these arguments all over the liberal blogosphere, if you can pick them out of all the hate-filled rants and ad hominem attacks. Here's one example of the techniques used by liberals to argue against DDT use, courtesy of the liberal blog Polianna.com:[10]

> What should not be done, however is returning to the utilization of DDT in order to control the mosquito population and stop the proliferation of malaria. Consider some of the facts about DDT—1) DDT is a close relative of Agent Orange, the chemical used during the Vietnam War by the United States in order to kill vegetation and reveal to locations [sic] of the enemy. In the years following the War, veterans and some Vietnamese have experienced a host of dangerous and undesirable effects, including cancer and birth deformities in off-spring; 2) DDT is fat-soluble, meaning that it stays in the body longer

and is able to accumulate over time; and 3) the U.S. does not use DDT and yet we want other countries to expose their populations to it. It is very important for developed nations, who themselves faced the threat of malaria at various times in the past, to fight this fight. But spraying a relative of dioxin all over the African continent is not the way. Would Americans want this for their own children?

This is a masterclass in obfuscation and stupidity. The argument that DDT is similar to Agent Orange is completely irrelevant. DDT is not Agent Orange and, as we have seen, is not harmful to humans in anything except massive doses. DDT is indeed fat-soluble, and people who were heavily exposed to DDT in its manufacture or application showed levels of DDT in their fat up to 1,000 times greater than normal in their blood. But even these high levels were of very little harm to the workers. Finally, the suggestion that Africa should not use DDT because America doesn't is a complete reversal of the true situation. As we have seen, Africans are crying out to be allowed to be able to use DDT without suffering penalties imposed by liberal environmentalists and their foreign aid donor allies.

It takes a very peculiar imagination to argue that America is trying to impose DDT on an unwilling Africa. One liberal blogger, Ed Darrell, even managed to suggest that the prevention of DDT use was yet another nasty plot by the evil President Bush and his corporate masters:[11]

> Since indoor spraying is authorized under current law, including international treaties, since the UN and the U.S. fund such spraying, and since most nations that could use DDT in such a fashion are already using it in such a fashion—except where industrialists or the Bush administration refuse to allow it for stated reasons that are completely absurd—I can only assume

that those who complain that we need to "loosen up" on DDT are advocating broadcast spraying once again.

I wonder what Dr. Zaramba would say to that.

Our friends at Polliana.com go further, though. In an argument worthy of Planned Parenthood Founder Margaret Sanger or Princeton's Peter Singer, they argue that DDT use would not help Africa, because children aren't productive:

> The United States should help poor, third-world nations get out of their bottomless amounts of debt they have amassed over the years from loans granted by international organizations, such as the World Bank and the IMF, to help them fight poverty. Did malaria cause this debt? No. Sadly, the fact of the matter in regards to the malaria epidemic is that the vast majority of its victims are children under age 5. These are not "productive" members of society. Contrasting this with the HIV/AIDS crisis, which strikes and kills adult people in their prime working stage of life, makes it easy to see which disease causes the bigger drain on the productivity of communities. A decrease in productivity means a decrease in wealth and a decrease in the ability for governments to cover their debts. Throw in a corrupt government and the problem gets even worse.
>
> It would be so easy if one could spray DDT over the continent of Africa and make the continent's poverty and debts go away. You can't. To suggest that you can is irresponsible and irrational, trademarks of conservative thinking.

The liberal environmentalist's mind is a funny place, isn't it? The clear and proven link between malaria and GDP (and therefore poverty) is not mentioned, because the focus is on suggesting that malaria is far less of a problem than AIDS. Nor, as I have emphasized above, is anyone talking about mass spraying. The plain fact is that judicious use of DDT alongside other methods of malaria prevention such as bed nets and better public sanitation would save hundreds of thousands of children's lives every year. These children will grow into productive members of society, increasing their nations' wealth. Failure to acknowledge that simple fact is probably the clearest example of liberals infantilizing society I've ever come across. Eradication of malaria in Africa is an unquestionable good, despite the twisted logic of our blogging friends.

Liberals even exaggerate the few genuine arguments they have about negative effects of DDT—Teresa Heinz and John Kerry, for instance, repeat in their latest book a bizarre story.[12] Mrs. Kerry told the story to a friendly blogger in April 2007:

> A few decades ago, the World Health Organization wanted to end a malaria epidemic in Borneo, so it sprayed DDT from airplanes to wipe out the indigenous population of mosquitoes. Unfortunately, the DDT also wiped out the wasps that controlled the local thatch-eating insects, with the result that everyone's roof caved in.
>
> Meanwhile, the DDT accumulated in the local lizard population, and wiped out the cats that ate the lizards, thereby unleashing a ferocious infestation of rats. Ultimately, the World Health Organization was forced to parachute in 14,000 new cats, to control the rats. This came to be known as Operation Cat Drop.
>
> This story is popular with environmentalists, but I share it now to make a point about unintended consequences. Much of what we do in life is not intended to come out the way it does.[13]

This bizarre story should set anyone's garbage detectors ringing. Parachuting 14,000 cats? In fact, Operation Cat Drop did take place, but only twenty cats were delivered, along with a crate of Stout for the local chieftain. Yet it is highly unlikely that the cats could have been killed by DDT in the first place, because the amount of lizards they would have had to eat to reach a fatal dose would have killed them through sheer over-eating long beforehand. Moreover, the original World Health Organization study of the effect on the thatched roofs found that the slight inconvenience to the villagers and their architecture was more than offset by the welcome benefit of malaria reduction. Every part of the story is exaggerated to the point of absurdity, yet it is presented routinely by the Kerrys and their ilk as conclusive evidence that DDT is uniquely evil amongst chemicals.

The liberal campaign against DDT provides an excellent example of why the liberal approach to the environment is so dangerous. Not only did it have direct effects related to its primary use, against the spread of malaria, and not only are their arguments in defense of the ban vapid, but they also ignore the collateral damage inflicted on the environment itself, never mind humanity. DDT, you see, was a primary weapon in the fight to save trees.

Treehuggers Against Trees

Dutch elm disease has ravaged the flora of most of the developed world. Possibly originating in the Himalayas, it was first noticed in the Netherlands in the 1920s. In 1930, it reached the United States. Wherever the disease has taken hold it has had a savage impact on native populations of elms, whether they be the majestic American elm or the noble English elm. The disease itself is a fungus, which kills a young elm in one or two months and older, established elms in a couple of years unless rapid and continuous corrective measures are taken.

The main way by which the disease is spread (its "vector" in the language of the disease specialists) is via bark beetles. These beetles look for dead or weakened elm wood, into which they then burrow, creating a space under the bark to lay their eggs. If the fungus is already there, massive amounts of fungal spores are produced in these spaces, which are then picked up by the hatched beetles and carried to other trees that the beetles feed on.

It should therefore be apparent that the best way to control the spread of Dutch elm disease is to control the beetles that spread it. That's exactly what happened in the United States in the 1940s, and the main control agent was DDT. As my colleague John Berlau summarizes in his book *Eco-Freaks: Environmentalism Is Hazardous To Your Health:*[14]

> Starting in the late '40s, dedicated foresters and groundskeepers in communities across America began spraying DDT on elms with amazing results. Not only were the trees unharmed by the DDT, but the beetles stopped attacking them nearly so much. It looked like the elms would survive and prosper—thanks to DDT.

Yet it was not to be. In the 1960s, a new fungus appeared. Early attempts to control the disease repeated the successful strategy of the 1940s by using DDT. However, after the publication of Carson's screed, DDT use declined considerably. Berlau relates the story of Yarmouth, Maine, whose "tree warden," Frank Knight, would spray the town's seven hundred elms root and branch with DDT every year. During the time he was allowed to do this, Mr. Knight lost only one tree to Dutch elm disease. However, as Berlau relates:

> [O]ne spring in the mid-1960s, when Knight was on vacation, an antipesticide activist influenced by Rachel Carson's 1962 book convinced the town council to stop spraying. The next year, the beetles destroyed one hundred elms. "When we didn't spray, we just lost them wholesale," Knight recalls sadly.

It was the same story across America. In 1967, a new group of well-heeled professionals, mostly lawyers, calling themselves the Environmental Defense Fund sued municipalities across America to stop using DDT to combat Dutch elm disease and were successful in fifty-five of them.[15] They also succeeded in persuading the Michigan Department of Natural Resources to cancel DDT usage across the state. This was actually the start of the DDT ban bandwagon described above.

DDT's usual replacement in protecting elms, methoxychlor, was much less effective. Several studies found no difference between Dutch elm disease spread in communities that sprayed and did not spray with the new insecticide. This may have been at least partly due to the fact that methoxychlor appears to be ineffective against the native elm bark beetle (although the more common European elm bark beetle is the main vector for the disease). DDT had no such compunctions.

Dutch elm disease was a global problem. In the UK, sources at the Forestry Commission told me that DDT was the benchmark against which pesticides were judged for effectiveness during the epidemic there in the 1960s, but that it was too environmentally and politically unacceptable to use itself. The other pesticides were all less effective and more expensive.

As Richard Campana summarizes:[16]

The loss of DDT for control of insect pests of shade trees and ornamental plants was a special blow to arboriculture. Perhaps most seriously affected were extensive and intensive control programs of Dutch elm disease and gypsy moth. Despite assurances from pest control authorities, none of the alternatives proposed could match the effectiveness of DDT against a wide variety of insect problems. This had a demoralizing impact on arborists, commercial and municipal, that led in time to the virtual abandonment of control programs for Dutch elm disease and other insect pests. Of even greater significance, the ban on DDT became the symbol for igniting the pesticide controversy as a dominant public issue that continues today.

The American elm was devastated. Perhaps Mrs. Kerry should reflect more deeply on her statement, "Much of what we do in life is not intended to come out the way it does." More than half of all elms in the United States have been destroyed, thanks to the concerns of environmentalists. In towns across America, the shade provided on so many streets has gone—a real *Nightmare on Elm Street.*

Environmentalism's Founding Myth

Not only was Carson the forerunner of Michael Moore and Al Gore in the faux documentary stakes, but she invented the environmental alarmist strategy that has been so successful in pushing a radical liberal agenda. As such, her paradigm has been disastrous for rational political discourse. It is a template for bypassing debate and ignoring consequences. Here's how it works.

First, identify your cause and the laws you want to see enacted. Like a horse wearing blinders, some liberal environmentalists can only see the problem directly before them. Other problems, connected problems, and complex dynamics are blocked from their view. At this point, a simple syllogism kicks in. For Rachel Carson, the syllogism was: (a) government should protect the environment; (b) banning DDT will save the lives of birds; therefore, (c) government should ban DDT.

The collateral damage caused by the DDT ban—such as the impact DDT restrictions had on malaria control or on arboreal life—is off to side, and the blinders keep them out of view.

We are currently seeing this principle in action in the push to reduce greenhouse gases at any cost—even burning corn, stunting the development of poor nations. Environmental action is all upside to the liberal environmentalist, no downside.

Second, create an apocalyptic scenario. The whole point of Carson's *Silent Spring*, embodied in the title, was to paint a picture of a world without avian life—that is, a world without birdsong. This simple, evocative message horrified readers, shocking them on a visceral level. Environmentalist-stoked fears about "Frankenfoods" resulting from out-of-control biotechnology follow this model. If Prometheus had had a liberal environmentalist as a neighbor, he would have been spreading tales about how Prometheus' secret of fire would burn the entire world to the ground.

Third, claim there's a threat to children. For those unmoved by fears of a birdless world, this should suffice. Carson said in her book that, "A quarter century ago, cancer in children was considered a medical rarity. Today, more American school children die of cancer than from any other disease." Her statistics were misleading—the actual rate of cancer among children is unchanged since the 1900s, but cancer's incidence relative to other diseases has increased as medical technology has vanquished many of those other diseases. If it takes a village to raise a child, at least one whole street is populated by shrill scolds warning the other villagers about how their actions might affect the child's development.

Fourth, don the mantle of science and dismiss any evidence that contradicts your position. Carson used statistics and scientific data to provide a seemingly empirical basis for her alarmist claims. As we have seen, she misstated the science repeatedly. Yet evidence doesn't matter; the authority of simply *claiming* to represent science "proves" action is needed. Even hotly disputed scientific claims can provide a seemingly invincible case when asserted in the right way. In a world increasingly devoid of moral authority, the supposed impartiality of science provides a seemingly objective source of authority. Yet it is little more than stolen lightning; science and statistics can be twisted to back up virtually any position or policy stance.

Fifth, use the previous four steps to create a clamor that rules out rational debate. With a potential catastrophe, a threat to the innocent, and a ream of supposedly empirical data on your side, you have a recipe for urgent action—though one based on emotion and uncritical acceptance of assertion. Public policy is not (nor should it be, when you stop and think about it) a rational process—emotion and acceptance of authority often drive it—so in recognition of that, modern democracies have created checks and balances to ensure that factors like emotion and prejudice don't stampede over other considerations. Yet, as the case of DDT shows, the alarmist model can often overcome these checks. If you can also destroy the credibility of your political opponents through ad hominem attacks, so much the better.

Finally, once your measures have been adopted, defend them ruthlessly. The alarmist model relies on its successes being unassailable. Critical examination threatens to reveal measures advanced by alarmists may be unwarranted, ineffective and, in many cases, positively harmful. Once one such measure is repealed, people may think twice about passing more like it. The techniques of ad hominem attack and appeals to emotion are once again central here. Rational discussion of an irrational policy is bound to lead to people realizing its weaknesses, so the liberal environmentalist can never allow that to happen. The opponent of the policy must be smeared as an evil polluter, a tool of big business, the bastard son of Sauron and Cruella De Ville.[17] The great advantage of such an approach is that it puts your opponents on the defensive, forcing them to refute the allegations rather than concentrate on the argument at hand. We'll see an excellent example of this later.

Chapter Two

Ethanol

Save the Planet, Starve the World

The streets of Mexico City were mobbed. An estimated 75,000 people marched, chanted, and carried banners. The target: the skyrocketing price of tortillas. Yet the target should have been American liberal environmentalists and their allies in big agribusiness.

Tortillas are a staple of the Mexican diet, especially for the poor-to-middle class. The flat breads are made from corn, the price of which had risen dramatically in recent months.

The result was a rapid price increase in a kilo of tortillas, from 63 cents in January 2006 to $1.81 a year later. It was a gut-punch to the lifestyle of many Mexican families. The *Washington Post* described the scene in Aurora Morales's tortilla shop in Nezahualcoyotl, Mexico, where Morales had been forced to increase her prices:

[A] 73-year-old woman named María Neri approached the counter. Neri has no pension and no savings, but she gets a few

pesos each month from a nephew and a daughter. She lives just
around the corner from Rosales's tortilla shop and has been buy-
ing two kilos a week for years. On this day, even with the Mexican government's new price control, she could afford only one.

The Mexican government, forgetting decades of economic
experience, imposed price caps, which have been largely ignored.
As the *Post* reported:

> With a minimum wage of $4.60 a day, Mexican families with
> one wage earner have been faced in recent months with the
> choice of having to spend as much as a third of their income
> on tortillas—or eating less or switching to cheaper alternatives.
>   Many poor Mexicans, [Mexican nutrition expert Amanda]
> Gálvez said, have been substituting cheap instant noodles,
> which often sell for as little as 27 cents a cup and are loaded
> with less nutritious starch and sodium.
>   "In the short term, the people who can buy food are going
> to get fatter," she said. "For the poor, the effect is going to be
> hunger."

So what had caused this dietary devastation? The Mexicans
knew full well:

> There is almost universal consensus in Mexico that higher
> demand for ethanol is at the root of price increases for corn
> and tortillas.

Given the cultural importance of tortillas, the effect of the
price rise has been destabilizing. Street vendors have been
accused of profiteering. The government has been accused of col-
lusion with big business interests. Tortilla makers have seen their
sales plummet. With more likely to come as a new congressional

mandate for more ethanol from corn sends prices ever higher, the prospect of food riots in America's southern neighbor becomes more likely. The prospects for pressure on the southern border should be clear. What is bad news for Mexico is certainly bad news for America in this case.

Many factors affect commodity prices, but here, the price of white corn (used to make the tortilla flour) rose in conjunction with the price of yellow corn. Arturo Puente, an economist at Mexico's National Institute for Forestry, Agriculture and Livestock Research, explained that "the price of white corn, which is used to make tortillas, is indexed in Mexico to the international price of yellow corn," according to the *Washington Post*.

Yellow corn was spiking internationally, not thanks to increased appetites for corn on the cob or even corn-fed cattle, but for the simple reason that Americans were increasingly burning the corn in their car engines.

U.S. ethanol consumption was causing tortilla chaos in Mexico. The cause of the ethanol consumption: central planning and environmentalism, including Al Gore's crusade against CO_2.

Tortilla consumers are far from the only victims, but liberals' appetite to push ethanol on U.S. consumers is growing.

Hating Oil

Liberal environmentalists hate the internal combustion engine. They despise the carbon dioxide it produces, the consumption of resources involved in its creation, and, it seems, the mobility it gives people and the goods they purchase. In 1992, Al Gore wrote of the need to establish "the strategic goal of completely eliminating the internal combustion engine over, say, a 25-year period."[1]

Fifteen years on, this goal looks as unachievable as it did when Gore wrote it, and so the liberals have changed tactics—somewhat. They have attacked the fuel source instead of the engine.

Gasoline is now the big enemy, a product that is uniquely evil both in its planet-destroying properties and its ability to start wars. Oil, then, provides the perfect common villain for the anti-American caucus of the Left and the environmentalists.

The idea that Americans only fight wars when their energy sources are under threat is one that has gained currency in liberal circles around the world. The cry of "No blood for oil!" was heard repeatedly during the run-up to the Iraq war. They point to the fact that major Republican figures have ties with the energy industry, such as Vice President Cheney's time as chairman of Halliburton. They insinuate or outright assert that the Iraq War was therefore fought in order to personally enrich senior Republican figures.

The argument has some lovely internal contradictions. They sometimes contend that the war was all about raising prices, thereby increasing their cronies' earnings. On the other hand, they say the war was about opening up Middle Eastern oil fields to U.S. markets, which, of course, would have downward pressure on prices.

Sometimes they point out that rising prices enrich the president's enemies in terror-sponsoring nations. Sometimes they argue that the president's friends in terror-sponsoring nations reduce their prices as a political favor to the GOP.[2] Whichever way prices go, it seems, the president benefits in some way from a "war for oil."

So antiwar activists have joined the environmentalists in a push for less oil burned in the nation's automobiles. Of course, gas taxes are unpopular, so they had to come up with another way to reduce our consumption of oil. Giant agribusinesses, which spend millions on lobbying Washington, offered the environmentalists one idea: corn ethanol.

Ethanol is a fuel just like gasoline. It can be burned to provide energy. It gives off fewer carbon emissions than gasoline, though, and is therefore to be favored by environmentalists. It can be made in several different ways, but the two most cost-effective ways to make it are from corn and from sugar. We'll come back to sugar later, but for the moment, we'll look at the corn ethanol industry that dominates in the United States.

Converting corn into ethanol has been done for most of mankind's history. It is, after all, the basis of much of the world's alcohol. Backwoods moonshine outfits in the Appalachian region of this country were, for centuries, a leading source of American ethanol. Industrial-scale production of corn ethanol as a fuel source, however, has happened only recently. It got its first big boost as a gasoline additive.

After environmental scientists decided that the lead that was added to gasoline to help engine performance was responsible for a variety of ill effects, and under government pressure, refiners traded out the lead for a substance called Methyl Tertiary-Butyl Ether, more commonly known as MTBE. From 1992 to 2006 MTBE was the primary oxygenate added to gasoline. However, MTBE was soon declared evil, as well. Gradually throughout the 1990s, environmentalists identified MTBE contamination of the environment following large gasoline spills and leaks of underground storage tanks at gas stations.

These activists alleged that MTBE was harmful to human health, despite the fact that it has never been classified as a carcinogen. It causes kidney lesions in animals at high doses. Also, it is an emulsifier, which means it makes other elements in gasoline—such as benzene, which is certainly harmful—more soluble, thus potentially increasing the possibility of health risks. On the basis of this slim evidence, the environmentalists began a campaign to ban MTBE. California and New York, to no one's great surprise, led the way, banning the substance from January 1, 2004. Those two states represented 40 percent of the market for MTBE.

Lead and MTBE now dubbed *bad*, the gasoline industry needed a new additive, and ethanol seemed the most suitable.

Ethanol, however, is expensive to produce. Corn must be planted, grown, and weeded. It must be gathered, ground, fermented, distilled, and transported. Almost all water must be removed from it before it can be used as a fuel, because otherwise it will separate out from the gasoline blend, settle at the bottom of the tank, and cause the engine to stall. This causes problems in transportation. It cannot be moved by pipeline and therefore must be moved by truck. It's easy to see that a lot of energy goes into getting a gallon of ethanol to market.

Once it's in your car, it turns out, ethanol is not as powerful as gasoline. The Department of Energy reports that a gallon of ethanol has only about two-thirds the energy content of a gallon of gasoline.[3] If my Saturn goes twenty-six miles on a gallon of gasoline, a gallon of ethanol would only take me seventeen and a half miles.

These high energy inputs (farming, distilling, transporting) combined with the low energy outputs, means it only yields about 34 percent more energy than was spent to make it.[4]

Because of the narrow margins, ethanol producers have demanded subsidies from the Federal Government. They got them in spades. As agronomist Dennis Avery sums it up:

> The real cost of U.S. ethanol must include the government subsidies to corn farmers, which USDA has recently estimated at more than $5 billion per year for about 12 billion bushels of corn annually. That is more than 40 cents per bushel, paid not just by consumers of corn but by *all* American taxpayers. In addition, refiners enjoy a federal excise tax forgiveness of 51 cents per gallon. Finally, the U.S. offers ethanol tariff protection from low-cost (Brazilian) imports of 2.5 percent—plus 54 cents per gallon. The refiner subsidy alone is equal to oil at $32 a barrel. Clearly, Congress was not trying to protect the public from high ethanol prices.[5]

The taxpayer is already paying through the nose for the privilege of having a less efficient fuel source added to his gasoline. It doesn't stop there, though.

In addition to the massive subsidies, ethanol producers have another little present from the Feds. Gasoline producers are *mandated* by law to buy a certain amount of their product. Under the Energy Policy Act of 2005, manufacturers must buy 4 billion gallons of the moonshine per year, rising to 7.5 billion gallons by 2012. That's why your gas pumps now say "contains up to ten percent ethanol." The Energy Independence and Security Act of 2007 went much further, massively increasing the mandate to 36 billion gallons by 2022, of which 15 billion would come from corn-based ethanol. That's despite current U.S. production capacity only being around 5.6 billion gallons. Ethanol producers are therefore eagerly applying for subsidies to build new plants, which state-level politicians quite happily provide.

Ethanol is clearly a gravy train for the producers. If the government pays you to produce something and then tells your customers they must buy it, you don't really have to do much except sit back and collect the checks.

This would be objectionable to any believer in the free enterprise system even if those were the only problems associated with corn ethanol. Yet corn ethanol is not just a pork boondoggle of epic proportions, but—as is so often the case with central planners' big ideas—it is shaping up to be an environmental and humanitarian disaster.

Burning Food

The primary use of corn up to now has been as a foodstuff, for man and for the animals he raises for food purposes. Given the recent demand for ethanol as a fuel additive, however, farmers have rapidly been turning away from raising corn to feed people and towards raising corn to fill gas tanks and collect subsidies. This has brought significant problems.

Corn is at the base of the food chain in many ways. It feeds us directly. It feeds the animals we raise to slaughter and eat. It feeds the animals we raise to provide us with milk and other dairy products like cheese, cream, and yogurt. Increasingly (and thanks to other harmful big-government programs), it has provided us with sweeteners for our treats and soft drinks in the form of corn syrup. Corn provides us with alcohol to drink after we have eaten our food. ABC News found that the price of virtually every ingredient in a slice of pizza is affected by the price of corn in some way.[6]

So, when farmers are converting corn into ethanol rather than using it for food production, there is only one thing that can happen: food prices go up across the board. As the congressional mandate calls for increasing corn ethanol use, food production is likely to suffer even more as the years go on. According to projections from the U.S. Department of Agriculture, the year 2007 will have seen farmers plant 90.5 million acres with corn: 12.1 million acres more than they did in 2006.[7] The Agriculture Department further projects that by 2016-17, ethanol will account for 31 percent of the corn crop, compared with just 14 percent in 2006.[8]

When farmers are planting more corn for ethanol, it's not only corn-for-food that gets crowded out. There is only so much farm acreage in this country. Corn for ethanol will increasingly displace acreage used for soybeans, cotton, and barley. Products based on those crops will also increase in price. For instance, the USDA predicts a drop of 8.4 million acres in soybean planting in 2007—11 percent of the total soybean acreage.

The price increase won't just affect grains. As the International Monetary Fund wrote:

Higher prices of corn and soybean oil will also likely push up the price of partial substitutes, such as wheat and rice, and other edible oils, and exert upward pressure on meat, dairy, and poultry prices by raising animal rearing costs, given the predominant use of corn and soymeal as feedstock, particularly in the United States (more than 95 percent). Furthermore, since corn is more energy intensive than soybean in production, high crude oil prices could also raise corn production costs.[9]

That's why high prices for corn translate into high prices for cereals, canned fruits and vegetables, snacks, juices and sodas, and much else besides.

The effect on food prices has already been seen. The livestock and poultry industries normally purchase over half the corn raised in the United States. With their supply curtailed, feed prices rose by 40 percent over the summer months of 2007. So, for example, the price of eggs followed, rising by 48 percent over one year:

Wholesale egg prices averaged $1.05 per dozen in the first quarter of 2007, compared with 71.4 cents a dozen a year ago and 89.0 cents in the fourth quarter of 2006. The almost-48-percent price rise in the first quarter of 2007 over the previous year largely reflects higher costs of corn and soybean meal.[10]

Grocers are not happy. In fact, the industry's trade group, the Grocery Manufacturers' Association, has called on congress to rethink its policies. Its president, Cal Dooley, said on May 18, 2007:

We urge Congress and the Administration to undertake a comprehensive study that evaluates the full impact—including any and all unintentional consequences—of expanding the use of biofuels. Such a study will enable policymakers and the public to make fully informed decisions when it comes to our nation's energy policy.

The grocery industry's worries are unsurprising. Far more surprising is the relative silence of the liberal "hunger" lobby. Grocery price rises affect the poor more than other classes for the simple reason that the poor spend a greater proportion of their income on food.

"Hunger" groups are typically a hypersensitive bunch, getting outraged about anything that might increase what they term "food insecurity." For instance, in 1991, the Survey of Childhood Hunger categorized a child as "hungry" if his parents answered "yes" to the question: "Did you ever rely on a limited number of foods to feed your children because you were running out of money to buy food for a meal?" This dubious methodology resulted in a commonly quoted figure of 11.5 million hungry children in America.[11] That's one in every four children. Of course, the real number is substantially lower than that, but if liberal activists are happy to use that number, you might expect them to be outraged by a substantial increase in grocery prices caused by ethanol.

That doesn't seem to be happening. America's Second Harvest—which issues alarmist reports about the extent of hunger in America—had no mention of ethanol on its Web site before late October 2007, when it put out a statement reading, "America's Second Harvest takes no position on ethanol use, nor do we suggest any linkages between ethanol and hunger."[12]

Search the Web site of Action Against Hunger, and you won't find the word "ethanol." The Food Research and Action Center mentions it in its news digest pages, but nowhere else. Bread For The World, to its credit, has expressed concern over ethanol, but mostly obliquely.

Given the large rises in the price of food over the past year (4.8 percent in the U.S. and 4.3 percent in Europe),[13] this silence is inexcusable from hunger advocacy groups. Hunger, while less endemic than some advocates make out, is a serious problem in the United States and needs to be tackled. Congressional mandates that increase hunger are particularly offensive, and rather than reacting with proposals to increase welfare, as is likely to be the case when people finally wake up to the ill effects of this ethanol scandal, it would be helpful for hunger advocates to call for the end of ethanol subsidies altogether.

In fact, the ethanol boondoggle is not just increasing hunger in America, but it is causing prices to rise all over the world. As discussed at the beginning of this chapter, one of the first casualties of the 2005 ethanol mandate was the Mexican tortilla. As the *Washington Post* reported as early as January 2007,[14] the rising price of white American corn had led to a rise in the price of yellow Mexican corn.

Nor is Mexico the only country to suffer. In China, pork occupies the cultural space the tortilla does in Mexico. It is central to the nation's cuisine. Yet, ironically in the Year of the Pig, accelerated use of ethanol has driven up feed prices and caused an acute shortage of pork. This is rattling the entire economy, as the *New York Times* reported in June 2007:[15]

> The most recent statistics from the agriculture ministry show that prices for live pigs rose 71.3 percent in April compared with the same month a year earlier, while pork prices climbed 29.3 percent in April from March. The price of pork followed pig prices higher in May as well, to the dismay of shoppers. . . .
>
> And just as higher gasoline prices can lead to a political reaction in the United States, the Chinese government is particularly worried about soaring pork prices because of their

impact on household budgets and the way they can exacerbate income inequality.

Pork is a critical source of protein for Chinese of all incomes, but particularly for low-income workers like those who keep American and European families well supplied with $49 DVD players and other popular consumer products.

And in Indonesia, in January 2008, a mob 10,000 strong took to the streets of Jakarta demanding that their government do something about the price of soybeans, inflated by the rush to biodiesel.

Fueling Famine

As damaging as the effects are in successfully developing nations like China and Mexico, ethanol hits much harder in the very poorest of the world. The misplaced desire to reduce carbon dioxide emissions by burning food instead of gasoline exacerbates famine. Many African nations are dependent on help from the United Nations' World Food Program, one of the United Nations' more effective agencies. Even that organization has seen a crisis develop as a direct result of the United States' ethanol foolishness.

The Program's executive director, Josette Sheeran, says that ethanol-fueled spikes in food prices have made it much more difficult for the organization to carry out its mandate. Purchasing costs have risen by 50 percent in the last five years, and the price it pays for corn rose by 120 percent in the six months prior to July 2007:[16]

Rising prices for food have led the United Nations programme fighting famine in Africa and other regions to warn that it can no longer afford to feed the 90m people it has helped for each of the past five years on its budget.

The World Food Programme feeds people in countries including Chad, Uganda and Ethiopia, but reaches a fraction of the 850m people it estimates suffers from hunger. It spent about $600m buying food in 2006. So far, the WFP has not cut its reach because of high commodities prices, but now says it could be forced to do so unless donor countries provide extra funds.

Josette Sheeran, WFP executive director, said in an interview with the *Financial Times*: "In a world where our contributions are holding fairly steady, this [cost increase] means we are able to reach far less people."

She said policymakers were becoming more concerned about the impact of biofuel demand on food prices and how the world would continue to feed its expanding population.

She went on to make an even starker warning: "We are no longer in a surplus world."

To be sure, we should not worry too much about agriculture's capacity to adapt to feed the world in the medium-to-long term. As fast as population grows, food production has always grown faster. As Action Against Hunger puts it, "The growth curve of food availability in the world continues to be higher than the increase in population, even in developing countries."[17]

Crop yields have increased substantially in the developed world over the past hundred years and will continue to do so all over the world as biotechnology and improved management techniques spread. Farmers will be able to grow food next year in places that last year were considered inhospitable. We also will get more per acre than we currently do in the best of circumstances.

However, in the short-to-medium term, for those who are suffering from genuine hunger as a result of the chronic misgovernment and wars that have plagued the developing world, the biofuels push is causing even more problems.

When Britain's premier automotive reporter, the curmudgeonly Jeremy Clarkson, arrived in Los Angeles for a motor show in April 2007, he was picked up in an "eco-limo." The driver, Clarkson related, proudly and at length expounded his scientific knowledge, telling Clarkson that the vehicle ran on fuel from "a bio-plant." Yet Clarkson knew exactly how to end the tedium:

> "But," I said, "you don't mind leaving all the world's normal oil in the ground and running your car on what could be an African's lunch?" Bzzz went his head. Then he twitched a bit. For a while he looked a bit like a sci-fi robot that had been given conflicting orders.[18]

The "eco-limo" that is making such a contribution to the world hunger problem gets sixteen miles to the gallon.

Recipe for Disaster

Yet even as the biofuels craze contributes to a short-term humanitarian disaster, it is also contributing to longer-term environmental disaster, which is precisely what it was supposed to avert. In three main areas—biodiversity, land use, and the atmosphere—it is causing major disruption.

Long ago, the environmental movement latched on to the idea that large animals, preferably cuddly (like the panda) or symbolic (like the American Bald Eagle) made great fundraisers. These "charismatic megafauna" were incredibly useful to them as long as their numbers were declining. How could anyone want to see a world without a panda, or an America without its national symbol? The polar bear has recently leapfrogged (that'd be an endangered tree frog) those other two animals as the endangered symbol *de nos jours*, presenting a misleadingly cuddly symbol of a world threatened by melting ice.

That is despite the fact that polar bear numbers are actually increasing and that all populations bar one appear to be unaffected by global warming—sorry, I'm getting ahead of myself. We'll come back to the polar bear later. To return to the matter at hand, if we were looking for an example of charismatic megafauna that would warn the world about the biofuel disaster, it would be the orangutan.

The orangutan is also known as the Wild Man of Borneo. It is a peaceful, highly advanced primate native to the rainforests of Indonesia. Yet it is now very much an endangered species. For years the main threat to the orangutan's natural habitat has been plantations producing palm oil. Palm oil has been a very useful substance, aiding in the manufacture of products as diverse as soap, chocolate, and lipstick. Now, however, there is a push to use it as a new biofuel akin to ethanol: palm oil can be mixed with diesel to make a fuel that emits fewer greenhouse gases and, given its source, makes biodiesel cheaper than ordinary diesel fuel.

So while palm oil has always been a feature of Indonesia's economy, and a lot of the blame for past recklessness with regards to the Orangutan's habitat can be laid at the door of the Indonesian dictator Sukarno and his successors, it is the current demand for biodiesel that is really accelerating the problem. Dr. Ian Singleton, scientific director of the Sumatran Orangutan Conservation Program, told Friends of the Earth:

> We have already lost huge areas of orangutan habitat and tens of thousands of orangutan to the palm-oil industry, and we are losing many, many more as I write. Indonesian newspapers have just reported that a kind of "oil-palm fence," stretching 845 kilometers along the border between Indonesia and Malaysia in Borneo, is to be established, crossing through orangutan habitat. The problem is truly immense.[19]

The new rush for biodiesel is causing a massive land rush in Sumatra and Borneo, the main islands of Indonesia. Is this ravenous capitalism at work? Hardly. On both the supply side and the demand side of the palm oil crisis, the culprit is state control of the economy.

The demand comes from the European Union—and not from its consumers. An EU directive, issued in a desperate attempt to come close to meeting greenhouse gas targets set by Kyoto, mandates that Europe replace at least 10 percent of its auto fuel with biodiesel by 2020.

Eager to supply the continent with the now-mandatory biodiesel, the Indonesian government has decided that 75,000 square miles of land should be converted to palm oil production by 2020. This allocation is being taken up at a ferocious rate, at least partly because the logging of lumber will be valuable even before the palm oil is manufactured.

Orangutans and other endangered species, such as the Asian elephant and Sumatran tiger, just get in the way of these clearances. They are therefore disposed of by force, as told in the *Guardian*:

> "In reality it's over for the tiger, the elephant and the orangutan," said Mr [Willie] Smits, who founded the Borneo Orangutan Survival Foundation. "Their entire lowland forest habitat is essentially gone already. We find orangutan burned, or their heads cut off. Hunters are paid 150,000 rupiah [$16.60] for the right hand of an orangutan to prove they've killed them."[20]

The Indonesian government claims that no trees are being cut down to provide palm oil space, but no credible conservation group believes this. Land is supposed to be "degraded" before being eligible for palm oil production, but corruption being what it is in the developing world, it appears to be easy to buy a reclassification from virgin forest to degraded land.[21]

Yet the Indonesian government also seems to realize that there is a problem, and has therefore called for subsidies from the developed world to help it meet its own development goals:

> "The Indonesian government simply doesn't have the capability or the capacity to do this alone without the support of the Europeans, the U.S., Japanese, or whoever," said Alhilal Hamdi, chief executive of Indonesia's biofuels development board. "It's no good other countries looking to us to help cut their CO_2 emissions without helping to support us in that effort."

To their credit, environmental groups have condemned the rush to biodiesel for its effects on Indonesian wildlife, yet they fail to realize that they are trying to square a circle. It is the environmental groups and their legislative liberal friends with their mania for subsidies and mandates that let this genie out of the bottle.

The orangutan is being crucified on a cross of green.

The Corning of America

The massive land clearances in Indonesia also provide a preview of what might happen in the United States if the current mandates for ethanol here are allowed to remain in place. The plain fact is that ethanol from corn and from other proposed sources will actually require a huge amount of American wild land to be converted to agricultural use.

Agronomist Dennis Avery of the Hudson Institute served for nearly a decade as Senior Agricultural Analyst with the U.S. Department of State, where he received the national Intelligence Medal of Achievement. He wrote the landmark report for

President Lyndon B. Johnson's National Advisory Commission on Food and Fiber. In 2006 he analyzed the land demands of ethanol mandates for the Competitive Enterprise Institute. His conclusions were sobering.

Dennis pointed out that in 2005, the U.S. harvested 280 million metric tons of corn—about half the world's corn crop and most of the world's corn *exports*. Yet, according to the University of Minnesota, if all of that corn were converted to ethanol, it would displace only about 12 percent of the national demand for gasoline.

This means that if the U.S. were to continue to feed itself and replace 10 percent of gasoline with ethanol, farmers would need to plant 55 million more acres with corn—above and beyond the 80 million acres currently devoted to the crop. That new land devoted to corn alone would be equivalent to half of the state of California.

Where would this land come from? The United States' Conservation Reserve amounts to only 30 million acres, and most of that land is too arid to grow corn. Therefore, in order to meet the ethanol demand, farmers will have to start clear-cutting forest. Unfortunately, forest land is of much poorer quality than crop land. As Dennis says, it is "steeper, dryer, poorly drained or somehow lacking—and therefore low-yielding." It is a reasonable assumption to say that such cleared land would be about half as productive as current cropland, which would mean that the additional land required could total about 110 million acres.

Yet is there even enough forest to cut down? In the major corn states, privately owned forest amounts to just 80 million acres, and most of that is in the northern parts of Minnesota, Wisconsin, and Michigan, where it is too cold currently to mature corn successfully.

Furthermore, there is political pressure on authorities not to permit any more use of energy-intensive nitrogen fertilizers.

Using less effective fertilizers doubles the amount of land needed to grow corn yet again, meaning that 220 million acres of land would be needed.

Now all this land clearance will come at a very high environmental price. Not only do trees absorb carbon dioxide from the air, they provide very important habitats for wildlife. The great plains that are now covered in crop land provided a home for a comparative handful of species, such as bison and prairie dogs. Forests, by contrast, shelter a cornucopia of fauna (like the orangutan). In the Peruvian Amazon, one national park is home to 1,300 plant species, 332 bird species, 131 different kinds of reptiles and amphibians, seventy species of non-flying mammals, and an unknown but substantial number of different bats, flying squirrels, and insects. North American forests are less diverse, but it is sure that clearing them would be devastating to vast numbers of native species.

Corn interests say this assessment of land requirements is overstating the case. They point to rising yields from crop lands. The yield point is certainly true: U.S. corn production went up from 115 bushels per acre in 1986-95 to 138 from 1996-2004. Yet this improvement was achieved at a time of very low costs for energy and materials. Today, the same pressures that are driving up the cost of oil are driving up the cost of diesel, fertilizer, and equipment like irrigation pumps. This means that the upward progress of corn yields is slowing. Moreover, as Avery points out, on recent trends it will take thirty-five years to increase corn yields by 50 percent. Biotechnology may well help out, but the liberal environmental movement is not known for its keenness to help speed the adoption of genetically modified crops (genetically modified human embryos, on the other hand, are quite all right according to their liberal allies).

What about other sources of ethanol? Even environmentalists who recognize the food and clearance problems relating to corn ethanol and biodiesel argue that it is a necessary step along the way to ethanol produced from biomass, like corn stalks, wood chips, and switchgrass. This "cellulosic ethanol" is the holy grail of the alternative fuels movement. Theoretically it provides the opportunity to turn waste into energy. Sadly, the technology is not there. There is no cost-efficient way to turn these materials into fuel on a commercial scale.

That is why they should be regarded as "miracle fuels," because it will take a major breakthrough in science to allow them to fulfill their potential. As the MIT *Technology Review* says:

> [R]esearchers at cellulosic-ethanol companies, national labs, and academic labs are engaged in continuing R&D both in converting biomass into ethanol and in growing more-productive strains of biomass. Right now the conversion is an expensive and water-intensive multistage process. Some groups hope to genetically engineer a single organism to both break down cellulose into simpler sugars and ferment alcohols, thereby simplifying the process. Others are working to improve methods for converting biomass into ethanol using heat and catalysts. . . . And companies such as Celunol are investigating better crops, such as the ancestors of today's sugarcane, that can produce more ethanol per acre. Some researchers have even given up on the idea of cellulosic ethanol, turning instead to sources such as algae for biofuels.[22]

Betting on cellulosic ethanol is betting on this breakthrough. President Bush and Congress seem to think we can pull this off: they have decided that these so far non-existent technologies should provide 21 billion gallons of ethanol by 2020. That's some gamble.

How are these technologies going to be developed? With taxpayer money, of course. President Bush's 2007 budget directed

$150 million at cellulosic ethanol. Various firms have succeeded in severely lowering the cost of enzyme fermentation, down from $5 a gallon to 30 cents. But this is still not enough to make cellulosic ethanol cost-effective. For thirty years we've been told switchgrass is the fuel source of the future. Yet it is as far in the future now as it was when Jimmy Carter made it part of his energy policy in the 1970s.

Oh, and how much land will this switchgrass require? The National Resources Defense Council says a mere 114 million acres. Exactly the same points about land clearance made above apply.

Do NOT Give Us Some Sugar

As it happens, there is a source of ethanol that does not come from U.S.-based corn and which could provide plenty of potential for increasing the ethanol element of gasoline without driving up the price. During the oil crisis of the 1970s, the military dictators of the South American nation of Brazil decided that it should use its own natural resources to reduce its dependence on foreign oil. In the right circumstances, ethanol can be made much more cost-effectively from sugar than it can from corn, and Brazil has an ideal climate for growing sugar. Brazilian land suitable for sugar cultivation is cheap and abundant, and Brazilian wages are much lower than American wages. This means that Brazil produces large amounts of ethanol from sugar.

Brazilian ethanol's production costs far undercut American costs. A Department of Agriculture study in 2006 found that the cost of a gallon of Brazilian sugar-based ethanol was a mere 81 cents.[23] This compares to just over a dollar for American corn-based ethanol (and $2.40 for American sugar-based ethanol).

The lesson from this should be obvious: the United States could import ethanol from Brazil to meet its mandate without sacrificing environmental quality or starving the world. As you might expect, such a common sense solution is just about the last thing likely to be adopted.

The problem is the cooperation between the powerful U.S. sugar industry and the protectionist government in Washington. They have seen the success of the Brazilian sugar ethanol industry and have decided that it could be replicated in the U.S.—with the right amount of subsidies and incentives of course. With such a cheap source of sugar-based ethanol already existing in Brazil (and the industry is rapidly expanding in the Caribbean, where sugar has been the basis of the economy since the early days of the rum trade in the seventeenth century), the U.S. sugar industry also argues that it must be protected from the competition. Subsidies and protectionism are of course central features of traditional left-wing economics, so the sugar industry's stance is unlikely to be challenged.

The sugar industry's position is entrenched. It got its first subsidies as a result of national security arguments following the imposition of sugar rationing during World War II. The industry was further protected by tariffs and import quotas—basically, the federal government keeps out almost all foreign sugar. The result has been a sugar industry able to charge a domestic price for sugar far more than the world market price.

This government-inflated U.S. sugar price is the main reason for the growth of corn syrup as a sweetener in soft drinks and other products. Pick up a can of Coke or Pepsi in most other countries in the world and you'll see sugar on the ingredient list where U.S. bottles list corn syrup. The difference is most of the world can buy sugar from all over the world. Here in the United States, however, we have very little access to that world market. Attempts to reduce sugar subsidies, lower tariffs, or abolish quotas have always failed in the face of massive lobbying from the sugar industry.

What this all means is that the sensible option of importing Brazilian or Caribbean sugar ethanol to help meet the ethanol mandate is unlikely to be taken up. As Dennis Avery says:

> Today, there are strong ethical and environmental reasons not to allow the already generously subsidized and protected U.S. sugar industry to get any part of any ethanol subsidies. Instead, U.S. sugar tariffs and import quotas should be eliminated, so that Brazilian and Philippine ethanol could be imported to help tamp down high gasoline prices.

Yet without anyone willing to take on the vested interests of the sugar industry, the prospects for sugar-based ethanol making a valuable contribution to American gasoline production are anything but sweet.

Biofuels' Noxious Byproducts

So biodiesel kills great apes, cellulosic ethanol doesn't exist, and corn-based ethanol is a gigantic wealth transfer to agribusiness. Yet what about the main argument for biofuels—that they reduce greenhouse gas emissions? This has been the chief justification for governments' pushes towards biofuels around the world.

Politicians may be willing to sacrifice the oranguntan, plow under forests, and spark tortilla riots if it will save us from the cataclysms and plagues global warming (or, more accurately, Al Gore) threaten to bring. Yet it is quite apparent from even a cursory look at the science that biofuels aren't even effective at reducing emissions.

All other things being equal, ethanol emits about a third less greenhouse gas than gasoline. All things, however, are *not* equal. To begin with, remember that ethanol isn't as efficient as gasoline.

This means that for every gallon of ethanol you burn, you get less energy than you would from a gallon of gasoline.

So even if a gallon of ethanol produces fewer emissions than a gallon of gas, the gap narrows the more ethanol you burn. A gallon of gasoline contains 115,000 BTUs of energy. A gallon of ethanol contains 75,700 BTUs.[24] So to get the same energy output as a gallon of gas, you need to burn one and a half gallons of ethanol. If you work through the numbers, that means that using ethanol instead of gasoline entirely might actually increase the amount of greenhouse gas emitted.

That's not the end of it, however. Producing gasoline is actually quite an efficient process. Once you've found it, you simply stick a pump in the ground, suck up oil, refine it and distribute it. Ethanol from corn, on the other hand, requires much more intensive work in planting, growing, weeding, reaping, fermentation, and distribution.

Tractors used in the farming burn gasoline. Some ethanol plants use coal fires to distill the ethanol. Trucks, not pipelines, must be used to distribute the stuff. So every gallon of ethanol already has burned a large amount of fossil fuel in its production.

How much? Cornell ecologist David Pimentel is unequivocal. His studies[25] find that corn ethanol uses 29 percent more fossil fuel energy in its production than it replaces. This is like someone charging you 29 cents to replace an old dollar bill with a new one. Other forms of ethanol are even worse. Switchgrass uses 45 percent more fossil energy, wood biomass 57 percent. As for biodiesel, soybeans are about the same as corn ethanol, using 27 percent more fossil energy, while sunflower plants require a staggering 118 percent more fossil fuel energy to produce than they replace. It's not exactly a good investment.

What does all this mean for greenhouse gases? It means that every gallon of corn ethanol has already had 1.3 gallons of gasoline worth of greenhouse gases emitted in its production. Add to that the emissions that still come from a gallon of ethanol, and one gallon of ethanol is actually responsible for the emissions of about two gallons of gasoline. Certainly, there's a small CO_2 reduction when the next bushel of ethanol corn is planted, grows, and absorbs some CO_2 from the atmosphere but all the energy used in planting, harvesting, and transforming that next bushel to ethanol is additional.

Not all agronomists agree with Prof. Pimentel, but even among those who think that ethanol actually produces more energy than it requires in its manufacture, ethanol doesn't escape environmental censure. Marcelo Dias de Oliveira and his colleagues conclude:

> The use of ethanol as a substitute for gasoline proved to be neither a sustainable nor an environmentally friendly option considering ecological footprint values, and both net energy and CO_2 offset considerations seemed relatively unimportant compared to the ecological footprint.[26]

It isn't looking good for biofuels, is it? Yet the story doesn't stop there. The massive land clearances we looked at above are themselves responsible for releasing greenhouse gases into the atmosphere, because trees store carbon. Taking this into account, Renton Righelato of the World Land Trust calculated that increased use of biofuels would release between two and nine times as much greenhouse gas into the atmosphere as fossil fuels would.[27] He told the conservation Web site mongabay.com:

> For reducing carbon dioxide in the atmosphere, maintaining our forests and restoring them is much more effective than using land for biofuels. When forest is destroyed more CO_2 is lost than can be saved in 50 years or more through producing biofuels on the cleared land.[28]

As for the United States, researchers found that ethanol, whether from corn or switchgrass, produced more carbon dioxide emissions than it saved:

> Using a worldwide agricultural model to estimate emissions from land use change, we found that corn-based ethanol, instead of producing a 20% savings, nearly doubles greenhouse emissions over 30 years and increases greenhouse gases for 167 years. Biofuels from switchgrass, if grown on U.S. corn lands, increase emissions by 50%.[29]

Moreover, that conclusion doesn't even consider the costs to the environment in terms of biodiversity. More forests, such as those that sprang up after the Green Revolution increased crop yields, provide more habitat for species. Fewer forests, as would be the case in a biofuel-centered world, mean fewer species. The environmental case against the liberal push for biofuels is rock solid.

So is the economic case. The Paris-based Organization for Economic Cooperation and Development released a report in summer 2007 called *Biofuels: Is the Cure Worse than the Disease?* [30] It concluded:

> Realistically, biofuels might displace 13% of petroleum by 2050. That would reduce energy-related CO_2 emissions 3% below baseline projections. The cost of obtaining these reductions is very high—well over $500 per tonne of CO_2 equivalent for corn-based ethanol in the United States, for example, with other researched countries not performing much better.

Let's recap. The push for biofuels is a victory for liberal economic command-and-control management, with subsidies, mandates, and pork resulting in an agricultural-industrial complex that couples agriculture to government. The government-dictated preference for crops as fuel rather than as food causes higher food prices, resulting in increased hunger in the poorest places and a politically destabilized world. Moreover, wildlife habitat disappears and the benefit in terms of greenhouse gas emissions reduction is at best microscopic and may be entirely illusory. Even green environmentalists are now complaining about it.

It's too late, however. Biofuels are now part of the liberal creed. On July 2, 2007, Hillary Clinton told a crowd in Des Moines, Iowa:[31]

> Now, Iowa is way ahead of the rest of the country. What you've done with ethanol . . . you're setting the pace.

Ethanol is a key part of Hillary's plans for energy and global warming. Barack Obama is alongside her. He supports a further subsidy for E85:—a vehicle fuel that is 85 percent ethanol and 15 percent gasoline—along with additional incentives for the production and sale of ethanol-capable vehicles.

How different this is from 2002, when Senator Clinton said during a Senate energy debate:

> We are providing a single industry with a guaranteed market for its products—subsidies on top of subsidies on top of subsidies and, on top of that, protection from liability. What a sweetheart deal.

That was in the days when subsidies to business were seen as subsidies to capitalist bosses and oppressive employers. Now, however, the ethanol industry is a mainstay of a new economic theory that replaces pretended concern for the worker with pretended concern for the planet. In the liberal world, the theory that biofuels are good triumphs the mountain of evidence that they are not. As with Marxist economics, the new environment-centered economics is a mere justification for a rejection of the free enterprise system. Biofuels will do to the planet what collectivization did to workers in Soviet factories. There is, however, no Radio Free Borneo broadcasting in orangutan.

II.

Blind Faith in the Green God

EcoPaganism

Religion plays a vitally important part in human life. For America, this is especially true, and America's religion, whatever the Founders might have to say about it, has always been Christianity. The Pew Research Center for the People and the Press found in 2004[1] that 71 percent of Americans agreed with all three of these central Christian statements: "prayer is an important part of my daily life," "we will all be called before God on judgment day to answer for our sins," and "I never doubt the existence of God."

For self-identified liberals, however, that figure is only 54 percent. For self-identified liberal Democrats it is just 52 percent. Liberal involvement with traditional religion has been falling for twenty years. In the last year of Ronald Reagan's presidency, 1988, Pew found as many White Evangelical Protestants identified themselves as Democrat as did Republican (33 percent each). By 2004, only 22 percent of such Protestants identified themselves as Democrats (compared to 43 percent Republicans).

Among Roman Catholics, affiliation with the Democratic party fell from 41 percent as recently as 1994 to just 28 percent in 2004.

Human nature abhors a religious vacuum. In any given group of people, you could probably count on the fingers of one foot the number of people who really, really don't believe in any kind of higher power. Sure, you might find a few if you got together a bunch of nuclear physicists or Marxist historians, but in general people feel the need to answer to some sort of higher power.

It is my contention that, just as environmentalism has replaced Marxism as the central economic theory of the Far Left, so too has environmentalism begun to replace liberal Christianity as the Left's motivating religious force. Were it not for the presence of powerful Black protestant churches in the liberal alliance, it might have completely supplanted Christianity already.

The causality works both ways: as a result of its growing influence, the environmental movement has taken on the facets of religion, and the increasingly religious tone has drawn in those thirsty for spiritual gratification, but averse to traditional religions.

Author Michael Crichton was one of the first to explicitly accuse environmentalism of becoming a religion. In a speech to the Commonwealth Club in San Francisco in 2003,[2] he set out why:

Environmentalism seems to be the religion of choice for urban atheists. Why do I say it's a religion? Well, just look at the beliefs. If you look carefully, you see that environmentalism is in fact a perfect 21st century remapping of traditional Judeo-Christian beliefs and myths.

There's an initial Eden, a paradise, a state of grace and unity with nature, there's a fall from grace into a state of pollution as a result of eating from the tree of knowledge, and as a result of our actions there is a judgment day coming for us all. We are all energy sinners, doomed to die, unless we seek salvation, which is now called sustainability. Sustainability is salvation in the church of the environment. Just as organic food is its communion, that pesticide-free wafer that the right people with the right beliefs imbibe.

Crichton's analysis is sound, but perhaps limits itself in its comparison only to Judeo-Christian theology. As anyone who has studied the ancient Indo-European religions, as I have, will know, there are two dominant mythical forces in their cosmologies: the Weather God (Zeus, Jupiter, Thor) and the Earth Mother (Gaia, Ceres, Freya). The Weather God resides in the sky and lashes down rain, hail, and thunder on those who do not propitiate him. The Earth Mother gives her faithful followers her bounty, but when they fail her in some way, she withdraws that bounty in famine. Frequently, the two are married.

Today, both Weather God and Earth Mother are central in the argument over global warming. The atmosphere is to be protected at all costs, its avatar propitiated by the closing of power stations and silencing of internal combustion engines, so that his hurricanes are averted and his beneficent winds drive turbines. The earth is to be worshipped by the returning to her ways, shunning biotechnology and nuclear power, so that she can provide her rewards to the faithful.

These two gods are supported by a variety of hierophants and augurs. What is shameful is that many of these are supposedly scientists. A scientist who says that the atmosphere is warming and this is probably because of certain physical processes is still a scientist. A scientist who goes further, saying the people must take certain acts to avoid disaster, has become instead a priest. It is no coincidence that words like prophet, seer, and sage, historically associated with religious figures, are routinely applied to leading alarmist scientists. The leader of the movement, the sermonizer supreme, Al Gore, is even adoringly referred to by his flock of true believers as The Goracle.[3]

That's the hierarchy. Who makes up the rank and file of the clergy, the hedge-priests as it were? That is where the Internet comes in. The role of a priest is to reveal mysteries, to speak the sooth to the faithful. No one fits this description these days better than bloggers. When some new scientific finding comes out which challenges their worldview, the blogs spring to defend the creed.

Take, for example, the release of a report by Senator Jim Inhofe's staff in December 2007 that chronicled how no fewer than four hundred academics working in the field of climate analysis had cast doubt during the year on the theory of man-made climate catastrophe. Despite the fact that the report contained the researchers' own words, the bloggers sprang to the task of discrediting the report and reassuring the faithful that their creed stood unchallenged.

Taking their cue from hierophant Al Gore, whose office condemned the report on the grounds that "twenty-five or thirty of the scientists may have received funding from Exxon Mobile (sic) Corp,"[4] DeSmogBlog was first to the fray, calling the report "bunk." Its carefully argued summary was that the list was made up of "deniers-for-hire." Forced to concede that many names were not on their usual list of enemies, the blog simply asserted that, "It seems fair to assume that this, too, is an ideologically driven document with no merit whatsoever, either as a piece of research or, even more laughably, a reliable comment on science."[5]

Next up was *Grist* magazine, where Andrew Dessler dismissed the report with a wave of a priestly hand.[6] He said that the report "provides a long list of names of people who disagree with the consensus, and I have no doubt that many on this list are indeed skeptics. The question is: does their opinion matter? Should you revise your views about climate change accordingly? Considering the source, I think we all know the answer to that." Indeed, faith sustains the alarmist. He also noted that Freeman Dyson, the great physicist, had made the list, but said that just as you would not take a sick child to Dyson to heal, so would you not take a sick planet to him either. The fact that no one has ever been in the business of healing planets does not matter in the relaying of this parable.

The list went on. The *American Prospect*'s blog simply contended that Senator Inhofe's staff were "still tirelessly plugging away at global warming denialism," so blaming the messenger rather than dealing with the arguments of the four hundred academics.[7] The blog also called the report "false" and "blatantly misleading." Former Clinton administration appointee Joseph Romm characterized the report as "recyc[ling] unscientific attacks on global warming."[8] When *New York Times* environment correspondent Andrew Revkin, interestingly one of the few reporters who covers the global warming debate even-handedly, mentioned the report on his blog, Romm slammed him for legitimizing it, calling his coverage "amazing" and even went on to suggest that Freeman Dyson was not a serious scientist. That's a bit like saying Tiger Woods isn't a good golfer.

The report was released on December 21, 2007. All those reactions had been posted and disseminated to the faithful by December 22. No one had any need to read the report to make up his own mind. The priesthood had done it for him.

Now religions need to sustain themselves in some way. Membership fees for environmental organizations act as a form of tithe, of course, but there is another form of payment liberal environmentalism extracts from the faithful. We mentioned the idea of carbon offsets as indulgences back in the introduction. For Johann Tetzel, the Dominican friar whose sale of indulgences to pay for the new St. Peter's in Rome annoyed Martin Luther so much, the point of indulgences was clear: "As soon as pennies in

the money chest ring, the souls out of their Purgatory do spring."
We've seen how committed environmentalists are the most likely
buyers of carbon offsets—the faithful, in other words, looking to
cleanse themselves of their sins of emission. At least Tetzel's customers got a uniquely beautiful cathedral out of the deal.

Yet if the offsets racket is pre-Reformation, another aspect of
liberal environmentalism is positively Lutheran.

Not by Works, but by Faith Alone

It was Martin Luther who first, from his reading of the Bible,
advanced the notion that it is not deeds that God loves, but
faith—that even the wicked can be justified in God's eyes through
their faith in Him. It was quite a revolutionary concept, and the-
ological debate about it continues to this day, but it is a creed
that seems to have been adopted wholesale as part of the liberal
environmentalist church.

Take, for instance, the Kyoto Protocol. Since it was signed in
1997, most nations that signed it have ratified it, but not the
United States. Al Gore and Bill Clinton never bothered putting it
before the Senate, in sure knowledge that they would lose the
vote in humiliating fashion. A few days before Gore negotiated
what came to be the final version of the protocol, the U.S. Senate voted 95–0 in favor of a resolution that said the Senate did
not want a treaty that would harm the American economy or
gave large emitters from the developing world like China and
India a free pass. Yet that is precisely what Gore agreed to. The
Clinton-Gore administration spent 801 days sitting on the treaty
before passing the hot potato to George W. Bush. Yet it is Bush
who gets the opprobrium from liberal environmentalists for failing to advance a treaty he neither negotiated nor signed. Clinton
and Gore showed faith, you see, even if their works did not
match their faith.

Now, the Kyoto Protocol committed developed nations to reducing their emissions to a set level by 2012. We know that liberal environmentalists regularly upbraid the United States for failing to match the zeal of the European Union in implementing the Protocol. Yet how have the European Union and the United States performed when it comes to emissions since the signing of the treaty? In his *Politically Incorrect Guide™ to Global Warming*, Christopher Horner revealed the truth:

> Using any benchmark but one, the EU-15's CO_2 emissions have gone up and faster than the United States'. The chart [below] details European CO_2 emissions from 1990 to 2004. Only when they use 1990 as the baseline can they claim superior performance to the U.S.... At some point, one might imagine a chastened Europe would dial the rhetoric down a bit—but not as long as the unquestioning media give them, and their enabling American politicians, a free ride on the issue.[9]

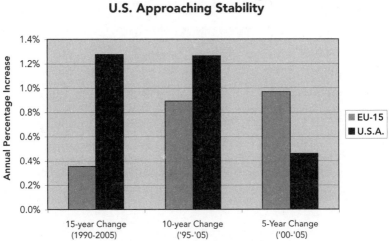

**Greenhouse Gases:
EU Emissions Accelerating,
U.S. Approaching Stability**

So the United States has performed more "good deeds" in terms of slowing emissions growth than the European Union since the declaration of faith that is the Kyoto Protocol. Yet the deeds count for nothing, because they are not done in the name of the faith. Those that fail to perform the deeds called for in the declaration, however, are justified by their profession of faith alone. You can't get much more religious than that.

By the way, it's not just critics of liberal environmentalism that contend that environmentalism has become a religion. *Grist*'s most influential blogger, Dave Roberts, thinks there's some truth in it.[10] He contends that the allegation is "rhetorically brilliant," because it appeals at once to that bugbear of liberals, the "religious right," but also to "the kind of rightie who fancies himself a tough-minded, rational realist." First of all, he says that the second charge has some validity, but doesn't think that's important:

> There's definitely some truth to the second charge—irrationalism—but that doesn't particularly set environmentalism apart. Take any issue on which there are strong feelings—civil rights, abortion, supply-side economics, the Iraq war—and you'll find a group of people for whom it has become a "religion" in that sense. They've made up their mind, it's never going to change, and they interpret all evidence through the heavy filter of their own preconceptions. They have a set of saints, a set of dogmas, a set of holy texts, even various identifying raiments. Environmentalism's been around for a long time, and it's accrued its fair share of such folks.

If that weren't damning enough coming from one of their own, Roberts concedes the first charge as well:

> But there's something more going on with environmentalism, and I think it has to do with the first charge, that environmen-

talism really does involve a form of spiritualism or worship. The graven idol, in this case, is nature itself. Deep ecology is what people have in mind.

Many folks, consciously or subconsciously, view the notion of valuing ecosystems or animals above people as a kind of fundamental *betrayal*. Say what you will about what's best for human beings, what social or political or moral arrangements, but saying human beings just don't *matter* as much as the rest of the natural world is in itself unnatural in some way. We are built—literally, genetically—to value our family first, then a series of overlapping, wider tribes, all the way up to abstractions like "nations." To cast that aside and say our natural setting matters more is viewed by many people, even many who would not consciously cop to it, as perverse, possibly evil.

Roberts says that to counter the allegation, he prefers to argue that environmentalism is in our self-interest, a sort of Pascal's Wager response,[11] and that environmentalism delivers better results than anything else, in itself a reaffirmation of the faith.

Yet there are some who go further than Roberts suggests, and actually have an object of worship.

The Gaia Movement

Animism is a fancy word for a familiar concept. Whenever we imbue an object or concept with the aspects and feelings of a living being, we are animizing it. For instance, if I were to say that a rain cloud looks angry, I'm doing it then. If I say that love showed me my wife the first time I saw her, I'm doing it then. And if I say that the Earth is a living organism, I'm doing it then too.

Amazingly, there are honored and respected scientists who have turned this animization of the Earth into a branch of ecological science. Sir James Lovelock and his followers called their idea,

"The Gaia Hypothesis," and it continues to be an actively debated part of science even though it infuriates many scientists. Back in the 1970s, James Lovelock, now (coincidentally, I'm sure) of Green College, Oxford, had been working on methods to detect life on Mars. He came up with the idea that the Earth and the life it supports are actually a complex system that is best thought of as one single organism. The Nobel laureate author William Golding lived in the same village as Lovelock and often went walking with him. It was Golding who suggested that Lovelock name his theory after the Greek name for the Earth Mother Goddess, Gaia.[12]

Introducing the naming of the concept in his book, *The Ages of Gaia*, Lovelock wrote:

> Most of us sense that the Earth is more than a sphere of rock with a thin layer of air, ocean, and life covering the surface. We feel that we belong here, as if this planet were indeed our home. Long ago the Greeks, thinking this way, gave to the Earth the name of Gaia.

I'll spend some time on Lovelock's views, here, but he is not alone in his quasi-religion. More importantly, many key environmentalists—while they would not agree wholesale with Lovelock—speak and act as if he were right, and the Earth were some sort of higher being.

Scientifically, Lovelock has defined Gaia as:

> A complex entity involving the Earth's biosphere, atmosphere, oceans and soil; the totality constituting a feedback or cybernetic system which seeks an optimal physical and chemical environment for life on this planet.

This is Darwinism taken to its extreme, a sort of survival of the fittest planet. Yet Darwinists themselves find it ridiculous. No lesser figures than Stephen J. Gould and Richard Dawkins have attacked his statement, "the quest for Gaia is an attempt to find the largest living creature on Earth."[13] Gould critiqued the hypothesis as a mere metaphor, wanting to know the mechanism by which the self-regulation Lovelock claims to have identified was actually regulated.

Despite strong scientific criticism, Lovelock has continued to develop his thesis. He accepted Dawkins' critique that global self-regulation could not possibly have evolved, but decided to develop a Darwinian computer model of a simple world covered with plants, which he called "Daisyworld." Lovelock believes that the model provides proof of "the evolution of the organisms and the evolution of temperature as a single, coupled process."[14] He also claims that the model has resisted falsification, and is therefore scientifically valid. James Kirchner, professor of Earth and Planetary Science at the University of California, Berkeley, contends that the model has simply come out with the results the programmers wanted because of the way they programmed it.

Lovelock's tenacity paid off, however. He stepped back a little from claiming that Gaia promotes life intentionally, arguing it was indeed a mere metaphor. With this concession, at a time when concern about man's interaction with the global temperature became overwhelming, it was bound to attract adherents. In 2001 at a global warming conference in Amsterdam, more than a thousand delegates signed on to the statement: "The Earth System behaves as a single, self-regulating system comprised of physical, chemical, biological and human components."

Yet more recently, the teleology—the idea of *intention*—has crept back into Lovelock's work. He has happily taken the global warming scare as evidence of humanity interfering with his beloved system and argued strongly that mankind will suffer as a result. In the tellingly named *The Revenge of Gaia*,[15] Lovelock talks about Gaia burying organic carbon "to keep oxygen at its proper level." He goes further with his animism than ever before, saying that Gaia likes it cool,[16] that Gaia is "angry" with us and that she will "eliminate those that break her rules."

Lovelock could easily be accused of cribbing from the Norse myth of Ragnarok, although preceded this time by a Great Summer rather than a Great Winter. It explicitly describes Gaia as a being that will take revenge on us for our actions. If that isn't the stuff of doom-mongering, I don't know what is.

Many scientists find the current language surrounding the Gaia theory deeply worrying, and well they should. In particular, they are beginning to realize its religious aspects are more than just a metaphor. Instead, they look like the founding doctrines of a new church. Tyler Volk, for instance, from New York University's Department of Biology, wrote in his review of *The Revenge of Gaia* for *Nature* magazine:

> Too often, Gaia here seems less like science and more like one man's mythology elevated into the service of deeply felt environmental concerns. Lovelock likens the incomprehensibility of Gaia to that of God, valorizes those who declare allegiance to Gaia, and claims that Gaia theory is a seed from which an "instinctive environmentalism can grow; one that would instantly reveal planetary health or disease and help sustain a healthy world." What does "instantly reveal" mean?

To anyone who has studied comparative religion, the meaning is obvious. Gaia and the Church of Environmentalism is a "revealed religion," and as such sets itself up in imitation of, and in competition with, the Abrahamic faiths of Christianity, Judaism, and Islam, which all reveal the truths of the world to their faithful. The truth of planetary health is only but instantly available to those who believe in Gaia.

The "cult" of Gaia is widespread. I should say here and now that I do not allege that many people actually *worship* Gaia, with rites, ceremonies, and vestments. Instead, it is a way of thinking about the world that partakes of religious norms. Propitiation of Gaia comes not in the form of libations or human sacrifices, but in the form of economic sacrifices performed out of fear of a non-human entity.

It could be described as a "meme," a unit of cultural information, were it not for the religious elements, especially those relating to propitiation. Those make it something different, something that makes the natural world something to be preserved because it is to be feared. Lovelock makes this clear when he says, "Even now, when the bell has started tolling to mark our ending, we still talk of sustainable development and renewable energy as if these feeble offerings would be accepted by Gaia as an appropriate and affordable sacrifice."[17]

The Gaia idea permeates modern environmentalism. Philosopher William Irwin Thompson views it as the yarn that could stitch together a global culture.[18] Australian global warming alarmist Tim Flannery "leans heavily on the Gaian view of Earth as a self-regulating entity," according to the Sierra Club's own blog.[19] The Natural Resources Defense Council helps sponsor the Gaia Festival, which calls itself an "annual community gathering, focused on Earth-centered spirituality and self-transformation through rhythm, dance, yoga, film and art."[20] The Greens of the Gaia Selene movement believe that the way to save the Earth is to colonize the moon.[21] The Sierra Club, Environmental Defense, and dozens of other non-profits and companies have formed a formidable investment/activism network named Ceres—the Roman goddess of agriculture, the seasons, and the harvest.

The bloggers, of course, use the terms instinctively.

Al Gore's use of the Gaia idea, however, is more insidious. In *Earth in the Balance*, Gore speaks approvingly of the idea in explicitly spiritual tones:

> Lovelock insists that this view of the relationship between life and the nonliving elements of the earth system does not require a spiritual explanation; even so, it evokes a spiritual response in many of those who hear it. It cannot be accidental, one is tempted to conclude, that the percentage of salt in our bloodstreams is roughly the same as the percentage of salt in the oceans of the world. The long and intricate process by which evolution helped to shape the complex interrelationship of all living and nonliving things may be explicable in purely scientific terms, but the simple fact of the living world and our place on it evokes awe, wonder, a sense of mystery—a spiritual response—when one reflects on its deeper meaning.

It is worth reflecting on that for a while, though not in the sense the vice president meant. Mr. Gore toys with intelligent design before rejecting it in favor of evolution and going further along the mystic path. He proceeds to tie the Gaia hypothesis to Christianity in a way that is unsettling for any orthodox Christian:

> If we are made in the image of God, perhaps it is in the myriad slight strands from the Earth's web of life—woven so distinctively into our essence—that make up the "resistance pattern"[22] that reflects the image of God, faintly. By experiencing nature in its fullest—our own and that of all creation—with our senses and with our spiritual imagination, we can glimpse, "bright shining as the sun," an infinite image of God.

For Gore, then, it seems the primary expression of revelation is not Holy Scripture nor the ministrations of the Church, but

Mother Earth. This is practically indistinct from the revealed truth of Gaia espoused by Lovelock. When we look at Gore's current crusades, we see he is advocating sweeping public policy changes dictated directly by this revelation. Someone should call the ACLU.

Revising the Bible

Al Gore is not alone in imposing the tenets of Gaian environmentalism on Christianity. Churches around the world have been quietly revising which parts of the Bible are "relevant" in their quest to be seen as environmentally friendly.

First to go have been verses 28–29 of Genesis, which state, in the majestic language of the King James Version:

> [28] And God blessed them, and God said unto them, Be fruitful, and multiply, and replenish the earth, and subdue it: and have dominion over the fish of the sea, and over the fowl of the air, and over every living thing that moveth upon the earth.
>
> [29] And God said, Behold, I have given you every herb bearing seed, which is upon the face of all the earth, and every tree, in the which is the fruit of a tree yielding seed; to you it shall be for meat.

These are obviously inconvenient for the liberal environmentalist as they imply that God has commanded that we use the Earth and its resources as we see fit to our advantage, "replenishing" it or "subduing" it as needs be.

So certain senior churchmen, my own Anglican/Episcopalian Church featuring prominently of course, have sought to revise the theology surrounding these plain words. The Bishop of Canberra in Australia, head of the Anglican Communion Environmental Network, is quite clear that the meaning does not give mankind dominion over the Earth, saying:[23]

Holy Scripture reminds us that, the earth is the Lord's and everything in it (Psalm 24:1). All of creation belongs to God, not to human beings. We are part of the created order, and our first calling by God is to be stewards of the earth and the rest of creation (Genesis 1:28–29).

So when we exploit God's creation to breaking point, we break the most fundamental commandment known to us: out of our greed and selfishness, we knowingly cause the degradation of the world's ecosystems instead of protecting the design that issues from the Creator's generosity. Willfully causing environmental degradation is a sin.

He goes further:

[I]f Christians believe in Jesus they must recognize that concern for climate change is not an optional extra but a core matter of faith. The Archbishop of Canterbury, Dr. Rowan Williams, has warned that our continued failure to protect the earth and to resolve economic injustices within and between societies will lead not only to environmental collapse but also to social collapse. One of the Millennium Goals was to make poverty history by 2015, but unless we stop climate change, this great aim will be just an empty dream. Indeed without action now, we will assuredly make poverty permanent.

In other words, Genesis suggests that if you are a global warming skeptic, you cannot be a Christian. That's quite a turn around from the traditional interpretation of the passage.

The leader of the global Anglican community, the Primate of All England, His Grace the Archbishop of Canterbury, appears to concur. In what Mark Steyn called "a desperate attempt to cut the Anglican Communion a slice of the Gaia-worship self-flagellation action," he told BBC's *Today* program environment correspondent Roger Harrabin that "coercion" was needed to save *billions* of lives:

> HARRABIN: Do you have a position on this in terms of what the Government's responsibility is, vis-à-vis the changes that will happen in other parts of the word that you mentioned earlier, the floods and the droughts.
>
> ARCHBISHOP OF CANTERBURY: I think this is something in the long run that Government simply has to be brazen out. I mean nobody likes talking about government coercion in this respect—whether it's speed limits or anything else. Nobody, for that matter, likes talking about enforceable international protocols. Yet unless there is a real change in attitude, we have to contemplate those very unwelcome possibilities if we want to the global economy not to collapse and millions, billions of people to die.

And who says Anglicans don't do the whole fire-and-brimstone bit?

The Archbishop also criticized, of course, the American lifestyle as the main threat to those billions of lives:

> ARCHBISHOP: [I]t's a question if you define morality as something which looks beyond just the interests of yourself and your immediate neighbors, then it's, I think, a profoundly immoral policy and lifestyle that doesn't consider those people who don't happen to share the present moment with us...
>
> HARRABIN: When you look at the international situation things are very, very difficult to achieve on an international level because the Americans simply will not agree to any cuts whatsoever. President Bush is a Christian; are his actions compatible with Christian ethics?

ARCHBISHOP: I don't think it's compatible with a Christian ethic to ignore the environmental degradation that we face; it is a long term moral—well not a long term, a medium term—moral question for everyone and therefore a present imperative. It's perfectly true that nearly a quarter of carbon emissions on the face of the globe are attributable to the usage of the United States, and the leadership of the United States has been very slow to catch up with this.

I once appeared in an Oxford Union debate on the same side as the Archbishop when he was the Lady Margaret Professor of Divinity at Oxford University. I found him to be a very intelligent and deeply thoughtful individual. I was so shocked by this exaggeration and willingness to embrace policies that will do such untold harm to the world's poor that I wrote to him as head of my church. I received no acknowledgment, let alone a response.

The Anglican Church isn't alone in its subordination of traditional teaching to the liberal environmental agenda. Even American evangelicals are subtly reinterpreting the Bible to fit to an environmental agenda. Take, for instance, the Rev. Richard Cizik, a charming man I've had the pleasure of meeting, who is vice president of governmental affairs for the National Association of Evangelicals. He told *Grist* magazine what he felt was the basis for Christian environmentalist activism:[24]

It is simply our articulation of a biblical doctrine, which is that we are commissioned by God the Almighty to be stewards of the earth. It is rooted not in politics or ideology, but in the scriptures. Genesis 2:15 specifically calls us "to watch over and care for" the bounty of the earth and its creatures. Scripture not only affirms this role, but warns that the earth is not ours to abuse, own, or dominate. The Bible clearly says in Revelation 11:18 that "God will destroy those who destroy the earth."

Notice no mention of Genesis 1 this time. Yet the reference to Genesis 2 is illuminating, as the paraphrase of "watch over and care for" is at odds with most translations. Here's a sample:[25]

KING JAMES BIBLE:
And the LORD God took the man, and put him into the garden of Eden to dress it and to keep it.

NEW AMERICAN STANDARD BIBLE:
Then the LORD God took the man and put him into the garden of Eden to cultivate it and keep it.

AMERICAN STANDARD VERSION:
And Jehovah God took the man, and put him into the garden of Eden to dress it and to keep it.

BIBLE IN BASIC ENGLISH:
And the Lord God took the man and put him in the garden of Eden to do work in it and take care of it.

DOUAY-RHEIMS BIBLE:
And the Lord God took man, and put him into the paradise for pleasure, to dress it, and keep it.

DARBY BIBLE TRANSLATION:
And Jehovah Elohim took Man, and put him into the garden of Eden, to till it and to guard it.

ENGLISH REVISED VERSION:
And the LORD God took the man, and put him into the garden of Eden to dress it and to keep it.

JEWISH PUBLICATION SOCIETY TANAKH:

And the LORD God took the man, and put him into the garden of Eden to dress it and to keep it.

WEBSTER'S BIBLE TRANSLATION:

And the LORD God took the man, and put him into the garden of Eden, to dress it, and to keep it.

WORLD ENGLISH BIBLE:

Yahweh God took the man, and put him into the garden of Eden to dress it and to keep it.

YOUNG'S LITERAL TRANSLATION:

And Jehovah God taketh the man, and causeth him to rest in the garden of Eden, to serve it, and to keep it.

Not much about "caring for" there, because the text doesn't say that. This is no modern bastardization of the text, either. The oldest Greek translation—from BC—uses the words ἐργάζεσθαι αὐτὸν καὶ φυλάσσειν, which literally means to *work* it and *guard* it, which is exactly what a man does with his private property.

As for the passage in Revelation, yes the text explicitly says God will "destroy those who destroy the Earth," but the context is quite clearly *not* about the environment. It is the context of the return of Christ following the Great Tribulation, the campaigns of the Antichrist and the Battle of Armageddon. It is hard to see how the use of DDT, the release of trace chemicals or a small change in the composition of the atmosphere can be counted as "destroying the Earth" when all that is going on around us. Even the liberal environmentalists at *Grist* seemed quizzical at the Rev. Cizik's citation here, asking, "Do you believe that polluters will literally be destroyed by God?" Cizik's reply continues to ignore the context:

It's very difficult to comprehend the full ramifications of this Bible verse, but I can tell you it's a warning: Destroyers

beware. Take heed. It was by and for Christ that this earth was
made, which means it is sinfully wrong—it is a tragedy of enormous proportions—to destroy, degrade, or despoil it. He who
has ears, let him hear.

One might note Paul's second letter to Timothy, chapter 4,
verse 3 at this point: "For the time will come when they will not
endure sound doctrine; but after their own lusts shall they heap
to themselves teachers, having itching ears. . . . "

There is, however, one major Church that has resisted the pressure to conform to liberal environmentalist doctrine. In his Message for the Celebration of the World Day of Peace 2008, His
Holiness Pope Benedict XVI declared as follows:[26]

We need to care for the environment: it has been entrusted to
men and women to be protected and cultivated with responsible
freedom, with the good of all as a constant guiding criterion.
Human beings, obviously, are of supreme worth vis-à-vis creation as a whole. Respecting the environment does not mean
considering material or animal nature more important than
man. Rather, it means not selfishly considering nature to be at
the complete disposal of our own interests, for future generations also have the right to reap its benefits and to exhibit
towards nature the same responsible freedom that we claim for
ourselves. Nor must we overlook the poor, who are excluded in
many cases from the goods of creation destined for all. Humanity today is rightly concerned about the ecological balance of
tomorrow. It is important for assessments in this regard to be
carried out prudently, in dialogue with experts and people of
wisdom, uninhibited by ideological pressure to draw hasty conclusions, and above all with the aim of reaching agreement on a
model of sustainable development capable of ensuring the well-
being of all while respecting environmental balances.

These are guarded comments in measured tones, as one might expect. Yet their import is clear. The head of the Roman Catholic Church is concerned that liberal environmentalist ideology places animals and "material nature" ahead of humanity. He recognizes that the Earth is there for our use (but not abuse) and that the poor need more access to that resource. His Holiness is also worried that certain decisions, almost certainly those pertaining to the global warming issue, are being taken imprudently under "ideological pressure" from the liberal environmentalist movement. These are sensible pronouncements, all the more remarkable given the way that liberal environmentalists are so adept at exerting moral pressure.

Despite the Pope's comments, the general trend among Christian churches is towards conformity with the liberal environmentalist doctrine. It is sad that some are playing such obviously unsound Biblical reference in aid of this trend, particularly as the liberal environmentalist movement has allied itself closely with forces whose agenda can only be described as anti-human.

Anti-Human

As we saw above, there is a very close relationship between the environmental movement and groups who think there are too many people in the world, amounting to an incestuous relationship in the case of the Sierra Club and Zero Population Growth. We are now beginning to see it at work in global warming alarmism. Chris Rapley, then director of the British Antarctic Survey and a prominent alarmist, wrote the following for the BBC under the headline, "Earth is Too Crowded for Utopia:"[27]

Although reducing human emissions to the atmosphere is undoubtedly of critical importance, as are any and all measures to reduce the human environmental "footprint," the truth is that the contribution of each individual cannot be reduced to zero.

Only the lack of the individual can bring it down to nothing.

That's a chilling conclusion. Rapley believes that the "optimum" size of the Earth's human population is two or three billion—less than half the current population. He also believes, in his new position as director of London's Science Museum, that emissions are not reducing fast enough. He wrote an article for *Science* magazine in September 2007, with James Lovelock, surprisingly enough, that argued that "geo-engineering" fixes were needed to remove carbon dioxide from the air and store it in the oceans. He told the BBC:

> It's encouraging to see how much serious effort is going into technical attempts to reduce carbon emissions, and the renewed commitment to finding an international agreement. . . . But in the meantime, there's evidence that the Earth's response to climate change might be going faster than people have predicted. The dramatic loss of ice in the Arctic, for example, poses a serious concern for the northern hemisphere climate.

Now, if population is a serious concern for the climate and population reduction is part of the solution, what does that mean if the problem is very urgent?

I'm not trying to suggest that Prof. Rapley would be happy to see gas chambers erected all over the world to solve the population "problem," but it does suggest a serious lack of thinking through the problem. If the professor is not going to advocate what the Archbishop of Canterbury might call "coercion" in order to reduce the human population of the Earth, then, by his own lights, any measure introduced will be too slow to have any effect on the climate issue. The question of population and climate is therefore irrelevant, and he should realize that.

Yet the subject of population growth is familiar to many liberals who cut their teeth on it during the 1970s. That was the era of Paul Ehrlich's *The Population Bomb*, a book that attained almost Biblical status on the left and yet which, unlike the Bible, has been proven comprehensively and extensively wrong.

Paul Ehrlich is an entomologist, a bug scientist, who currently holds the position of Bing Professor of Population Studies in the department of Biological Sciences at Stanford University. In 1967 he wrote in *New Scientist*, "the battle to feed all of humanity is over.... In the 1970s and 1980s hundreds of millions of people will starve to death in spite of any crash programs embarked upon now." He added, "India couldn't possibly feed two hundred million more people by 1980," and "I have yet to meet anyone familiar with the situation who thinks that India will be self-sufficient in food by 1971." In 1968 he expanded these thoughts into his bestseller, *The Population Bomb*. His concern for the world led to him being awarded numerous academic prizes and he became a regular guest on *The Tonight Show*. The MacArthur Foundation gave him a "genius grant."

He was, of course, spectacularly wrong. Humanity discovered new ways of feeding and supplying itself, which means that the Earth can easily support a growing population even now. India's population has continued to increase linearly, and is now over 1 billion. Ehrlich's failure was that he did not recognize that use of resources is not simply a matter of arithmetic, but that it involves the human mind performing mental jiu-jitsu to solve seemingly intractable problems. The University of Maryland's Julian Simon, who wrote the book *The Ultimate Resource*,[28] famously challenged him to a bet on future resource availability as demonstrated by the price of metals on the commodity exchange. Simon won. Ehrlich graciously paid up.

Nevertheless, Ehrlich remains wedded to his beliefs. In 2004, when the *New York Times* comprehensively debunked fears of the "population time bomb,"[29] he told the newspaper of record:

> I have severe doubts that we can support even two billion if they all live like citizens of the U.S. The world can support a lot more vegetarian saints than Hummer-driving idiots.

So in order to drive population down, we should move away from the "idiotic" pursuit of liberty and standards of living (ironically, higher standards of living drive population growth down as families become more comfortable with fewer children) and instead return to a "saintly" agrarian lifestyle (which, in fact, drives population *up* as more manual labor is needed and children are the best source of it)? The man truly is a genius.

Now who is the latest to raise the issue from the generation whose well-thumbed copies of *The Population Bomb* presumably lay on the floor as they experimented with not increasing the population? Step forward former president William Jefferson Clinton. During the early stages of his wife's campaign for the presidency, he made several references to the subject, explicitly tying it to the environment. In April 2007 he delivered a speech at Harvard, where he said the following:[30]

> I think it is highly likely that before we see the worst consequences of climate change, we will reap the consequences of the combined impact of resource depletion and population explosion. It is projected that the world will grow from six and a half to nine billion in the next forty-three years, by 2050—with almost all the population growth coming in the countries least able to handle it.
>
> Meanwhile, if you look around the world we have substantial loss of topsoil, substantial loss of forest cover, and certainly

the biggest loss of plant and animal species in human history—
for the last 150,000 years—and many people think for the last
half million years. This is a combustible mix. It raises the
prospect of places all over the world having a modern version
of that old Mel Gibson-Tina Turner *Road Warrior* movie.

Trust it to Bill to use popular culture to emphasize his point.
By October, he was warming to the theme. The *Washington
Post*'s Anne Kornblut noticed it:[31]

> Last week at his library, in a speech at a *Slate* conference hon-
> oring top philanthropists, Clinton sounded almost critical of
> the presidential candidates, including his wife.
>   His complaint? None has put the subject of population con-
> trol in a world with shrinking resources on the 2008 agenda.
>   "Now, nobody's going to talk about this in the election this
> year—in either party—but I ain't running for anything, I can
> do it," he said, saying the world population will be 9 billion by
> the year 2050.

It's pure Ehrlich. Not only do liberals like Clinton think there
are too many people in the world, but they also don't think those
people can improve themselves or the conditions around them.
As I mentioned, Ehrlich was wrong because he failed to recognize
that humanity could devise new methods of feeding itself. Clinton is wrong because he fails to realize that it is perfectly possible for humanity to devise new methods of powering its
civilization, thereby supporting larger numbers with lower emissions. The dogma of environmentalism is that more people will
have more impact. It is fundamentally wrong.

As an aside, it is controversial to do so, but we must consider
the racial implications of what Clinton is saying. Most developed

nations have a fertility rate below the so-called "replacement rate" of 2.1 children per woman. In countries like Russia, the fertility rate is so low that they face demographic collapse. This means that the western nations are not adding to the population "problem" as the liberals see it. When you ask which nations are contributing most to population growth, you see Mali with 7.38 children per woman, Uganda with 6.84, Yemen with 6.49 and even Iraq with 4.07.[32] To put it bluntly, when liberals say there are too many people in the world, what they are really saying is that there are too many brown people. They will be the ones on whom population controls will need to be enforced in the liberal environmentalist utopia. Once again, liberals are being either disingenuous or just not thinking through what they say. Neither interpretation reflects well on them.

To return to the point, for Clinton, like Al Gore and the rest of the Liberal Environmentalist Church, the effect of population, wealth, and technology are all bad. This is summed up in the famous, seemingly impressive, and quite wrong-headed equation:

$$I = PAT$$

For this Church, man's impact (I) on our planet is only exacerbated by:

P population (as mentioned, environmental activists have led the population control fight, including frequent praise for China's one-child policy)

A affluence (America, they note, consumes a grossly disproportionate share of the world's resources, while they fail to note that we contribute a grossly disproportionate share of the world's wealth)

T technology (nuclear, biotechnology, chemicals, cell phones, whatever—they worry about them ceaselessly)

You might ask who designed the I=PAT equation. It was, of course, Paul Ehrlich, in conjunction with eco-socialist Barry Commoner and Harvard professor of Environmental Policy, John Holdren.

If you accept this dogma, there can be only one, integrated, solution. There must be population controls so that there are fewer people. There must be rationing and taxing of resources so as to control and reduce consumption. And there must be technology controls whereby bureaucrats can hold in check the innovative genius of entrepreneurs. Government must control and oversee this process and enforce it when voluntary action is inadequate or not swift enough.

As an example of the sort of anti-population measures liberals propose, one Australian professor used the day when Al Gore received his Nobel Prize (December 10, 2007) to call for a $4,400 "baby tax" to be inflicted on any couple so uncaring enough about the environment as to give birth to a child.

Professor Barry Walters, clinical associate professor of obstetric medicine at the University of Western Australia and the King Edward Memorial Hospital in Perth, also proposed an $800 fine—sorry, "annual carbon tax"—per child. He further suggested that purchasing condoms and undergoing voluntary sterilization should earn carbon credits. He even likened babies to pollution, saying, "Far from showering financial booty on new mothers and rewarding greenhouse-unfriendly behavior, a 'baby levy' in the form of a carbon tax should apply, in line with the 'polluter pays' principle." The proposals were published in the prestigious *Medical Journal of Australia* and endorsed by high-profile Australian doctor Garry Eggar, who wrote, "One must wonder why population control is spoken of today only in whispers." Perhaps because referring to children as pollution is outrageously offensive, Dr. Eggar? In any event, Australian Family Association spokeswoman Angela Conway had the perfect response. She told Adelaide newspaper *The Advertiser*, "I think self-important professors with silly ideas should have to pay carbon tax for all the hot air they create."[33]

In fact, from Erlich's equation, *P, A,* and *T* represent the three great triumphs of modernity. We have been able to feed without famine, spread wealth to the many not just the few, and achieve a pace of technological progress undreamed of before. To demonstrate the rate of change, Pat Michaels of the University of Virginia often points out how he is today able to move across the country in a matter of hours in a thin aluminum tube while in his pocket sits a small device the size and shape of a credit card that contains on it all the greatest works of music ever composed by man. Even the iPod was inconceivable just ten years ago. Just as the foolishness of including *P* within the equation has been demonstrated by the failure of Ehrlich's theories, so the digital download replacing CDs (or digital cameras replacing film) has demonstrated that *T,* technology, often consumes fewer resources. Moreover, it was *A,* affluence, that enabled this.

These simple truths are ignored by the Liberal Environmentalist Church. Population, affluence, and technology are all evils of the modern world, not boons. As my boss Fred Smith has said:[34]

> In many ways, the modern environmental movement resembles the Counter-Reformation within the Catholic Church of the sixteenth century, a revitalized faith that a professional priesthood must retain control over the fate of this earth, of mankind itself. There can be no salvation without the cleansing of society of the evils of modernity (evils, it might be noted, that were often directly the product of the policies and programs of the earlier progressive movement).

Of course, the conservative recognizes what these controls really mean: fewer people, fewer goods and services, and less innovation is actually the path of death, poverty, and ignorance. It is this realization that clearly demonstrates the wrong-headedness of the equation. How much differently would I=PAT be respected if it were cast as

$$Es = D \times P \times S$$

Where *D* is the Death of 4–5 billion people, *P* is the Poverty of those that remain, and *S* is the technological Stagnation that they live within. *Es* is, however, Environmental Salvation. It's a pity that only around two billion people will ever experience it.

In the end, no one has summed up the way in which liberal environmentalism denigrates the human being as well as Mark Steyn, who compares the environmental faith unfavorably to the Christianity it is infiltrating:[35]

> Environmentalism doesn't need the support of the church, it's a church in itself—and furthermore, one explicitly at odds with Christianity: God sent His son to Earth as a man, not as a three-toed tree sloth or an Antarctic krill. An environmentalist can believe man is no more than a co-equal planet dweller with millions of other species, and that he's taking up more than his fair share and needs to reduce both his profile and his numbers. But that's profoundly hostile to Christianity.

As we shall see, there are traditional and profoundly Christian ways of respecting the environment, but adopting the liberal disdain for humanity is most certainly not one of them.

. . . but Pro-Immigration

If you want to reduce the global population, and if you subscribe to the I=PAT model, curbing immigration should be a main goal. When people enter the U.S., they are upgrading in affluence, technology, and electricity, have more access to cars, and are better able to have more children.

You would think the liberal environmentalists would be down there building the wall along the Mexican border. But, in another sign of how environmentalism has fused with liberalism, environmental groups appear to have done a deal with their pro-immigration colleagues, just as they have in the case of contraceptive pollution (see next chapter).

The environmental groups used to lobby to restrict immigration. Roy Beck and Leon Kolankiewicz have charted the greens' retreat from this position,[36] suggesting the environmental movement was placed in a quandary when immigration began to emerge as the main driver of American population expansion in the 1970s. A variety of factors, most notably increasing affluence as well as the effect of public acceptance of contraception and abortion, had pushed the native-born fertility rate in the U.S. down below replacement level. As a result, the only thing that was keeping American population expanding was immigration. This forced the environmental groups into a choice. They could either a) continue working towards their population goals by advocating immigration controls or b) abandon the goals.

As Beck and Kolankiewicz say, "Such a choice surely was a shock to many environmental leaders. Left to future historians is a determination of how many made the choice consciously and how many passively chose option "b" simply by refusing to choose."

Many undoubtedly did choose. Zero Population Growth, whom we have mentioned before, was initially quite aggressive. Beck and Kolankiewicz cite a story from the *Washington Post* in 1977 about their position on the issue:[37]

Under the headline, "Anti-Immigration Campaign Begun," the story began: "The Zero Population Growth foundation is

launching a nationwide campaign to generate public support
for sharp curbs on both legal and illegal immigration to the
United States." It quoted Melanie Wirken, ZPG's Washington
lobbyist, saying the group favored a "drastic reduction in legal
immigration" from levels which were then averaging about
400,000 a year. The article reported that ZPG was adding
another lobbyist so that Wirken could devote all of her time to
immigration issues.

The Sierra Club, closely linked with Zero Population Growth,
also took an aggressive stance, as recently as the late 1980s:

[I]n 1980, the Sierra Club testified before Father Hesburgh's
Select Committee on Immigration and Refugee Reform: "It is
obvious that the numbers of immigrants the United States
accepts affects our population size and growth rate. It is perhaps less well known the extent to which immigration policy,
even more than the number of children per family, is the deter-
minant of future numbers of Americans." The Club said it is
an "important question how many immigrants the United
States wants to accept and the criteria we choose as the basis
for answering that question." In 1989, the Sierra National
Population Committee confirmed that, "immigration to the
U.S. should be no greater than that which will permit achievement of population stabilization in the U.S.," a policy confirmed by the Club's Conservation Coordinating Committee.

Yet in the next seven years or so, what Beck and Kolankiewicz
call the "full formula" environmentalists within the Sierra Club,
those who wanted to tackle all three aspects of the I=PAT equation, began to lose ground to other factions. The emerging
"environmental justice" movement, which believed there was a
racial element to environmental degradation in that polluters

were deliberately targeting racial minorities, and more blatant "immigrant rights" advocates began to gain positions of influence. Beck and Kolankiewicz reveal just how far the pendulum had swung:

> In February, 1996, the Club's National Board of Directors declared that no one speaking in the Club's name at the national or local level could call any longer for immigration reduction to reach U.S. population stabilization; henceforth, the Club would "take no position on immigration levels or on policies governing immigration into the United States." In effect, the board had ceased the Club's work for U.S. stabilization, which, at a practical level, is all but impossible given current immigration levels. For example, the only way to achieve immediate zero population growth without reducing immigration would be to cut the number of U.S. births in half.

The old "full formula" environmentalists, in credit to their consistency, did succeed in forcing a vote of the membership to dispute this new stance. They were, however, defeated by a margin of 60 percent to 40 percent.

This swift turnaround is testament to the power of political correctness and the fusion of environmentalism with liberalism in general. Just as environmentalists are unable to argue against the environmental problems caused by contraceptive pills, they are unable to argue against unchecked immigration, even when it is clearly linked to their beloved I=PAT equation. The power relationships within liberalism are just too important to upset.

Some might contend that this argues against my contention that environmentalism is the driving faith of liberalism. That is clearly not the case. There are few religions that do not trim their sails when facing the winds of politics. Those that refuse to are generally labeled "fundamentalist." Far from being a fundamentalist religion (although it certainly has some fundamentalist followers), environmentalism is the Established Church of Liberalism.

Blind Faith

Misplaced faith is a dangerous thing, as the two following chapters show. Faith provides certainty in the face of doubt, and allows belief to persist even when visible evidence may point in the opposite direction.

Well-placed faith allowed Job in the Old Testament to continue his belief in God even amid injustice, catastrophe, and suffering. It allowed Saints Peter and Paul to withstand persecution. Misplaced faith, on the other hand, is better described as destructive stubbornness, and it can have dire consequences.

In the following chapters we see how faith in the Established Church of Liberalism can be destructive. "Environmentalists" are willing to pollute the environment if higher dogmas of liberalism—such as population control—require it. They are willing to handicap "consumer safety" in the name of "conservation." They are even willing to offer up a sylvan sacrifice of one of America's greatest national treasures in order to abide by the dogma of central management and anti-capitalism.

Chapter Three

The Pill as Pollutant

And Other Environmental Menaces the Left Ignores

I n 2002, thanks to soccer star David Beckham, the world was introduced to the "metrosexual." Two years later, and with less mainstream media attention, we got our first exposure to "Intersex."

Intersex is not some new perversion or a weird combination of science fiction and pornography. It is an unfortunate condition that is affecting freshwater fish all over the developed world. It occurs when fish of one sex also exhibit sexual characteristics of the other sex.

In 2004, for example, researchers on the Potomac River, downstream from Washington, D.C., found large-mouth bass that in most respects were males, but who had eggs in their sexual organs. Quite often when this happens to fish, they find themselves unable to reproduce. When it happens primarily to male fish, the fish population in general suffers.

The cause of intersexuality among fish, scientists speculate, is pollution in the water, particularly hormones. Why don't we have more outcries about hormones, and campaigns to save the fish populations? Why aren't environmentalists lobbying on Capitol Hill to keep these chemicals from being dumped into our rivers?

Maybe because the source of these chemicals is not some corporate polluter, but something a little more dear to the Left: human birth control pills, morning after pills, and abortion pills. The environmentalists' silence on this topic and their willful distortions when they do talk about it show how, for many of them, the environment is more a tool for advancing favored policies than a real cause in itself.

There are other examples that demonstrate the same point, revealing liberal hypocrisy about human health and the environment, and showing the dangerous side of liberal policies. In this chapter, we also discuss the automobile, and how crash-worthiness—when it could spur more law-suits and regulations—was the rallying cry for auto regulation, but once crash-worthiness got in the way of other regulations, it was brushed aside.

The Feminization of Fish

You may remember learning in school about the "endocrine system," a network of glands and organs that regulates the body's production of hormones. Some chemicals can mess with that system, and they are called "endocrine disruptors." Whenever the endocrine system is disrupted, hormone disorders occur.

So when anglers start reporting large numbers of fish suffering from the intersex problem, academic researchers descend on the lake or river in an effort to find out what exactly is causing it. Take Boulder Creek in Denver, for instance. Scientists from the University of Colorado in 2005 examined the trout and other fish that populate the river. They netted 123 fish downstream of Boulder city's sewage plant and found a tremendous imbalance: 101 female, 12 male, and 10 intersex fish. One researcher told the *Denver Post*, "It's the first thing I've seen as a scientist that really scared me."

So what caused this systemic hormone imbalance in the river? As I've indicated, the Boulder sewage plant had something to do with it. The researchers found:

> [The c]ause of the intersex condition remains speculative but appears to be associated with endocrine-active contaminants, including 17β-estradiol and 4-nonylphenol, identified in the waste water treatment plant effluent of Boulder and other municipalities.

Now where does this chemical contaminant known as 17β-estradiol come from? It's actually a natural hormone: estrogen. So it comes out of human bodies and is flushed through the sewage system to the nation's rivers. Yet this natural hormone is not the only one that floods our freshwater resources. Also common is the *synthetic* estrogen used in oral contraceptive pills. This too comes out of human bodies and is flushed through the sewage system.

Recent research has proven that this synthetic estrogen causes significant problems for fish. A study by Univerity of Exeter researcher Amy L. Filby[1] found that the "estrogen . . . caused feminization of male fish, and altered DNA integrity, immune cell number and ability to breakdown pollutants."[2] The estrogen, moreover, reacted with other common contaminants of waste water to have even more potent effects. Other surveys of fish exposed to water from waste water treatments have found the same results.[3] One seven-year research project found that chronic exposure to the specific synthetic estrogen of birth control caused "a near extinction of [a fish] species from the lake."

The potency of synthetic estrogen is also very important. One study found that the potency of synthetic estrogen is ten to fifty times higher in fish than natural estrogen.[4] This means that its disruptive effect will be that much greater. Moreover, as one might expect given its source, synthetic estrogen is present in rivers in massive amounts all over the developed world. European studies have found surface waters generally have concentrations between 0.5 and 7 nanograms per liter. A study of 139 American streams found that 5 percent have concentrations above 5 nanograms per liter. This may not sound much, but studies have shown that concentrations between 2 and 10 nanograms per liter affect reproduction in fish. Life-long exposure to 5 nanograms per liter "caused a 56 percent reduction in fecundity and complete population failure with no fertilization."[5] As the researchers say: "[o]ur findings raise major concerns about the population-level impacts for wildlife of long-term exposure to low concentrations of estrogenic endocrine disruptors."

So one would expect that such scientific findings would alarm liberal environmentalists. At least one of the Boulder researchers initially thought so. David Norris of the University of Colorado was surprised by their lack of interest. He told the *National Catholic Register*:[6]

"Nobody is getting passionately concerned about it," Norris said. "It makes no sense to me at all that people aren't more concerned."

When the story of his finding hit Denver and Boulder newspapers, Norris anticipated an immediate response from environmentalists, who define the politics of Boulder and are known to picket in the streets demanding ends to questionable farming practices, global warming and pesticide treatments.

To the professor's surprise, however, the hormone story was mostly ignored.

Two years later, environmental groups have failed to take up the cause of saving Boulder Creek and its fish from hormone pollution.

As it happens, the liberal environmentalist position on endocrine disruptors is a case study in doublethink. It's worth looking first at the noise they make about other, non-contraceptive, synthetic endocrine disruptors. After all, if they are upset by one set of artificial chemicals that they say affects the environment, surely they should be upset by another set that also has a clear environmental effect, shouldn't they? Well, of course not. What we'll find is that the liberal environmentalists yell loudly from the rooftops about chemical by-products of industrial processes, but when the source of the chemicals is the contraceptive pill, you can sit back and listen to the crickets chirp.

Read these accounts and ask yourself: are the environmentalists really upset about the *effects* of industrial activity, or simply the *fact* of industrial activity? This reflects the moral teachings of the religion of environmentalism: while, objectively, industrial hormones and contraceptive hormones are identical, they must be treated as distinct morally. Industrial hormones are the result of development and profit-making, which makes them sinful; contraceptive hormones are the result of empowering women and reducing population, which makes them salutary—even if the fish can't tell the difference.

A Lot of Noise over Nothing. . . .

When endocrine disruptors were first identified in the early 1990s, the environmental movement went into overdrive. Here was a new thread that seemed to fit perfectly into their storyline: industrial chemicals ruin our health and threaten the very existence of our species.

Identifying synthetic chemicals as the main culprit, they attacked on all fronts, hoping to ban these industrial chemicals because of the possible effect on human reproductive and child health. Theo Colborn of the World Wildlife Fund waxed lyrical

on the subject at a meeting organized by the U.S. Department of
the Interior in 2001:[7]

> ...these chemicals can undermine the development of the
> brain, and intelligence and behaviour, and the endocrine,
> immune and reproductive systems....There is now a growing
> collection of studies revealing that some of these chemicals can
> affect our children's ability to learn, to socially integrate, to
> fend off disease and to reproduce.

Yet there is little substance to these allegations. Even calling
the substances endocrine disruptors when it comes to their effect
on humans is over the top. The American Council on Science and
Health prefers to call them "endocrine modulators," which certainly seems to be more accurate. The National Academy of Sciences is even more careful, calling them "hormonally active
agents."

Scientific studies have not found that endocrine modulators in
the environment affect human health. Even so, we know that
there are other, more significant sources of endocrine modulators
than industrial chemicals, indicating that the risks of industrial
chemicals are tiny in comparison. Industrial chemicals, it
appears, *have* had an impact on wildlife, but they are isolated
events resulting from high-level exposures, rather than widespread phenomena.

Finally, the limited cases of potential wildlife impacts have
declined considerably as the level of industrial endocrine modulators in the environment has declined, reducing problems for
wildlife. The one case where we have substantial evidence of sustained and perhaps increasing effect on the environment is the
case of synthetic estrogen.

Take, for example, the case of diethylstilbesterol, or DES, an
estrogen drug used between 1940 and 1970 to prevent miscar-
riages. When it was found that the children of women who used

this drug were suffering a higher incidence of reproductive tract problems than normal, the liberal environmentalists tried to parlay this into an attack on industry. Greenpeace, for instance, called the discovery "a critical piece of evidence which showed that the human body could mistake a man-made chemical for a hormone."[8]

Greenpeace's argument was this: if this manmade chemical could disrupt the endocrine system, then other synthetic chemicals are dangerous to humans, as well.

That argument is quite a stretch. DES was so much more potent than the endocrine disruptors in industrial chemicals the liberal environmentalists are so keen to finger. Toxicologist Steven Safe notes, "DES is not only a potent estrogen, but it was administered at relatively high doses.... In contrast, synthetic environmental endocrine-disrupting compounds tend to be weakly active."[9] But Greenpeace's reaction is understandable when you realize their job is to look for excuses to attack big business.

But, returning to the matter at hand, scientists have found the synthetic chemicals DDT (yes, it's our old friend again) and PCBs (the chemicals claimed to be endocrine disrupters that have been most studied by scientists) have as little as one one-millionth the potency of even human-produced estrogen,[10] which, remember, is far less disruptive than synthetic estrogen found in birth control pills.

Still, wherever they can, liberals use hormone problems as excuses for attacking and regulating industry. One "proof" routinely trumpeted is a Danish study that found male sperm counts had declined significantly between 1940 and 1990. The researchers, mind you, explicitly stated that they had not determined whether endocrine modulators were involved. Still, this study quickly became a "go to" document for those wanting to regulate industry out of existence. Greenpeace, for instance, claimed this was evidence of "a dramatic increase in the incidence of several reproductive disorders in men" over the last fifty years.[11]

This study has come under withering critique, for using too-small samples, omitting unhelpful data, and offering dubious interpretations of the data cited.[12] Since then, studies on sperm count have had mixed findings.[13] Even Richard Sharpe, one of the strongest advocates of potential sperm declines, notes "it is only a hypothesis."

The idea that industrial chemicals are bringing down the male sperm count is persistent, though. A recent *Guardian* article pushed the idea that "potentially dangerous chemicals are linked with falling sperm counts,"[14]

Now if artificial hormones and industrial chemicals are supposed to be affecting the male of the species, it'd be impossible for the scare merchants to leave the females out. In place of declining sperm counts, endocrine modulators are supposed to give women breast cancer. Once again, the allegations started after just one study in the early '90s, and, surprise surprise, it was DDT that was the villain.

A 1993 study led by Mount Sinai Medical School professor Mary Wolff compared DDT levels in the body fat of 58 women diagnosed with breast cancer with 171 control subjects.[15] Although still a small sample, the Wolff study was larger than prior studies, only one of which had more than twenty subjects. Wolff et al. found higher levels of DDE (the metabolite of DDT) in women with breast cancer, indicating an association between the two phenomena.

While including phrases of caution ("these findings are novel" and "require confirmation"), the study was chock-full of more explosive rhetoric that overwhelmed the nods to scientific responsibility. In the conclusion, the authors made strong statements about their "findings" and, of course, make a plea for government action:

Our observations provide important new evidence related to low-level environmental contaminants with organochlorine residues to the risk of breast cancer in women. Given widespread dissemination of organochlorines in the environment, these findings have immediate and far-reaching implications for public health intervention worldwide.

As Stephen S. Sternberg, pathologist with Sloan-Kettering Cancer Center, noted, "With these statements, one can hardly consider that the investigators reported their conclusions cautiously." The result was media hype about breast cancer risks. "The jury isn't in, yet you would never know it from the media reports," said Sternberg.[16]

Real scientists quickly ripped the study to shreds. One group was particularly scathing:

Their literature review excluded substantial conflicting evidence, their discussion of the Serum DDE and PCB measurements and the case-control analysis excluded important details, and their dose-response analysis, given their data used an inappropriate method. Also we do not believe that their data support their conclusion of a relationship between breast cancer and organochlorines as a class.[17]

The National Academies of Sciences also took a careful look at the study and noted the following problems. The size of the study was too small to provide much conclusive information; methodological problems could mean that the disease was causing higher levels of DDE rather than the other way around.

The National Academies concluded that the Wolff study and all the ones published before 1995 "do not support an association between DDT metabolites or PCBs and the risk of breast cancer."[18] Subsequent studies further undermined such cancer claims.[19] Key among these was a study of 240 women with breast cancer and a control group of the same size, which could not find a link.[20] Another study of more highly exposed populations in

Mexico, where DDT was still being used for insect control, found no significant difference in DDE levels among control and breast cancer groups.[21] Accordingly, the National Academies concluded the following about the studies conducted after 1995: "Individually, and as a group, these studies do not support an association between DDE and PCBs and cancer in humans."

When you come down to it, there doesn't appear to be any real evidence that human-engineered hormones have any real effect on human health. Ironically, the entire theory that industrialization is causing severe endocrine disruption falls completely apart when exposures to naturally occurring endocrine modulators are taken into account. Plants naturally produce endocrine modulators called "phytoestrogens" to which human beings are exposed at levels that are thousands and sometimes millions of times higher than those of synthetic chemicals. Humans consume these chemicals every day without adverse effects; some even contend that these chemicals promote good health.

Laboratory experiments have shown that there are so-called "endocrine disruptors" present in forty-three different foods common in the human diet, including corn, garlic, pineapple, potatoes, and wheat.[22] Most amusingly, soybean, that product so beloved of the vegetarian liberal environmentalist, is a particularly potent source of phytoestrogens. One study found that, even ten years ago, the U.S. soy harvest was producing about 230 million pounds of those natural endocrine modulators annually.[23] Given that soy flour, soy protein, and soybean oil are now ubiquitous in the western diet, these hormones are being consumed in hundreds of products every day.

Given all the sources of these natural phytoestrogens, it appears that on average human beings consume just over 100 micrograms of estrogen equivalents a day from natural sources. Compare that to the amount of industrial chemical amount of

2.5 micrograms. Yet all the environmentalists' attention has been focused on that tiny number.

Even that, however, doesn't tell the whole story. Phytoestrogens are actually much more potent than the chemicals that act like estrogens. Our friend DDT, for instance, has a relative potency to natural estrogen of 0.000001, meaning that it takes a million molecules to have the same endocrine effect as one molecule of real estrogen. So the actual equivalent to that 100 microgram number is not 2.5 micrograms, but an infinitesimal 0.0000025 micrograms of estrogen equivalent from industrial chemicals. The title of this subsection, "A lot of noise over nothing," is almost literally true.

But Silence Speaks Volumes

Let's get back to our main point, the silence of environmentalists over the synthetic estrogen from contraceptive pills. How much are humans ingesting daily from those sources? Brace yourselves. The medicines used in hormone replacement therapy contribute about 3,350 micrograms per day. The birth control pill contributes about 16,675 micrograms per day. The so-called "Morning After Pill" weighs in at a whopping 333,500 micrograms per day.[24]

These are massive amounts of fully potent estrogen, and they are passing into the environment, causing the problems in fish that we have already discussed. We've also seen how much effort the environmentalists have put into attacking the sources of the much less significant industrial estrogen mimics. Therefore, there's a problem, and it's similar to phantom problems the liberals have made a big fuss over. Put two and two together and you should get four, but math was never liberal environmentalists' strong point.

First of all, they deny that contraceptive pills are necessarily the source of the problem, continuing to pin the blame on the much smaller, far less potent endocrine disruptors in DDT and other industrial chemicals. One of the leading British researchers into the intersex problem, Susan Jobling, had this exchange with an Australian radio reporter in 2004:

> ALEXANDRA DE BLAS: Is the synthetic steroid from the contraceptive pill the main cause of the problem?
>
> SUSAN JOBLING: That's very unclear. The synthetic steroid from the contraceptive pill which is ethanol estradiol, is an extremely potent oestrogen [sic], and therefore it only needs to be present in water in minute quantities to cause effects. And certainly it's a contributor to the problem, but in terms of steroid oestrogens, there are also natural steroids which we excrete, and therefore which enter sewage treatment works, and so what you've got there, is you've got a cocktail of those steroid oestrogens, and in addition to that, you have chemicals which have been made by man to serve other purposes, for example, some RB breakdown products of industrial detergents, some are from the manufacture of plastics, and these chemicals are not steroid oestrogens in the true sense of the word. What they are is chemicals which by virtue of their chemical structure can mimic the effects of oestrogens; by fooling the body into thinking that they are oestrogens, and interacting with the specific receptors that we have in our body, via which oestrogens exert their effects. So really, what you're looking at is a cocktail effect.[25]

As we've seen, the research shows that there is such a cocktail effect, but that estrogen by itself affects the fertility and sexual characteristics of fish. Contraceptive pills would continue to have a significant effect by themselves, even if the environmentalists' dreams came true and the tiny amounts of industrial estrogen mimics were eliminated from the world's water supplies. Moreover, without the "cocktail effect," the tiny amounts of industrial chemicals would have even *less* effect than they already do. Once again, we must ask, why the lack of action?

Al Gore might call this "contraceptive denial," but, by his repeatedly stated logic, uncertainty is no excuse for inaction. So why have his disciples in the environmental movement not made a big deal out of this? One answer is that the poor dears just don't have the time. Back to Boulder, where the *National Catholic Register* reports:

> As nonviolence coordinator for the Rocky Mountain Peace and Justice Center, Betty Ball has taken to the streets with signs in protest of genetically modified crops. She lobbies Boulder's city and county officials to stop spraying mosquitoes in their effort to fight the deadly West Nile virus—a disease that killed seven Boulder residents and caused permanent disabilities in others during the summer of 2004.
>
> "Right now we're worried about weed control chemicals and pesticides," said Ball, when asked whether her organization would address the hormone problem in Boulder Creek. "The water contamination is a problem, but we don't have the time and resources to address it right now."

Well, a genuinely small group like the Rocky Mountain Peace and Justice Center (annual revenue for 2004 $245,000) might indeed face that problem, but what about the big groups like the Sierra Club? They can't use that excuse, can they? No, they don't. For them, it's something different:

> Curt Cunningham, water quality issues chairman for the Rocky Mountain Chapter of Sierra Club International, worked tirelessly last year on a ballot measure that would force the City of Boulder to remove fluoride from drinking water,

because some believe it has negative effects on health and the environment that outweigh its benefits. But Cunningham said he would never consider asking women to curtail use of birth control pills and patches—despite what effect these synthetics have on rivers, streams and drinking water.

"I suspect people would not take kindly to that," Cunningham said. "For many people it's an economic necessity. It's also a personal freedom issue."

Aha. Now we're getting to the meat of the issue. Many would regard the use of an affordable, safe automobile as an economic necessity and a personal freedom issue, but that doesn't stop the liberal environmentalists seeking to curtail their use. As I've noted before, the liberal principle of "pro-choice" applies to a very narrow collection of choices.

Population Control vs. the Environment

By any standard typically used by environmentalists, the pill is a pollutant. It does the same thing, just worse, as other chemicals they call pollution.

But liberals have gone to extraordinary lengths in order to stop consideration of contraceptive estrogen as a pollutant. When Bill Clinton's Environmental Protection Agency launched its program to screen environmental estrogens (a program required under the Food Quality Protection Act), the committee postponed considering impacts from contraceptives. Instead, it has decided to screen and test only "pesticide chemicals, commercial chemicals, and environmental contaminants." When and if it considers the impacts from oral contraceptives, the Agency says that its consideration will be limited because pharmaceutical regulation is a Food and Drug Administration concern.

As a result, the EPA's program will focus all energies on the smallest-possible part of endocrine exposure in the environment and the lowest-risk area. If regulators did screen for estrogen from contraceptives or for estrogen from plants (phytoestrogens), these two sources would dwarf the impact of pesticides and other chemicals.

These findings would highlight the fact that low-level exposure to commercially related endocrine disruptors is relatively insignificant, a fact that would undermine the agency's ability to regulate commercial products on the allegation that they are a significant source of endocrine disruption.

So government bureaucrats, the enforcement wing of liberal environmentalism, officially refuse to do anything about the contraceptive pollution issue in the United States. All this is in marked contrast to the United Kingdom's Environment Agency, which at least has the decency to label the contraceptive pill a pollutant,[26] even though it appears powerless or unwilling to do anything about it.

What about the activist wing? Well, this is where the story gets really interesting. Environmental groups have a long record of promoting contraceptive use—not *availability*, but *use*. The current head of the Sierra Club, Carl Pope, was once political director of the group Zero Population Growth. Back in 1970, the Sierra Club adopted the following resolution, which is worth quoting in full:

> Whereas, every human being and every American, present and future, has a right to a world with a healthy environment, clean air and water, uncluttered land, adequate food, sufficient open space, natural beauty, wilderness and wildlife in variety and abundance, and an opportunity to gain an appreciation of the natural world and our place in it through firsthand experience, and

Whereas, population growth is directly involved in the pollution and degradation of our environment—air, water and land—and intensifies physical, psychological, social, political, and economic problems to the extent that the well-being of individuals, the stability of society, and our very survival are threatened, and

Whereas, human populations are making ever increasing demands upon irreplaceable natural materials and energy sources, and

Whereas, the protection of the quality of our environment is impossible in the face of the present rate of population growth, including that in the United States, despite the advanced state of technology and the growing affluence of some segments of human society,

Be it resolved by the undersigned organizations...

That we must find, encourage, and implement at the earliest possible time the necessary policies, attitudes, social standards, and actions that will, by voluntary and humane means consistent with human rights and individual conscience, bring about the stabilization of the population first of the United States and then of the world;

That pursuant to this goal, families should not have more than two natural children and adoption should be encouraged;

That state and federal laws should be changed to encourage small families and to discourage large families;

That laws, policies, and attitudes that foster population growth or big families, or that restrict abortion and contraception, or that attempt to constrict the roles of men and women, should be abandoned;

That comprehensive and realistic birth control programs should be available to every member of our society;

That environmental, population, and sex education should be readily available;

That there should be increased research into the sociology of population stabilization and into the improvement of contraceptive technology;

That private and governmental departments, commissions, and committees should be created to deal effectively with the population problem; and

That the foreign policy of the United States should reflect the urgent realities of the population-environment crisis.

This proposal was reaffirmed and amended to the text above in 1995.

The Sierra Club isn't some outlier in the liberal environmental movement. They all believe this. Take, for instance, the World Wildlife Fund's senior campaigns officer, Norman Myers, who said in an interview on the WWF UK's Web site:[27]

This new wave [of claimed species extinctions] is being created partly by pressure of ... big deep breath ... too many people, still increasing at quite a rapid rate, an extra 72 million per year. That's one factor, and we know how to fix it, we know it will not cost the Earth. We could supply contraceptives to all those 180 million people in the developing world who don't want any more children but they lack the contraceptive hardware. We should supply them as a basic human right even if there was no population problem.

The list goes on. Environmental Defense advocates "access to contraception" as a vital element in the fight against global warming.[28] The Earth Policy Institute also calls contraception a "vital service."[29]

It's not just environmentalists campaigning for contraception, of course. Their colleagues in the liberal movement use environmental arguments in favor of contraceptive use all the time. Take, for example, the Guttmacher Institute, which in 2006 issued a detailed policy report with the ironic title, "Environmental Justice Campaigns Provide Fertile Ground for Joint Efforts with Reproductive Rights Advocates."[30]

Marie Stopes International says on the environment page on its Web site:

> There are many pressures on the environment and natural resources, but the environmental challenges humanity faces will become harder to address as the world's population continues to increase. Worldwide, there is still a vast unmet need for contraception. Around 200 million women world wide who want to access contraception, can't.[31]

Planned Parenthood of America says:

> For the past decade, prominent women in the global environmental movement have been advancing an environmental agenda based on feminism and human rights. They believe there are strong links between the health of the environment, the ability of women to engage and lead their communities, and their ability to exercise their inherent reproductive rights. Women have a stake in a clean environment because they are often the main providers of food and water, and their reproductive health can be adversely affected by environmental degradation.[32]

In other words, in the liberal world, the environment and unrestricted access to contraception are inextricably linked. We therefore have an answer to our question why liberal environmentalists are silent on the synthetic estrogen from contraceptives that is undoubtedly causing real environmental disasters. Because they helped cause them!

Now I'm not an anti-contraception activist by any means. Yet it seems clear to me that there is a real problem here. The problem could probably be solved by a few lawsuits under common law by owners of fishing rights against water treatment plants, who would then presumably be required to develop means of stopping the estrogen reaching the fishing grounds. However, in the world we live in, people have been stripped of property rights in favor of collective ownership, and the politicians who are supposed to represent our ownership are terrified of doing anything that might be seen as infringing on contraception. That's where environmental groups could be doing a valuable job balancing out interests. Yet because they're in cahoots with the contraception lobby, that isn't going to happen. The environmental groups should be part of the solution. Actually, they're part of the problem.

When Safety Doesn't Matter

Contraceptive contamination isn't the only area where liberals and environmentalists are happy to sacrifice a general principle for another, "greater" principle. We see the same storyline in automobiles.

Ralph Nader is probably the quintessential liberal activist, and he made his name as a champion of auto safety. It is therefore illuminating to see how auto safety has gone from being a central organizing principle of the Far Left to being yet another inconvenient truth. Safety is now almost an enemy of the environment.

When he was a student, Ralph Nader became interested in how automobile manufacturers were seemingly oblivious to minor improvements that could have made their cars much safer, such as a reduction in the amount of chrome on dashboards that appeared to have a blinding effect on drivers when the light shone the wrong way. In particular, he became interested in a

General Motors model called the Corvair, which he felt was inherently unsafe. Bizarrely, General Motors chose not to defend its product but instead to hire private detectives and prostitutes in an effort to smear the young activist. The resultant court case and award of damages helped Nader finance much of the early liberal campaigning establishment. As it happened, independent tests later showed the Corvair to be as safe as any other vehicle on the road at that time.

In 1965, Nader wrote the bestseller, *Unsafe at Any Speed: The Designed-In Dangers of the American Automobile*. In 1970, he founded the Center for Auto Safety. In all Nader's efforts the goal was the same: government regulation. By the time Nader was campaigning for airbags to be installed in all vehicles, a dogmatic vision of safety seemed to have replaced actual balanced assessments of safety.

Airbags are a very good example of what is known as a risk/risk trade-off. In essence, when you introduce a measure aimed at cutting one risk, sometimes you increase other risks in consequence. The end result might actually be an overall increase in risk. Airbags might decrease deaths among large, healthy males, but they actually appear to be very dangerous to small women and children. In fact, anyone who saw Ralph Nader in 1977 demonstrate an airbag going off with a three-year-old child receiving the blast full in the face would not be surprised at that.

The auto companies realized that compulsory airbags would result in a significant increase in risk for some of their customers, and sought to point out their dangers. Nader and his colleagues would have none of this, deriding the industry's attempts to wriggle out of installing an obvious safety improvement on all vehicles. In fact, the airbag battle was not over the devices themselves, but over the federal government's decision to mandate them, depriving consumers of choice, while introducing a new risk.

In the late 1990s, as cars with the first generation of mandated airbags became widespread, it became clear that the industry had been right and that Nader was wrong. The devices proved to be a net danger to children, killing approximately 150 of them through 2002. The government had to revise both its specifications for airbags and its warning labels in order to reduce the hazard. Several Nader-affiliated organizations opposed these revisions.

None of this is to say that airbags have been a disaster. They have certainly saved many lives, but, as we saw with DDT and the sacrifice of African children and American elm trees, the dogmatic approach to eliminating one hazard introduced new hazards. As my colleague Frances Smith, then executive director of the consumer advocacy group Consumer Alert said in 1997, "The lethal effect of air bags on children and small adults is dramatic evidence of what happens when policymakers adopt a 'one size fits all' approach that disregards individual differences and choices."

Now, when it comes to auto safety, consumer choice has been quite clear over the past couple of decades. As automobiles became more efficient in using energy, many American consumers showed that they wanted to cash in that efficiency in terms of safety and space rather than other considerations such as fuel efficiency or speed. Therefore, the SUV became the vehicle of choice for large numbers of Americans.

I used to be a determined foe of the SUV. When I arrived in the U.S. from England in the late '90s, I was astonished by the low gas mileage they got and how their greater size could lead to their headlights blinding the occupants of smaller cars. Indeed, I wrote several articles decrying them. Several took aim at the supposed safety features of SUVs, including one called "Armored Cars or Deathmobiles?" that alleged that SUVs were highly dangerous to other road users.

I was wrong. I had allowed myself to be misled by a study that purported to show that SUVs were no safer on the road, including to their own drivers, than most other cars on the road.[33] This study, by Lawrence Berkeley National Laboratory energy analyst Tom Wenzel and University of Michigan physics professor Marc Ross, was merely an analysis of traffic fatality statistics. Having worked in the UK Department of Transport, I should have known to go instead to the actual empirical data, from the people who crash cars repeatedly to test their safety.

The chief operating officer of the Insurance Institute for Highway Safety did not mince words when told about the study. He told the *Daily Californian:*[34]

> Any claim that vehicle weight is unrelated to safety is inconsistent with empirical evidence and inconsistent with the physical laws of nature.
>
> There are inherent advantages of additional vehicle weight in crashes with other vehicles, heavier vehicles experience less velocity change because of the laws of momentum and in single vehicle crashes, heavier vehicles may deform or break objects that would stop lighter vehicles.

Wenzel and Ross claimed that "quality" attributes correlated much more closely with safety than did vehicle size. Lund was not impressed. He said:

> I am even more concerned that their measure of "quality" is heavily influenced by the price of the vehicle. There are large differences between the populations of drivers that buy expensive cars and those that buy cheaper cars.
>
> It is likely that the effects which Ross and Wenzel attribute to quality are actually caused by differences in the driver populations. In any case, there are mountains of data demonstrat-

ing the safety effects of vehicle size and weight; there is virtually nothing to support the effect of "quality."

In other words, the study was outside the scientific mainstream. Yet who paid for the study? Why, it was the American Council for an Energy Efficient Economy, a small but influential environmental organization, which touts the supposed "scientific consensus" about global warming in its lobbying efforts[35] on energy efficiency. The Sierra Club also gleefully reported the news in its *Sierra Magazine* under the title, "Bigger Isn't Better: Dispelling the Myth of the Safe SUV."[36]

Now there are times that a single, groundbreaking study can undermine a scientific consensus and shift the ruling "paradigm," as Thomas Kuhn called it, to a new theory. This is clearly not one of them. What those people, including myself, who leapt on the Wenzel and Ross study displayed was not scientific open-mindedness, but something called "confirmation bias," where you automatically think things that support your views are correct.

That shouldn't be surprising. It is quite clear that SUVs today are one of the *bêtes noires* of the liberal environmentalist. Once again, the reason is global warming. SUVs, being larger, tend to have much lower gas mileage than the average car. Accordingly, the SUV is viewed as evil, because it emits much more carbon dioxide over its lifetime than the average vehicle.

One of the reasons for this is that SUVs, as light trucks, are exempt from fuel efficiency requirements. When Congress created the corporate average fuel economy (CAFE) standards in 1970s, they understood that not all vehicles serve the same purpose. Anything that is designed for hauling boats, farm equipment, tools, or materials, can't be subject to the same fuel economy rules as passenger cars, because those have the effect of reducing weight and therefore power (and we'll come back to this point in a minute).

Accordingly, Congress made a separate category, with lower standards, for light trucks. The CAFE rules made it very burdensome for carmakers to produce station wagons, which were classified as cars, but if you just turned that family car into a "light truck," the regulations were not as stringent.

Thus was born the sport utility vehicle, or SUV, designed for sporting activities and therefore eligible for the light truck fuel standards. Americans simply substituted the SUV for the station wagon, liking its space and safety features, effectively pulling off a consumer end-around run past the fuel economy standards.

Again, the liberal environmentalists hate this. They have embarked on a massive campaign of attempting to shame the American consumer for subverting gas mileage to other considerations. The Left has tried to force Detroit to stop making them, or at the very least, to make much more expensive vehicles, by imposing more stringent fuel economy standards. Here's what the Sierra Club has to say on its Web site:[37]

> When it comes to wasting energy, SUVs are unrivaled. Built with outdated, gas-guzzling technology, many SUVs get just 13 miles per gallon. And the higher gas prices are, the more money they waste.
>
> Auto-industry advertising portrays SUVs as the ticket to freedom and the great outdoors. Commercials depict them climbing massive snow-capped mountains or tearing through desert sand dunes, taking their owners into the wild. In reality, the only off-road action many of these vehicles see is accidentally driving through a flower bed next to the driveway.
>
> Missing from these ads are other contributions from SUVs—the brown haze of air pollution hanging over many of our national parks, images of weather disasters linked to global warming or the oil derricks and tankers needed to feed gas-guzzling SUVs. In contrast to Detroit's carefully crafted

image, SUVs have a dark side. They spew out 43 percent more global-warming pollution and 47 percent more air pollution than an average car. SUVs are four times more likely than cars to roll over in an accident and three times more likely to kill the occupants in a rollover. They also cost the owner thousands more on gasoline.

Yes, you, the American consumer, are a dupe for thinking that an SUV provides you any benefits at all.

By the way, notice the way the Sierra Club attempts to scare you by concentrating on rollovers. They don't tell you that rollovers occur in only 2 percent of vehicle crashes or that the rates of rollovers per vehicle mile traveled or per licensed vehicle have decreased in the past decade.[38] Rollovers are a serious issue, to be sure, but chances of fatality in a rollover are significantly reduced by the occupants simply wearing a seatbelt. But wearing a seatbelt doesn't help fight carbon emissions, so the Sierra Club isn't going to tell you that.[39]

On the most important question, the SUV shines. According to the Insurance Institute for Highway Safety's 2005 numbers, the average death rate for occupants of an SUV was forty-seven per million, compared to eighty-six per million for passenger cars. The SUV is almost twice as safe as a passenger car, in other words.

The thing is that the liberal movement used to recognize that vehicle weight was an important factor in securing occupant safety. In a 1989 interview, Mr. Nader had the following exchange:[40]

Q: If you were to buy a car today, what would it be?
NADER: One with an airbag.
Q: What size?
NADER: Well, larger cars are safer—there is more bulk to protect the occupant. But they are less fuel efficient....

Q: Which cars are least safe?

NADER: The tiny ones such as the Corvette, Yugo, Hyundai.

That's not all. In a 1972 book, he argued that the low weight of the Volkswagen Beetle was a clear indicator of its poor crash-worthiness:[41]

> The total weight of the Beetle's four replacement parts is the lowest in this study, a hint of the VW's abysmal crush characteristics. What may be an economy in a minor collision may lead to a staggering loss in a more serious crash.

In fact, a major theme of the book on the Beetle is that small cars are inherently less safe than larger ones. My colleague Sam Kazman brought this up during my testimony before the National Academy of Sciences CAFE panel in February 2001. When one of the book's authors, Clarence Ditlow, testified after Sam, he claimed that the Center for Auto Safety didn't even exist in 1972.[42] That seems to be the very opposite of confirmation bias: denying the very existence of something you yourself wrote as evidence.

Yet here's the greatest part of what the liberal environmentalist would ordinarily call "denialism": there is significant and substantial evidence that the introduction of fuel economy standards significantly increased the number of road accident deaths above what would have been expected. In 1992, my organization, the Competitive Enterprise Institute, won a federal appeals court victory finding that the National Highway Traffic Safety Administration had illegally ignored the lethal effects of the fuel economy program. In 2001, a National Academy of Sciences panel concluded that the fuel economy program has contributed to between 1,300 to 2,600 traffic deaths each year, by restricting the production of large cars.

More recent investigation from the NHTSA has confirmed this effect and actually found it to be "substantially larger" than previously thought. It also found that each relative one hundred-pound reduction in the weight of a light truck or van increased that vehicle's occupant fatality rate by about 3 percent, while negligibly decreasing risk to occupants of other vehicles. The study is unequivocal in its summary of the benefits of vehicle weight:

[H]eavy vehicles had lower fatality rates per billion miles of travel than lighter vehicles of the same general type. When two vehicles collide, the laws of physics favor the occupants of the heavier vehicle (momentum conservation). Furthermore, heavy vehicles were in most cases longer, wider and less fragile than light vehicles. In part because of this, they usually had greater crashworthiness, structural integrity and directional stability. They were less rollover-prone and easier for the average driver to control in a panic situation. In other words, heavier vehicles tended to be more crashworthy and less crash-prone. Some of the advantages for heavier vehicles are not preordained by the laws of physics, but were nevertheless characteristic of the [model years] 1991-99 fleet. Offsetting those advantages, heavier vehicles tended to be more aggressive in crashes, increasing risk to occupants of the vehicles they collided with.

So those who are demanding an increase in fuel economy standards are also to all intents and purposes arguing for more deaths on the road.

The blood toll cannot be dismissed as an unforeseen consequence. The effect of fuel economy standards on safety has been well known for over twenty years. Liberals who press for higher fuel economy standards do so in full awareness of the extra lives that will be lost on the road as a result. The inescapable conclusion is that 2,000 deaths a year is a price they are willing to pay for less oil consumption. If a tougher standard of forty miles per gallon were to be adopted, studies suggest the death toll could be over 5,000 extra lives lost per year.[43] The Energy Independence and Security Act of 2007 took us some way towards this level of carnage, mandating a standard of thirty-five miles per gallon by 2020. Thank you, Congress; think about that the next time you hear a liberal say that the Iraq death toll is all about oil.

There are those who counter that Detroit should be able to build an affordable, life-preserving, high-mileage SUV and that it is the American automobile industry that is stopping this for some nefarious, profit-making reason of its own (presumably so it can continue to pay it labor union retirees their exorbitantly expensive pensions). Yet it isn't just the American manufacturers who are finding this difficult. As Barry McCahill, president of the SUV Owners of America lobby group, told a U.S. Senate hearing in May 2007:[44]

> So why can't somebody just make a light truck that gets thirty-five miles per gallon? As complex as all of this is it really boils down to one simple concept: Gasoline has been five and six dollars a gallon in Europe for years and yet the fastest growing vehicle segment in Europe is SUVs. In the U.S. we have had sustained high gas prices and light trucks are still selling strong. The marketplace is begging for an ultra-high-mileage fullsized vehicle that meets the utility niche. Since market pressures have not already resulted in such a vehicle(s), legislation forcing its arrival surely must come with negative tradeoffs consumers would not accept if they knew. As a matter of basic fairness and sound policy, potential tradeoffs need to be anticipated and explained up front to the American people.

The tradeoff the liberal environmentalists demand is actually safety for gas mileage. In other words, blood for oil. The auto safety veterans of the liberal establishment should be hanging their heads in shame.

Liberal environmentalism causes disasters through its hypocrisies. It happily encourages the literal pollution of rivers in the name of women's sexual freedom and thousands of deaths on the road in the name of negligible effects on global warming. There's no logic to it at all. One might suspect that the movement was motivated by something other than rational analysis. The sacrifices at the altar of the green god are great, indeed.

Chapter Four

Yellowstone in Flames

The Dangers of Liberal Dogma

You could see the smoke more than an hour away. In a few days, it would cast an eerie pall over New York State, 1,500 miles away, but in late August 1988, it was billowing up in black columns, punctuated occasionally by a burst of orange flame as the fire swallowed another lodgepole pine.

Yellowstone had been burning for months, and half a million acres had been torched. Then it got worse. In a single day, August 28, or "Black Saturday" as it came to be known, 160,000 acres were consumed by the fires.

By September, parts of the glorious national park resembled less a peaceful retreat and more a war zone. *Washington Post* reporters Cass Peterson and T.R. Reid described the scene: [1]

> The road signs say this is Wyoming and the calendar says this is 1988, but the sights, sounds and smells here amid the raging, windblown wildfires of the Yellowstone Basin bring to mind other times and places—say, Danang in 1968.

The mountain roads are full of camouflage-green Army transports carrying firefighters to the front lines. Above the acrid, soupy pall of smoke that hangs low over the treetops can be heard the whup-whup-whup of Chinook helicopters, tracking the advancing foe with infrared imagery and dropping napalm-like jellied gasoline to start backfires at strategic points.

Through it all, residents of besieged towns continue to evacuate, with suitcases, tricycles and even prize moose heads strapped to the tops of their cars.

This was government come to the rescue, but as angry local residents said at the time, government policies—specifically the policies of busy-body environmentalists and conservationists—had lit this fire.

National Parks

America's National Parks are well regarded as glorious national treasures. They provide aesthetic pleasure and wonder to millions of Americans every year, as well as sources of recreation and exploration. We are lucky to have them. Yet from the beginning, many bureaucrats, politicians, and activists have viewed the parks as a tool to protect America from Americans.

Very early on in their existence, their management was captured by people who distrusted America and its free enterprise system (by liberals, in other words). Moreover, their custodians' antipathy to the American way has led to disaster far worse than has happened where free enterprise has been applied to preserve natural wonders.

This is especially true in the case of the shining jewel of the national park system, Yellowstone, which nearly burned down in the late 1980s. To understand why requires a detailed examination of the history of mismanagement, incompetence and liberal environmentalist dogma that contributed to the disaster. The trail goes back to Yellowstone's very founding, the story of which is actually a collectivist myth, designed to exclude the free enterprise system from involvement in the park.

The traditional story of Yellowstone's founding was well established by 1940, when the official history of the National Parks Service related it as follows:[2]

> Cornelius Hedges had looked deeply into American character and was not disappointed. He counted upon the altruism which marked that character, and planted in it the ideal which instantly took root and has since flowered as one of America's greatest treasures: the national park system. Thus was a new social concept born to a Nation itself reborn.
>
> The man who broached the national park idea to those men of courageous spirit who comprised the Washarn-Langford-Doane Expedition for exploration of the Yellowstone was indeed the most courageous of all. . . .
>
> As they sat around their campfire the night of September 19, 1870 near the juncture of the Firehole and Gibbon Rivers (now called Madison Junction), the members of the party quite naturally fell to discussing the commercial value of such wonders, and laying plans for dividing personal claims to the land among the personnel of the expedition. It was into this eager conversation that Hedges introduced his revolutionary idea. He suggested that rather than capitalize on their discoveries, the members of the expedition waive personal claims to the area and seek to have it set aside for all time as a reserve for the use and enjoyment of all the people. The instant approval which this idea received must have been gratifying to its author, for it was a superb expression of civic consciousness.
>
> As the explorers lay that night in the glow of dying embers, their minds were fired with a new purpose. In fact, some of

them later admitted that prospects of the campaign for establishment of the Nation's first national park were so exciting
that they found no sleep at all.

This, then, was the birth of the national park idea.

A stirring tale indeed—one worthy of memory and celebration. In fact, the spot of the campfire is today marked with a
memorial. The tale is redolent of the frontier spirit, yet at the
same time deeply appealing to East Coast altruists and philanthropists. It could almost have been designed to appeal to them.
Perhaps indeed it was, because it is almost certainly not true.

The fact is not one of the members of the expedition mentioned this poignant tale until almost forty years after the fact.
N.P. Langford first mentioned the event when his diaries were
published in 1905. Langford is an important figure in the history
of Yellowstone, as he was the park's first Superintendant in 1872,
but what is less well known is that he had significant interests in
the Yellowstone area beforehand.

In *Yellowstone: The Creation and Selling of an American Landscape, 1870-1903*, author Chris Magoc describes how Langford
introduced the glories of Yellowstone to the American public in a
series of magazine articles. Central to his narrative was the progressive's desire to "civilize the place," as Magoc puts it. Langford
talked of how this "marvelous freak of the elements" needed to
be added to the "family of fashionable resorts." Wealthy tourists
would be able to be among the first to see the natural wonders,
the exotic sights, the awe-inspiring majesty of nature.[3]

This was the 1870s, however. How were these tourists to get
to the wonders? It was certainly more than a carriage ride from
New York. The answer was obvious to Langford:[4]

By means of the Northern Pacific Railroad, which will doubt-
less be completed within the next three years, the traveler will

be able to make the trip to Montana from the Atlantic seaboard in three days, and thousands of tourists will be attracted to both Montana and Wyoming in order to behold with their own eyes the wonders here described.

Now Langford had more than just an altruistic motive in so publicizing the Northern Pacific. As Magoc points out:

[Langford] presented Yellowstone not only to *Scribner's* [the magazine's] readers but, more importantly, to audiences on a grand speaking tour funded by the Northern Pacific. Langford's brother-in-law was Minnesota governor William Marshall, a developer of Northern Pacific lands, who would soon influence the passage of the Yellowstone Park Act. With such personal and political relationships, N.P. (later self-designated as "National Park") Langford was perfectly positioned to become the park's first superintendent in 1872. At that time a nonpaying, patronage position, the superintendency did enable Langford to further the NPRR goal, one the Park Act itself initiated: the protection of Yellowstone from speculative commercial development—until the railroad could reach its borders and acquire the tourist franchise

This peculiar combination of interests should be familiar enough by now. Hedges may have genuinely been motivated by altruism, but Langford, with his Northern Pacific links, was motivated by profit. Like the proverbial "Baptist and Bootlegger," the businessman makes common cause with the altruist, and the tool is government restrictions on freedom. In the case of the Baptist and the Bootlegger, both seek laws limiting the legal sale of alcohol. In the case of the conservationist and the developer, both want to make sure nobody else is allowed to cash in— yet—on Yellowstone.

Still the amazingly altruistic campfire story as told by Langford, is the official founding myth of Yellowstone. Langford's tale
has been doubted for a while. Yellowstone historians Paul
Schullery and Lee Whittlesey explain exactly why in their 2003
article, "Yellowstone's Creation Myth: Can We Live with Our
Own Legends?":[5]

> Academics have long doubted the campfire tale, and as early as
> the 1930s, historians began to reinterpret the park's origins,
> observing that the story ignored known pre-1870 proposals to
> set aside Yellowstone as a public park. At the same time schol-
> ars also pointed out that the process by which the park was
> established did not seem to spring directly or indirectly from
> any such campfire conversation and that the public-spirited
> sentiments attributed to the park's founders were only one of
> the impulses driving their actions.
>
> Additional arguments discrediting the campfire tale followed.
> In 1948, in a short history of Yosemite National Park, historian
> Hans Huth referred to the campfire story as a "sentimental leg-
> end." Huth, aware of the precedents established by other pre-
> serves, such as Yosemite Valley in 1864, saw the campfire story
> as a violation of the complex richness of historical events.
>
> If things really had happened this way, it would indeed have
> been something of a miracle. It would have meant that public
> opinion had been prepared for this supposedly new and unique
> idea in little more than a year, and that Congress was ready to
> act favorably "to set apart the vast territory of Yellowstone as
> a public park or pleasuring ground for the benefit and enjoy-
> ment of the people." Ideas of such far-reaching consequence do
> not ripen over night; they develop slowly.

Yet the campfire story has become ingrained in the conscious-
ness of those to whom the National Parks are an important bul-
wark against private ownership of land. Despite being doubted

from the 1930s, it is repeated again and again as a story of vision and altruism. Schullery and Whittlesey cite, for instance, Peter Raven of the Missouri Botanical Garden, a prominent conservationist, hailed by *Time* magazine as a "Hero of the Planet" in 1999, as relating it uncritically in a speech in 2000 during which he lamented the rise in the world's human population. And our old friend Al Gore mentioned it approvingly for its symbolism, admittedly with a question mark over its veracity, during his speech to mark the park's 125th anniversary at Mammoth Hot Springs in 1997.

Why does the story continue to appeal to liberal environmentalists, despite its repeated debunking? For the simple reason that it contrasts the unselfishness of the environmentalist with the implied greed of those who would manage land in any other way than by government bureaucracy. Yet this distrust of private ownership fails to recognize the selfishness and indeed greed inherent in managing a resource using methods that contribute to the degradation of the resource, rather than transferring ownership to those who can manage it better. For the simple fact is that government bureaucracy has proven to be an inefficient, destructive, and indeed disastrous custodian of the land resources of the American West.

How Liberals Set the West on Fire

When the pioneers first entered the great forests of America, they found that the Native Americans had been managing the forests for centuries. They found that the forests contained very few big trees—maybe fifty such trees per acre. It became apparent that the Indians had set regular, low intensity fires. These fires burned away accumulations of undergrowth, deadwood, dying trees and particularly small trees growing between the big trees. The larger trees were unharmed. The thick bark of the pine tree, for example, means that small fires are of little harm to mature trees. This, in turn, kept the forest healthy, providing a barrier to disease, for example.

The pioneers, however, used much more wood in their civilization than did the Native Americans. They needed it for housing, for boats and river ships, for railroad sleepers, for carriages, and for town infrastructure. To them, therefore, fire was an enemy. Quick growth of new trees was important. Therefore, fire policies were put in place that suppressed any fire at all. This policy culminated in the creation of the iconic figure of Smokey Bear in 1945. Three years later, his catchphrase was born: "Another 30 million acres will burn this year—unless you are careful! Remember— only you can prevent forest fires!" The United States Forest Service gives out Smokey Bear awards, "To recognize outstanding service in the prevention of wildland fires and to increase public recognition and awareness of the need for continuing fire prevention efforts."

The price for this creation of an American icon was, however, a degradation of the health of American forests. Private logging firms continued to keep forests healthy where they operated, by clearing out the underbrush and deadwood and harvesting trees to clear spaces between other trees. Where they did not operate, undergrowth and deadwood began to accumulate. In particular, small trees proliferated. In the event of a forest fire, small trees are particularly dangerous, because they provide ladders, as it were, for the fire to climb up to reach the crown of mature trees, where the fires can take hold instead of being shrugged off by the thick bark below. Meanwhile, more and more land came to be controlled by the federal government, and therefore came under the control of an under-funded bureaucracy. Despite this, for a hundred or so years, this anti-fire system of management delivered reasonable results.

In the 1970s, however, the birth of the environmental movement changed American forest policies for the worse. As we have seen repeatedly, the environmental movement is dogmatically opposed to man's interference with nature (except where certain liberal sensibilities are concerned). It objected, therefore, to the "unnatural" control of forest fires created by natural means—by lightning strike, for example. A new policy, therefore, replaced the previous one of suppression of any fire. Under "natural regulation" and "natural burn" policies, such natural fires were to be allowed to burn until they burned themselves out. This was felt to be a return to a natural cycle of death and regrowth. One environmental activist put it succinctly: "Save a forest; let it burn."[6]

All very well, because such natural fires were indeed part of the management process that had served the indigenous population so well. But here we see yet another example of how environmental dogma combines with liberal collectivism to create disaster. Superimposing natural-burn policies on top of a hundred-year accumulation of fuel was bound to lead to disaster. It was like leaving a tinderbox out in the sun.

In the hot summer of 1988, a few natural fires sprang up in the environs of Yellowstone National Park. The officials sat back and did nothing, as was their policy. One Park Service official even predicted "no ecological downside" from the fires. Where it was felt fire control was needed, in most cases the firefighters were required to operate with as little impact on their surroundings as possible. This meant that the oldest and most effective technique in large scale firefighting—creating a firebreak by removing swathes of flammable material—was out of the question because bulldozers and so on could not be brought in. This hesitation proved disastrous.

The fires grew and grew. The huge fires that resulted took on a life of their own, becoming "a kind of self-sustaining mobile world of destruction," in the words of Micah Morrison, who wrote the definitive history of the fires and their real causes, *Fire in Paradise:*

The Yellowstone Fires and the Politics of Environmentalism. The wind would blow burning embers up to half a mile away from the main fire, creating new "spot fires" which would join up with the main fire, frustrating efforts at curtailment.

Then came Black Saturday in late August, when 160,000 acres of forest—three times the area of Boston, or equal to the size of Baghdad—were lost in a single day. Before it was over, more than a million acres (the size of Rhode Island) would burn. By mid-September, you could see the smoke on the East Coast, which was fitting, because some of the blame rest in Washington.

To begin with, there were two federal services involved, with contradictory policies. Many of the fires began outside Yellowstone, in national forests managed by the United States Forest Service, while others began inside the park, where they were the responsibility of the National Park Service. The National Park Service had gone completely over to the policy of "natural burn," while the Forest Service recognized the need for controlled management of fires when things got out of hand. The two services were less than accommodating towards each other. One of the fires that swept up from the southwestern corner of the park and narrowly missed Old Faithful had been started by a lightning bolt (a natural event) that struck a high-voltage power line (a man-made event). There are suggestions that the park service debated for twenty-six hours whether they should treat it as natural or man-made. During that time, of course, the fire continued to burn.

Morrison describes how at one point in July there were no fewer than thirteen "generals," each trying to oversee the fire control efforts, "all of them hammering for attention, resources and clear marching orders." The firefighters on the front lines were therefore often confused as to their objectives and what they were actually allowed to do in the circumstances.

Moreover, given the federally owned nature of the lands, the officials were not the only ones involved. Congressmen, administration officials, and of course the representatives of the Fourth Estate, all shoved their oars in the choppy waters. Speaking for their constituents, congressmen demanded an immediate end to the crisis, while the Park Service director attempted to defend the approach he was using. The level of confusion became immense.

The "let it burn" policy had already been abandoned in July, when the scale of the problem became clear. It was far too late by then. Park Service Director William Penn Mott told the *Washington Post*, "every firefighting technique available has been used to attempt to control these fires with very limited success." Chief Ranger Walt Dabney was more forthright. He told the *Post*,

[T]he more serious damage was done by the service's pre-1972 policy of suppressing all fires, which has allowed tinder-dry brush and dead trees to build up in the park. "We're living with a hundred years of fuel buildup now," he said.

Dabney said park officials adhered to the "let it burn" policy this spring because heavy May rains suggested that the summer would be unusually wet, as it has been for the past seven years. "Without a crystal ball or higher connections than we have, we had no way of knowing that it wasn't going to rain in June and July in Yellowstone," he said.

In August, the park received only .14 inch of rain—less than one-tenth of normal. As a result, Mott said, dead trees clogging the park have a moisture level of only 2 percent. "Kiln-dried lumber comes out of the mills at 12 percent," he said firefighters had been forced to battle the blazes by "flanking" them.

With such admissions, you would be forgiven for thinking that the liberal environmentalists who had foisted the flawed policy on the park would have been looking on with faces as ashen as their surroundings. This was far from the case.

One of the authors of the "let it burn" policy was Don Despain, a research biologist with the National Park Service. In *Scorched Earth: How the Fires of Yellowstone Changed America*, author Rocky Barker describes his reaction as he observed the approaching fires, one whole week after Black Saturday:

> Suddenly they began hearing trees torching in the distance as the fire moved toward them. Firebrands began raining on them and the plot. Lodgepole pines lit up as the fire climbed immediately from the ground into the crowns. Despain, usually calm, collected and reserved, was now excited. For the first time he was watching on of his test plots burn. He was there. He couldn't help himself.
>
> "Burn, baby, burn," he said.

The phrase Dr. Despain used was redolent of the language of the Black Panthers. It was the slogan of the Watts Riots of 1965 in Los Angeles, which saw thirty people killed, a thousand injured, and hundreds of buildings burned as a result of arson.[7] To be sure, Dr. Despain was probably referring just to his scientific test plot, but the choice of words was impolitic, to say the least.

Perhaps more indicative of the attitude of the liberal environmentalist crowd to the fires in general was the reaction of one senior figure. R.J. Smith recalled the incident in an interview with Glenn Beck on CNN in July 2007:[8]

> One of the Audubon Society board members who teaches children for the Audubon Society said the biggest disaster of the Yellowstone fires was that they did not destroy the town of West Yellowstone, which is the entrance to the park, because it was all ticky-tacky and neon cluttered and it should have been reduced to ashes.

R.J. suggests that this sort of attitude is widespread among liberal environmentalists. National Parks, they believe, should be reserved for those who can properly appreciate them, and a good indicator of this is choosing to stay at an expensive bed and breakfast rather than a Motel 6.

In any event, Dr. Despain's language was reported to the press. The *Denver Post* used his words to headline a front page article and furor ensued. While the bureaucrats of the Park Service fought to keep Dr. Despain in his job, they were unable to defend his "let it burn" policy. On August 29, when almost 9,000 people, including 2,000 army personnel, were still frantically fighting the fires, the *San Francisco Chronicle* ran a story that painted a poignant picture:

> The [let it burn] principle is summarized in a memo still posted on a bulletin board at a campground now ringed by fire in Yellowstone: "Only lightning fires are allowed to burn in Yellowstone."
>
> The memo is bitterly appropriate. Eight of the nine fires now raging in the Yellowstone country were started by lightning.

Wyoming senator Malcolm Wallop, who had earlier advocated the use of bulldozers when that was still prohibited, summed up the view of most rational observers. He told the *Chronicle*, "Once we get it [the fire] out, you have to take a good look at some things. You don't abandon 75 years of one policy of fire suppression and go to another policy of 'let it burn.'" President Reagan agreed. When he learned about the "let it burn" policy he was outraged that the crown jewel of the park service could be jeopardized so, and he ordered the army in to help. His administration insisted that the policy be jettisoned.

It was too late for Yellowstone, however. The baby did burn. By the time the last fire was extinguished and the smoke literally cleared, over a million acres had been burned, and the cost of the disaster came to $120 million. Yellowstone faced a long, hard journey back from this disaster.

In the meantime, however, it became clear that the schizophrenic approach of the Forest Service to fires over the past hundred or so years had led to more and more Yellowstones just waiting to happen. The Forest Service realized that it would have to start controlled burns to clear out the tinder that had collected for so long. The trouble was that controlling the fires under such conditions proved a difficult business. There is always a chance with each one that it might slip out of the government's control and become another wildfire. Eventually another disaster would occur.

Logging Saves Forests

So it proved. Over the next ten years or so, the National Park Service set rising numbers of managed fires. Between 1990 and 1999 the number rose by 75 percent, going from 182 fires affecting 83,000 acres to 319 fires affecting 132,655 acres. The number of acres subject to managed fires between 1995 and 1999 was three times that covered from 1986 to 1994.[9] Yet this was a candle in the wind; the scale of the problem was massive. A report from the General Accounting Office in September 1998, titled "Western National Forests: Catastrophic Wildfires Threaten Resources and Communities,"[10] indicated the extent of the accumulated problem and the expense of solving it:

> Our preliminary analysis of the Forest Service's fuels reduction costs—which according to agency data average about $320 per acre for the combination of burning and mechanical removal that is necessary in the interior West—indicates that as much as $12 billion, or about $725 million a year, may be needed to

treat the 39 million acres at high risk of uncontrollable wild-fire by the end of fiscal year 2015.

Yet just as the scale of the problem became clear, environmentalists intervened again. Liberal environmentalists hate the idea that anyone should ever make a profit from a collectivized national resource like the forests. Before the 1990s, commercial logging companies had been allowed access to the national forests for a fee that was placed in a trust fund, something that helped keep the forest service budget in the black and provided extra funds for fire control when needed. In the 1990s, however, environmentalists put a stop to this. Using the Endangered Species Act and various other legislative devices, they reduced the amount of logging in national forests by some 80 percent. As a result, the forest service's budget has been squeezed just when it needed extra money. In 1991, a worrying 13 percent of its budget was spent on fire control, but by 2006 that had ballooned to 45 percent as a result of the drying up of the logging fees.[11] There is more to say on this, but for the moment ponder how once again environmentalist dogma has endangered the resource they claim to protect.

In 2000, the chickens came home to roost. Two fires set by the Forest Service burned out of control. The stories of both fires provide excellent examples of the ways in which liberal environmentalist dogma had endangered the land.

The fire everyone remembers from 2000 took place in New Mexico, burning 48,000 acres and threatening the vital historic and scientific resources of Los Alamos National Laboratory. Four hundred homes were consumed, all as a result of a spectacular display of incompetence at Bandalier National Monument. After setting the fire, the wind blew fire beyond the planned boundaries, converting it into a wildfire that the personnel were unable to contain.

The Park Service investigation into the fire found that fire personnel had made repeated critical mistakes, including failure to take account of the local surroundings, failure to make any enquiries as to wind strength and direction, and failure to provide adequate contingency resources to fight any resulting wildfire.[12]

Interior Secretary Bruce Babbitt was candid on an appearance on the *Today* show. Declaring a thirty-day moratorium on managed fires, he called it a "systemic failure in the park service," and said, "I think we are going to have to go back as a result of this investigation and revamp the fire program from A to Z." Yet he also admitted something that to a liberal environmentalist like Babbitt must have felt like heresy. He said, "These forests are too thick. They're explosive, they're dangerous and the reason is that fire has been excluded for one hundred years and there is too much fuel in the forests, too many trees." Indeed there were. In the 1890s, the average Ponderosa pine stand would have held twenty to sixty trees per acre. A century later, it holds three hundred to nine hundred trees. The increased fire risk should be obvious.

Yet there is an alternative to controlled burns, one that is even more anathema to environmentalists than managed fires. It involves tree thinning by logging and the mechanical removal of deadwood and underbrush. In the Los Alamos fire, logging would have been a much better way to reduce the risk than any managed burn. Frank Gladics, president of the Independent Forest Products Association, was forthright in his criticism of how the Clinton-era forest officials dogmatically refused to consider logging as an environmental protection:

First [Interior] Secretary Bruce Babbitt and Chief of the Forest Service Mike Dombeck refused to utilize thinning or timber harvesting to reduce [forest] fuel levels, then they go ahead and have their employees strike a match. We hope Congress will

look to the root causes of these fires and hold the top leadership responsible for their dangerous strategy. The events of the
last several weeks have convinced us this administration hasn't
matured enough in their resource decision-making process to
be allowed to play with matches.

And in answer to any objection that logging is not environmentally friendly, Gladics had this to say:

[W]hen was the last time anyone heard complaints about loggers rampaging through neighborhoods indiscriminately burning down homes and destroying communities?

An even more specific story pertains to the second major fire
of 2000, when a managed fire got out of control on the North
Rim of Grand Canyon National Park and burned down substantial acreage in the Kaibab National Forest. I am indebted, once
again, to my friend and colleague R.J. Smith for this cautionary
tale.

As was the case in so many other places in the country, all timber harvest in the Kaibab had been stopped years earlier by radical environmentalists and compliant federal bureaucrats. The
stated reason was that logging might cause some unspecified
harm to the federally threatened Mexican spotted owl, of which
a few had been reported, and the northern goshawk, which was
not on the Endangered Species List, but which environmentalist
groups were lobbying to place there.

The elimination of the timber supply led directly to the closure
of the only timber company and saw mill in northern Arizona.
That devastated the community of Fredonia, Arizona. Soon the
only trace of the company was its abandoned foundations,
although the Forest Service office was still fully staffed and maintained a sizeable fleet of its unique pale green vehicles.

Not long before the Kaibab fire, the former president of the Fredonia timber company received a phone call from one of the officials in the Kaibab National Forest, remarking that the health of the forest was rapidly deteriorating without any management, thinning, or harvest. Young growth was increasing in density to the point where an unhealthy and unsustainable number of "stems" per acre were weakening all the trees as they competed ever more intensely for available water and nutrients. Could the company, the Forest Service wondered, restart its mill in Fredonia, bid on some of the trees and through selective harvest help improve the health of the forest?

The former president responded that the mill was now a hole in the ground. The buildings, equipment, and saws had long been sold, and the workers had moved to other parts of the nation where forestry jobs still existed. Even if all that were replaceable, there was no guarantee that the Forest Service would ever actually permit any of the Kaibab trees to be harvested, or enough of them, or of a large enough size, to be profitable. Furthermore, nothing could or would prevent the environmentalist radicals from going to court, prospecting for a sympathetic judge who knew that harvesting trees would destroy Mother Earth, and enjoining any potential sale.

The result was that the forest became even less well managed, with increased fuel loads. When the "prescribed burn" swept into the Kaibab, not only did forest burn—but along with it went the habitat and homes of the very species that the termination of timber harvest was designed to preserve.

That sad, deplorable, and irrational saga has been regularly repeated in recent years. In the most recent fires in California in 2007, there was much talk about the homeowners whose houses were destroyed being at fault in some way. The president of the Los Angeles water and power commissioners even suggested that "Nature never intended to support this many people here,"[13] as if nature had some sort of zoning rules and an allocation plan for human habitation. The *Times* of London picked up this ball and ran with it, saying, "Nature never intended us to build cities in deserts."[14] Somehow this was not construed as an attack on Arabs. Yet the untold story of those fires is actually that of the kangaroo rat.

When Californian farmers adjacent to the national forests found the kangaroo rat, which graces the Endangered Species List, on their property in the 1990s, they soon found that the rat had destroyed their livelihoods. They were unable to develop their properties in any way without paying a fine for every acre of land they owned, even if they only wished to develop a small portion of it and even if the rat habitat would be unaffected. So they sold their land to property developers, who were easily able to afford the fees. As a result, homes stood next to national forests where previously there had been a buffer zone of farmland.

Meanwhile, the forest service was unable to carry out controlled burns in those forests adjacent to the homes because the underbrush they wished to clear was also home to, you guessed it, the kangaroo rat. Even building a firebreak could get landowners into trouble under the Endangered Species Act. This problem was already apparent. After similar fires in 2003, California's Blue Ribbon Fire Commission, created by then governor Gray Davis and whose members included Democratic senator Dianne Feinstein as well as state legislators of both parties, concluded that "habitat preservation and environmental protection have often conflicted with sound fire safety planning."[15]

Liberal environmentalist dogma, however, prevented any action being taken to ensure that sound fire safety planning was enabled, far less that logging companies be allowed to do their bit to protect landowners and the environment. Instead, the contradiction was allowed to stand and when the fires swept through California, the environmental "protections" of the

Endangered Species Act led directly to the destruction of the very habitats and animals they were meant to save.

Congressmen should know about these problems and the best available solution. In September 2000, the late and much lamented Congresswoman Helen Chenoweth-Hage of Idaho, chair of the Forests and Forest Health Subcommittee of the House Resources Committee, held hearings on private conservation and the lessons the nation could learn from exemplary private landowners.

Skeet Burris, a South Carolina tree farmer and the American Tree Farm System's "National Tree Farmer of the Year," was asked if he practiced controlled burns on his private forestland. He replied that he did because it was necessary to protect the health of his pines and that fire was an integral part of the ecosystem of the southern pine forests. He said he burned about one-third of his forest annually.

Chenoweth-Hage asked if, before he began his burns, he waited until there was a huge fuel build-up, a long drought, and an especially hot spell with low humidity and high winds. To some laughter, Burris responded that such a policy would be insane. When he was told that such conditions were characteristic of prescribed burns on the national forests, he explained that he couldn't afford to take such risks.

His forests and home were all that he owned and that his children and grandchildren would inherit. Furthermore he couldn't risk his controlled burn destroying his neighbors' forests and homes because he would personally be held liable. There would be no taxpayers to foot the bill, no transfer to another forest, no early retirement on a taxpayer pension, no other golden parachutes. As the landowner he would personally bear the costs— and that drove his behavior.

As R.J. Smith says: "As long as man is part of nature, we can only have a sound and healthy environment by the exercise of caring stewardship and management. For guidance in that we must now look to the nation's successful private conservationists." Liberal environmentalism, on the other hand, has set the forests ablaze.

Yellowstone's Problems Continue

Yet it wasn't just the devastating fires of 1988 that demonstrated the futility of liberal environmentalist dogma in protecting and nurturing Yellowstone National Park. Just about everywhere one looks, the principles of collectivization and green environmentalism stand in the way of sound management of the resource. Before the fires, philosopher Alston Chase wrote a book titled *Playing God in Yellowstone*, where he concluded, "rather than preserved, [the park] is being destroyed." Those wider problems remain.

One question Chase raised is that of why there are so few beavers in the park. The answer to the question parallels the Smokey Bear/"let it burn" dichotomy. There are few beavers in Yellowstone because the vegetation had been depleted (even before the fires). The reason for the depletion was an over-abundance of elk in the park. There were too many elk because there were few predators: the rangers had killed most of the wolves, mountain lions, and coyotes, just as they suppressed any fires. When "natural regulation" came into vogue, there were too few predators to rebound, and the elk population, freed from the occasional cull, saw its numbers explode. Chase suggests that there are far many more elk and bison in the park than ever before in history (and the elk may not even be native to the park). Yellowstone is essentially preserving an environmentalist-approved illusion of the natural state. The actual natural state is long gone.

It has been a similar story with bears. Initially, the bears were a great attraction, and so the feedlots immortalized in cartoon lore as Yogi Bear's prime hang-out were institutionalized. When "natural regulation" became the policy, the feedlots were abolished. This hurt the bear population severely, forced the animals to roam further in search of food, and increased human contact with grizzlies, especially outside the park. The possibility of selective feeding of bears to avoid the problem of their dumpster-diving was discounted as against the natural regulation doctrine.

Even the Reagan administration played the environmentalists' game in Yellowstone. The Carter administration had rejected, as a waste of taxpayer dollars, a cherished park proposal to build a new development at Grant Village. To his discredit, the new interior secretary James Watt approved the project, despite it's being right on top of prime grizzly bear habitat. This was, once again, a case of the environment sacrificed in the name of anti-commercialism. The main reason for the project was to create a new, Park Service-run lodge hotel, competing with the private sector operators in the area. It is ranked number five out of five hotels in Yellowstone by the voters at tripadvisor.com.

The bighorn sheep was another victim of "natural regulation" following aggressive human control. With the elk population unnaturally large, the bighorn sheep were stressed. In the winter of 1981–2, the herd developed pinkeye. That is a minor disease, easily treatable, but the doctrine of natural regulation meant no interference at all. As a result, the blinded sheep fell off ledges, where at last some small mercy was shown to them, as rangers were allowed to intervene and shoot the incapacitated animals. The population of bighorn sheep dropped from 500 to 180.

Chase has an explanation for this schizophrenic approach to wildlife and land management. The problem is that liberal environmentalism is itself schizophrenic. We have seen repeatedly how a central tenet of liberal environmentalism is that mankind must have no impact on nature. Yet we have also seen how this faith is revealed through contact with nature. Therefore, for the environmental faith to spread, humans must be brought into places like Yellowstone while at the same time their very presence must be somehow ignored. The result is a philosophy of non-interference that actually interferes in the worst possible way. It treads lightly where a heavier step is required, as in culling elk, and treads heavily when a lighter touch would suffice, as in the case of the unnecessary and destructive Grant Village Lodge.

Chase points out that humanity is actually a part of nature, in Yellowstone as much as anywhere else:

> Natural areas were not made less natural by human presence. The worlds of nature and culture overlapped. We had tried to draw too fine a line between the two.
>
> Yellowstone was not just a natural area. It was not natural to see elk grazing on the mown bluegrass lawn of the adminis-tration buildings at Mammoth, to wake in the morning at the Lake Hotel to find a bison asleep under one's window, to meet a moose walking through the parking lot, to see a bear along the road. It was not natural, but it was nice. The park was a place where nature and culture mixed, a community of animals and people, a laboratory where we could learn to coexist with other creatures.

Even that possible fraud N.P. Langford would probably have appreciated that. Yet today, the commercialization of the park that he publicly opposed (while benefiting from in so many ways) is still anathema to the liberal environmentalist mindset.

Take, for example, a court case brought by a small band of environmental groups a few years ago. Since the mid-1990s, biotechnology firms have been interested in the potential medical properties of "thermophile"[16] microbes that reside in Yellow-stone's mud-pots and geysers. In 1997, one corporation that had been examining the microbes without any charge from the park agreed to pay the park for the privilege. Diversa Corporation of

San Diego pledged to pay the park $175,000 over five years and also agreed to give the park royalties from any future products generated as a result. The deal was not exclusive, and about twenty other companies expressed interest in similar deals.

Yet far from seeing this agreement as a potential source of funds to clear the park's maintenance backlog, environmental groups were horrified. A small faction[17] took the park to court, and a federal judge found, in the words of J. Bishop Grewell of the Property and Environment Research Center in Bozeman, Montana, "that while bioprospecting in Yellowstone is not illegal, compensating the park for it is."

The ruling from U.S. District Judge Royce C. Lamberth held that while Yellowstone might allow scientists to do research on its lands, "commercial exploitation of that same parkland may reasonably be perceived as injurious." That's right. The first penny that drops into Yellowstone's pot as volunteered compensation for scientific research harms the park by its very nature of being "commercial." To avoid the charge, the scientists would have to review the environmental impact of their research and consult with the public about it (and guess who would pretend to speak for the public if that occurred?).

The environmentalists' double standards are revealed once again by this case. As Bishop says:

Realistically, any Yellowstone visitor who has bought a moose-head hat, paid a lobster-dinner price for a scoop of ice cream at Old Faithful, or simply paid the park's entry fee has commercialized Yellowstone. Dan Janzen is a scientific adviser to Costa Rica's Guanacaste Conservation Area and a University of Pennsylvania biology professor. He observes that nature-oriented tourism "has been conducting commercial development of biodiversity and ecosystems in, and downstream from, national parks since the first train tracks were laid to Yellowstone's front door more than 100 years ago." Yet, somehow we don't find tourism as evil as biotech. Why?

The answer is the one we've already explored. People have to come to Yellowstone to experience *revelation*. They cannot come to it to seek medical breakthroughs for the betterment of mankind, which will only mean more human beings to destroy the environment. Yet even in this case, the schizophrenia of the liberal environmentalist mindset is revealed. The Park Service's chief of public affairs David Barna told Bishop, "You and I as tourists on the boardwalks probably carry more of these thermophiles home on our sneakers than the researchers take out."

The schizophrenia also extends to the vexed question of user fees for national parks. Under a program called the "fee demonstration program" that lasted from 1996 to 2004, parks and the forest service were able to charge park users for recreational access. Eighty percent of the revenue from these charges was kept by the local managers, allowing them to directly address local problems. Freeing the managers from the Washington game of pork-barrel politics was a huge boon. For example, Yellowstone had an outmoded sewer system that fed raw sewage straight into trout streams, but was unable to get Congress to pay for upgrading, while Congress happily acceded to the Montanan delegation's requests to rebuild a little-used backcountry chalet system at Glacier National Park.[18]

The fees were problematic to environmentalists, though. As with the microbial payment plan, this plan where visitors directly benefited the national parks was not good enough for the liberal environmental movement. As we've seen, they want people to visit the parks for their own reasons. They contended it dissuaded visitors. Yet the research evidence showed that the fees were so low that they dissuaded no one from visiting the parks. Most people were happy to pay them.

The Sierra Club tried a different tack. Their real objection was knee-jerk anti-commericalism, as we've seen. For instance, when the Forest Service decided to raise entry fees at the Angeles National Forest, where a thousand people at a time go for a hike in the woods, the Club suggested that "Charging fees has the potential to turn recreational management of public lands from a public service to the taxpayer into a commercial enterprise." This argument wasn't going to address the funding problem, however. So the Club argued that if Congress simply increased the amount of money given to the national parks and forest service, fees would not be needed. Yet we've already seen how weak that argument is. As Bishop Grewell put it in a different article:[19]

> For the past four decades, increases in staff and operating budgets for the land agencies outpaced visitation, even when adjusted for inflation, but dilapidation accelerated.
>
> The land agencies are not under-funded; they are mis-funded. Congressional members prefer to appropriate dollars for sexy projects that allow them to cut ribbons and reward contributors with lucrative construction contracts. Labor-intensive projects, including trail work, most maintenance, and on-the-ground research (things that Fee Demonstration can support) don t produce photo opportunities or political kickbacks.

Opposition to the fee demonstration program also came from a surprising source. Normally conservative Republican senator Larry Craig of Idaho suggested that taxpayers should have free access to public lands as they owned them. This argument is superficially attractive, but ignores realities. As Bishop also said, "Lumberjacks and ranchers are Americans too but they don't expect to use the public lands for free. Hikers and backpackers apparently think they should be different."

The fact is recreational use does impose maintenance costs on public lands just as surely as mining and logging do. Environmental groups make a big deal out of subsidies paid to loggers (who, as we've already seen, actually provide a vital service), but they essentially demand subsidies for hikers in the form of free access that does not reflect the costs they impose. Senator Craig, on the other hand, has important constituencies in loggers and ranchers. If user fees cause land managers to favor recreation as a better source of income over loggers and ranchers, his constituents could lose business. Senator Craig represents the bootleggers in this argument just as surely as the Sierra Club represents the Baptists.

In other words, the subsidy to hikers dissuades park managers from setting aside land for hiking, because they have nothing to gain. This leaves more land for loggers.

In the end, this case study illustrates exactly why the liberal solution of public ownership of land to protect the environment is inherently flawed. When you have a publicly owned commons, the commons becomes prey to considerations other than its well-being. This is known as the Tragedy of the Commons

The Tragedy of the Commons

The phrase "Tragedy of the Commons" was coined by controversial[20] ecologist Garret Hardin in a paper in *Science* magazine in 1968.[21] Hardin was arguing from an Ehrlich-like concern at overpopulation, but his theory went much further than that. As he put it:

> The tragedy of the commons develops in this way. Picture a pasture open to all. It is to be expected that each herdsman will try to keep as many cattle as possible on the commons. Such an arrangement may work reasonably satisfactorily for centuries

because tribal wars, poaching, and disease keep the numbers of both man and beast well below the carrying capacity of the land. Finally, however, comes the day of reckoning, that is, the day when the long-desired goal of social stability becomes a reality. At this point, the inherent logic of the commons remorselessly generates tragedy.

As a rational being, each herdsman seeks to maximize his gain. Explicitly or implicitly, more or less consciously, he asks, "What is the utility to me of adding one more animal to my herd?"....

Adding together the component partial utilities, the rational herdsman concludes that the only sensible course for him to pursue is to add another animal to his herd. And another; and another.... But this is the conclusion reached by each and every rational herdsman sharing a commons. Therein is the tragedy. Each man is locked into a system that compels him to increase his herd without limit—in a world that is limited. Ruin is the destination toward which all men rush, each pursuing his own best interest in a society that believes in the freedom of the commons. Freedom in a commons brings ruin to all.

As might be expected given the nature of this example, the insight that common ownership is thwarted by individual action is a very ancient one. Even Aristotle recognized it in the fourth century BC when he said:[22]

For that which is common to the greatest number has the least care bestowed upon it. Every one thinks chiefly of his own, hardly at all of the common interest; and only when he is himself concerned as an individual. For besides other considerations, everybody is more inclined to neglect the duty which he expects another to fulfill; as in families many attendants are often less useful than a few.

Hardin, as I said, was from the Ehrlich school of demography. He believed that the only solution to the tragedy was "mutual coercion, mutually agreed upon" and must involve "relinquishing the freedom to breed." In some ways, Hardin might be the ecologist with the most influence in modern times, as it appears the Chinese government has followed his advice.

Yet for those who prefer to think beyond Chinese Communist solutions, there is a tradition readily apparent in Anglo-American political thought, going back to John Locke. We have already touched on it. It is the institution of property rights.

The thing about common ownership is that it generally lacks incentives for good management beyond the hortatory or punitive. We see this in the realm of deep-sea fishing. With a common-owned fish stock, no individual fisherman has any incentive to stop fishing. If he doesn't take more fish, someone else will, and so the next time he comes back, there will be fewer fish to take. The only constraint is the size of his hold or any fines that may be imposed on him for exceeding a "quota." Yet holds can be expanded, laws broken, and fines paid or avoided.

What is missing in the commons is a positive incentive for good management. In the case of fish stocks, that is some incentive to allow the stocks to grow. In the case of forests, that is some incentive to keep the forest healthy and to maintain tree levels. In the case of rivers, that is an incentive to keep the river free from pollution, and so on. The best source of incentives that man has so far been able to develop is property rights.

Thus, the owners of artificial reefs can fish, but have incentives to keep the fish stocks there opulent. The owners of forests can log, but have incentives to keep the forests from burning down and to keep them replenished. The owners of rivers have the incentive to keep the rivers clean so that they can use it as a source of useful water, sell angling rights or allow other recreational activities (no one wants to water ski on a polluted watercourse).

Moreover, property rights encourage long-term thinking, while common ownership promotes short-term thinking. This is completely the opposite of what most collectivists assert, but a moment's thought establishes its truth. A property right is transferable, which means it can be passed on to another as an inheritance, a gift or a transaction. In any of these cases it is in the current owner's interest to ensure that the property remains as valuable as it can be. In the case of an inheritance, the owner will under normal circumstances wish the best for his or her heirs, and will therefore ensure the property is worth as much as he can ensure. Someone who gifts something to someone else will wish to obtain the recipient's goodwill, and therefore will wish the property to be as valuable as is feasible. The owner exchanging his property for something else will want to get the most he can for it. All of these considerations require an ongoing source of value. The owner who exploits all he can get from his property and then discards it has been very short-sighted. That is why land has, for generations, been the best and safest investment. People generally don't over-exploit their own property, whatever the collectivist might tell you.

Common ownership, on the other hand, is a very risky proposition. Most governments, local or national, are only in power for a few years at a time. There is also the chance that they might not be voted back into power. They therefore have incentives to maximize the short-term, not the long-term, value of the property. What do they care if they hand over an over-exploited asset to their opponents when they leave office? We see this in the annual appropriations round in Congress, where short-term considerations predominate, and all round the world. The annual public expenditure survey in the United Kingdom, for instance, estimates future needs only three years in advance. Long-term thinking cannot thrive in this environment. Moreover, commonly owned resources have to compete for funding in the public square. This inevitably results in the under-funding of unglamorous projects. This is why Yellowstone's sewers discharged into trout streams. Regular upkeep and maintenance is absolutely, positively the last priority on any list of public projects. Far better to construct a brand new, shiny building, with all the jobs and prestige that involves, than ensure a few trout don't get poisoned. The collectivist model ensures that happens.

The great philosopher Ludwig Van Mises realized what common ownership really meant; it meant that no one owned a resource. As he said:[23]

> If land is not owned by anybody, although legal formalism may call it public property, it is used without any regard to the disadvantages resulting. Those who are in a position to appropriate to themselves the returns—lumber and game of the forests, fish of the water areas, and mineral deposits of the subsoil—do not bother about the later effects of their mode of exploitation. For them, erosion of the soil, depletion of the exhaustible resources and other impairments of the future utilization are external costs not entering into their calculation of input and output. They cut down trees without any regard for fresh shoots or reforestation. In hunting and fishing, they do not shrink from methods preventing the repopulation of the hunting and fishing grounds.

As G.K. Chesterton said of secularism, when man ceases to believe in God, he doesn't believe in nothing, he believes in anything. So, when property rights are no longer the preserve of the individual, they are not the preserve of the government, they are the preserve of no one.

Common ownership clearly not only fails to *protect* the environment; it is a positive *danger* to the environment. The liberal approach of collectivization cannot benefit the environment.

Only private property rights can do that. And that is something our Founding Fathers recognized, so long ago.

Mr. Jefferson's Bridge

In Southwestern Virginia stands one of the natural wonders of the world. It is a giant natural arch of limestone, one hundred feet wide and crossing a canyon some three hundred feet deep. It is strong enough to carry a United States highway across it. The native Indian tribes called it the "Great Path." In the early days of the republic, it gave its name to Rockbridge County, Virginia. Today it is known as the Natural Bridge. Its long history is testament to the way in which private ownership can protect and preserve a natural resource.

It is indeed an impressive formation. The key to its formation was the shallow sea that covered the area 500 million years ago. The organisms that inhabited the sea died, leaving calcium-rich shells and bones that hardened into limestone and dolomite, which are easily dissolved by water. This means that the region is home to spectacular caverns, like the famous Luray Caverns. In the case of Natural Bridge, just such an underground cavern was created by the water course now known as Cedar Creek, which runs below the bridge. Eventually, the cavern roof collapsed, but one stretch of thick, resistant limestone survived and became Natural Bridge.

Its dimensions are astonishing. It holds fast 215 feet above the creek below (the equivalent of twenty-two to twenty-three stories). As such, it is fifty-five feet higher (or one third taller) than Niagara Falls. The span between the walls is ninety feet long. The "bridge" averages about one hundred feet wide and fifty feet in thickness. The stone arch contains some 450,000 cubic feet in volume and is estimated to weigh around 36,000 tons. A United States Geological Survey benchmark taken in 1905 atop the bridge places its altitude at 1,150 feet above sea level.

It was important to the native Indian tribes of the area, so much so that they invested a piece of their mythology in it. The peaceful Monocan tribe related its creation:[24]

[The Monocans] were being pursued by the Shawnee and Powhattan tribes. Hungry, tired and desperate, the Monocans fled through forests that were strange and menacing. Then, they came upon a huge canyon. The canyon was more than two hundred feet deep, one hundred feet wide, and stretched as far as they could see to the east and to the west. There was no way to cross. All hope gone, the Monocans knelt and called upon the Great Spirit to save his children. When they arose and looked again a great stone bridge spanned the chasm!

The women and children of the tribe were sent across to test its strength. When the arch supported them, the rest of the tribe crossed to the other side in safety. Buoyed by their experience, the Monocans held the bridge against their enemies and conquered many times their own number. The Monocans considered this a gift and called this revered bridge "The bridge of God."

The early visitors of the colonial era were no less impressed. Its first recorded mention is by one Andrew Burnaby in 1759, who mentions it as a natural curiosity. There is evidence to suggest that George Washington himself surveyed the bridge in 1750 while undertaking his survey of Lord Fairfax's grant of territory in Western Virginia. Yet it was another Founding Father who became synonymous with the bridge, deeming it, "the most sublime of Nature's works."

Thomas Jefferson's Monticello is eighty miles northeast of the bridge. His second home at Poplar Forest, near Lynchburg, Virginia, was only forty miles away. It was therefore nearly inevitable that he should encounter the bridge. His description in *Notes on the State of Virginia* demonstrates the awe he felt:

The Natural Bridge, the most sublime of Nature's works, though not comprehended under the present head, must not be pretermitted. It is on the ascent of a hill, which seems to have been cloven through its length by some great convulsion.... Though the sides of this bridge are provided in some parts with a parapet of fixed rocks, yet few men have resolution to walk to them and look over into the abyss. You involuntarily fall on your hands and feet, creep to the parapet and peep over it. Looking down from this height about a minute, gave me a violent head ach. If the view from the top be painful and intolerable, that from below is delightful in an equal extreme. It is impossible for the emotions arising from the sublime, to be felt beyond what they are here: so beautiful an arch, so elevated, so light, and springing as it were up to heaven, the rapture of the spectator is really indescribable!

His first visit to the bridge appears to have been in 1767. It seems that he decided quickly that he should purchase the bridge from the Crown in order to maintain its nature. In 1774, he achieved his goal. In a grant from King George III dated July 5, 1774, and signed by Virginia Governor Dunmore, Thomas Jefferson became the first patentee of the Natural Bridge of Virginia. The grant read:

Know you that for divers good causes and considerations, but more Especially for and in Consideration of the sum of Twenty Shillings of good and lawful money.... We Do give, Grant and confirm unto Thomas Jefferson, one certain Tract or parcel of land, containing 157 acres, lying and being in the County of Botetourt, including the Natural Bridge on Cedar Creek, a branch of James River.

A few years later, Jefferson wrote back to King George disputing his right to claim any title to land in what thereby became the

United States of America. With other things to busy himself with, and lengthy spells out of the country, Jefferson returned to pay attention to his property in 1802, when he surveyed the bridge in its entirety. The next year he built a cabin next to the bridge for himself, with two rooms, one for guests, in which he kept a log book that visitors could sign with their appreciations of the bridge.

Throughout his presidency and his retirement at Monticello, Jefferson would bring statesmen and dignitaries to view his wonderful property, among them John Marshall, James Monroe, Henry Clay, Sam Houston, Daniel Boone, Andrew Jackson, Martin Van Buren, and Thomas Hart Benton, who all signed the log.

One of the earliest visitors to the bridge during Jefferson's ownership was the Marquis de Chastellux, a French officer in the staff of the Comte de Rochambeau and member of the Academy, who made the first known drawings of the bridge. He published them in his work, *Travels in North America in the Years 1780–1782*, which gained international attention when released in France and England in 1786 and 1787, respectively.

Jefferson viewed his ownership of the bridge as a duty of stewardship, writing, "I view it in some degree as a public trust, and would on no consideration permit the bridge to be injured, defaced, or masked from public view." He also regarded it as important that as many people as possible could see it, saying, "Natural Bridge will yet be a famous place, that will draw the attention of the world."

Yet such stewardship did not preclude prudent use of the bridge as a resource. It contributed to the Revolutionary War effort as a "shot tower:" Molten lead was poured off the top of the bridge. On its descent, gravity and surface tension pulled the lead into spherical form, and the lead solidified into bullets when it hit the cold stream below. During the next clash with the British, the War of 1812, Jefferson opened a mine a few hundred feet from the bridge that provided saltpeter for gunpowder.

On Jefferson's death on July 4, 1826, ownership of the bridge passed to his heirs, Martha Randolph and Thomas Jefferson Randolph. It remained in the family until 1835, when it was sold for $1,500 (a handy profit on 20 shillings) to the contradictorily named Joel Lackland.

The Natural Bridge has remained in private ownership ever since. The new owner erected the Forest Inn to accommodate the growing number of visitors. In the 1880s, when it was owned by Colonel Henry Parsons, it attained resort status. In the 1920s, lighting engineer Phinehas Stephens installed a *son et lumiere* array that was opened by President Calvin Coolidge. The show, "The Drama of Creation," still plays every sunset, allowing the lights and the music of Verdi, Rossini, Wagner, Liszt, and Debussy to mingle with the sights and sounds of nature. Today, the bridge is owned by a consortium of eight owners, three of them in their eighties.

To go by liberal environmentalist caricatures of private stewardship, one would expect the bridge to have been so badly maintained that it would have collapsed,[25] or that it would have been carved out of the living rock and shipped to Arizona to stand alongside London bridge. Nothing could be further from the truth. Natural Bridge remains strong enough to carry U.S. Route 11 over it, which before the construction of Interstate 81 was the main north-south highway in these parts. That meant the bridge used to regularly carry eighteen-wheelers.

And the bridge is a tourist destination in its own location. It attracts 300,000 visitors a year. Again, liberal environmental cant would suggest that the place would have become a tacky tourist trap, with gaudy, inappropriate buildings and scant regard for the surrounding nature and wildlife. Again, this is not the case. The facilities associated with the bridge are unobtrusive, all designed in a colonial style. R.J. Smith describes his impressions of the site:

All the buildings in the Natural Bridge center follow the same colonial architectural scheme and color scheme with red brick, cream wood and grey roofs. There are red brick walls and natural wood fences. And signage in the complex, whether wooden or cloth banners, also fits in with green backgrounds with rufous trim and white and yellow lettering.

The grounds are landscaped with lawns, shrubbery and flowering trees including native redbud and dogwood. Little detracts from the viewsheds. There is only one tall sign, a ten foot by five foot green, cream and white old-fashioned metal sign atop a twenty foot green metal pole that says "Natural Bridge." The entire complex is remarkably unobtrusive and blends tastefully into the topography. In fact, other than the Natural Bridge pole sign the only other identification inside the triangle is a small metal plaque-like sign placed by the Virginia Conservation Commission in 1940 which identifies the site as: "Natural Bridge of Virginia. Legend says that the Monocan Indians called it 'The bridge of God' and worshipped it. Thomas Jefferson was the first American owner, patenting it with 157 acres on July 5, 1774, 'for twenty shillings of good and lawful money.' Millions of years old, Natural Bridge is considered one of the seven natural wonders of the world." Hardly a traffic stopper.

Yet this unassuming façade masks a busy, profitable use of the property. It contains a major corporate conference center and a family vacation hotel with rain-or-shine facilities. Its value is approximately $32.5 million.[26]

As for the flora and fauna surrounding the stone feature, that too has been conserved. The great naturalist John James Audubon traveled there to observe the birds and a hundred and fifty years later the Eastern Phoebes he sketched still nest there. Also prominent is a stand of particularly ancient trees. R.J. again relates:

The most interesting part of the trail—and most telling of the care of its owners over the last 250 years, is that the trail also passes through a stand of ancient arborvitae trees, the fabled "tree of life." It's an evergreen in the pine family, with unusual flattened, scale-like "needles" that are usually seen as a low ground cover or ornamental hedges. But here one passes through a stand of towering trees with strikingly deep, bowed and crooked branches, with benches and an information sign. This stand of giants includes a 56-inch diameter, 1,600 year old arborvitae—the oldest and largest known in the world. The species puts on growth rings very slowly, adding about an inch every 30 years or so. This little microclimate on the cool shaded limestone banks of Cedar Creek Canyon has sheltered this glen for nearly two millennia. The earliest Indians in the Shenandoah may have visited the spot to gather bark for traditional medicinal uses.

Wildlife and plant life alike flourish in this pleasant corner of southwestern Virginia. The owners of Natural Bridge have demonstrated for over 230 years that private management can maintain and enhance natural resources for the mutual benefit of themselves and the American people.

The contrasting cases of Yellowstone and Natural Bridge provide a useful reminder that liberal environmentalist dogma provides no guarantee of environmental protection, whereas the American tradition of respecting private ownership does. Jefferson and his compatriots recognized that an overbearing government that seized and abused property and disregarded local sentiments was an evil thing. His friend and protégé, James Madison, in particular regarded property and respect for it as centrally important to the nature of the United States' government. He particularly despised the expropriation of property by taxation, but his arguments apply equally well to regulation and government ownership:[27]

> A just security to property is not afforded by that government, under which unequal taxes oppress one species of property and reward another species: where arbitrary taxes invade the domestic sanctuaries of the rich, and excessive taxes grind the faces of the poor; where the keenness and competitions of want are deemed an insufficient spur to labor, and taxes are again applied, by an unfeeling policy, as another spur; in violation of that sacred property, which Heaven, in decreeing man to earn his bread by the sweat of his brow, kindly reserved to him, in the small repose that could be spared from the supply of his necessities . . .
>
> If the United States mean to obtain or deserve the full praise due to wise and just governments, they will equally respect the rights of property, and the property in rights: they will rival the government that most sacredly guards the former; and by repelling its example in violating the latter, will make themselves a pattern to that and all other governments.

Madison would regard his friend's stewardship of Natural Bridge as the model for his own environmental policy. He and the other Founding Fathers would find the National Parks model an insult to the "keenness and competitions of want" and would not at all be surprised that it had paved the way to environmental disaster.

III.

The Best Laid Plans...

The Green Lobby

I f your neighbor calls himself "an environmentalist," he may be speaking about his lifestyle. Maybe he drives a Prius—or even a Schwinn. He might bring his own coffee mug to the corner café to save paper. He recycles everything and buys recycled paper.

For this "environmentalist next-door" his cause is to reduce his negative impact on the planet, maximize his positive impact, and convince his friends and neighbors to do the same. This is environmentalism for many people, but it is not what the "environmental movement" is about.

The environmental movement is only minimally about encouraging individuals to live a "green" life. It is even less about actually doing "green things." It is primarily about lobbying governments to regulate, mandate, and prohibit individual behavior, supposedly helping the planet. It's also about lobbying governments to spend taxpayers' dollars toward that same end, or occasionally pressuring public companies to "do good" with shareholders' money.

"Sacrifice" is a favorite word of environmentalists, but sacrifice—the willing surrender of one's own wealth, time, or pleasure—has nothing to do with the environmental movement. The heart of the environmental movement is a lobby, one aimed at getting powerful people to do things with the freedom or property of others.

The green lobby is not interested in planting trees as much as it interested in getting its hands on the levers of central planning. Environmental "leaders" do not want to lead by example or by persuasion—they want to *manage*.

Past instances of mismanagement don't prompt them to give up the game. No, the green lobby keeps growing in size and influence.

The Size of the Green Lobby

The most influential conservative organization in the United States is probably the Heritage Foundation. Founded in 1973, it has an annual budget of around $40 million. It employs about two hundred people and has a membership of 200,000. It works on a variety of areas, including national security, social issues, energy policy, and some environmental work. It is the largest conservative think tank in the world. It is also dwarfed by any number of liberal environmental groups.

Take the Natural Resources Defense Council, for instance. Founded in 1970, about the same time as Heritage, it had a legal focus. It now has an annual budget of $70 million, about three hundred employees, and 1.3 million members/supporters.[1] Heritage doesn't look so big any more, does it?

Here are the biggest environmental groups, in alphabetical order, with their size and budgets where known.[2]

CENTER FOR SCIENCE IN THE PUBLIC INTEREST, founded by
  three veteran allies of Ralph Nader in 1971. It has a budget
  of around $15 million and 900,000 supporters.

CERES (COALITION FOR ENVIRONMENTALLY RESPONSIBLE ECONOMIES), founded in 1989, it has an annual budget of around $2 million.

ENVIRONMENTAL DEFENSE (formally the Environmental Defense Fund), founded in 1967 to campaign against DDT, it now says it "brings together experts in science, law and economics to tackle complex environmental issues that affect our oceans, our air, our natural resources, the livability of our man-made environment, and the species with whom we share our world." It has an annual budget of around $50 million, has 300,000 members and employs 247 full-time staff.

ENVIRONMENTAL WORKING GROUP, founded in 1993, supposedly provides "cutting edge research on health and the environment." Much of this research appears to be aimed at promoting organic foods (Michelle Malkin commented in 2002 that its agenda is "to cripple agribusiness altogether in favor of organic alternatives.) It has an annual budget of around $2 million and boasts of its "bang for buck" in getting better results than groups twice its size.

FRIENDS OF THE EARTH, founded in 1967, has an international presence, with its headquarters in the Netherlands and groups in over seventy countries. It claims to represent more than a million people worldwide. It has a U.S. budget of around $2 million. In the UK, it has two organizations, the Friends of the Earth Trust, with an annual income of £5,566,000 (more than $11 million) and Friends of the Earth Limited, which has a similar income.

GREENPEACE was founded in 1969 and is certainly the largest environmental organization in the world, with 5 million members and staffed offices in twenty countries. Its total annual budget is reckoned by activistcash.com to be in the order of $360 million. Its U.S. presence is more modest, about $10 million. Greenpeace's finances are so complicated that former Enron finance officials would find them mystifying (see below).

NATURAL RESOURCES DEFENSE COUNCIL, as mentioned above, was founded in 1967 and has an annual budget of $70 million, about three hundred employees, and 1.3 million members/supporters.

PEOPLE FOR THE ETHICAL TREATMENT OF ANIMALS, was founded in 1980, claims 750,000 members and has a budget of around $25 million. It is the largest animal rights organization in the world.

THE SIERRA CLUB is one of the oldest environmental groups, having been founded in 1960. It has over one million members, organized in sixty-five chapters and four hundred local groups across America. It funds projects to the tune of $20 million a year, but in some years spends much more ($73 million in 2002).

WORLD WILDLIFE FUND, otherwise known as the Worldwide Fund for Nature or WWF, was founded in 1961 and famously uses the panda as its logo. It is a massive organization, with its U.S. branch alone having a budget of over $100 million.

These are conservative estimates, not including some of the more innovative funding methods or a host of smaller groups. It also does not include more staid, but still leftist, environmental groups such as the Nature Conservancy ($731 million in revenues) and the Wildlife Conservation Council ($311 million) that are not as politically active.

Even so, the annual resources available to environmental groups amount to well over half a billion dollars. Taking into account the other groups, the figure might be as large as $1.9 billion. As Hugo Gurdon wrote in the *National Post* in November 2002, "Only 725 of the United States' 20 million companies can boast such magnificent cash flow." The green lobby is a massive financial operation. As one might expect, that leads to some innovative financial arrangements.

Greenpeace's finances are a case in point. Back in 2003, a nonprofit watchdog organization, Public Interest Watch, after investigating Greenpeace's finances, filed a complaint with the IRS alleging that Greenpeace had "illegally solicit[ed] millions of dollars in tax-deductible contributions."

What? How could an ethical organization like Greenpeace be accused of such activities? Surely all they are interested in is saving the earth? Well, Greenpeace has changed a great deal since its founding in the early 1970s. It began as a group dedicated to ensuring conservation by confronting people with the facts while maintaining a neutral position politically. It has now become a different beast entirely. Greenpeace co-founder Patrick Moore left the movement after fifteen years so that he could "switch from confrontation to consensus...to stop fighting and start talking with the people in charge." However, he noted, this brought him "into open and direct conflict with the movement I had helped bring into the world. I now find that many environmental groups have drifted into self-serving cliques with narrow vision and rigid ideology.... The once politically centrist, science-based vision of environmentalism has been largely replaced with extremist rhetoric." Greenpeace's founder, that is, rejects the organization's current tactics.

Moore is not alone. Greenpeace began as several different organizations, most of which consolidated into Greenpeace USA and Greenpeace International. However, one of the original bodies, Greenpeace Foundation, Inc., based in Hawaii, refused to do so. Like Moore, Greenpeace Foundation is openly critical of Greenpeace USA and Greenpeace International, whom they accuse of deceptive fundraising tactics, anti-Americanism, and failure to do much for wildlife preservation (especially in the case of dolphins).

It is this consolidation that was at the core of Public Interest Watch's complaint. Greenpeace USA is in fact two different organizations. Greenpeace, Inc. is the main entity conducting Greenpeace operations in the United States. As a tax exempt organization under section 501(c)(4) of the internal revenue code, it is free to lobby for legislation "germane to the organization's programs" and to engage in other advocacy activities, but because of these freedoms, it may not accept tax-deductible contributions. Greenpeace Fund, Inc., on the other hand, is a 501(c)(3) organization, and can accept tax-deductible contributions but cannot engage in lobbying or advocacy. Any funds it spends must by law be spent on strictly defined charitable purposes, such as education.

However, Greenpeace Fund's definition of "education" stretches to include advocacy and activism—and so does its money. Public Interest Watch, citing Greenpeace Fund's tax forms, alleged that, in 2000, the organization passed *all* of the money that it raised on to Greenpeace Inc, based in Washington, D.C., Greenpeace International, based in Amsterdam, and a few other affiliates. In 2000, according to its IRS returns, Greenpeace Fund raised $7.5 million, while disbursing $4.5 million to Greenpeace, Inc., $3.7 million to Greenpeace International for "general support," and $0.8 million to other Greenpeace organizations and projects around the world.

According to the complaint, Greenpeace Fund acts solely as "a shell corporation established for the purpose of enabling tax-deductible contributions from big donors and from foundations to flow illegally to Greenpeace, Inc. and Greenpeace International."

The law states that a 501(c)(3) organization will not retain its tax-exempt status, "if more than an insubstantial part of its activities is not in furtherance of an exempt purpose." Given the activities of Greenpeace, Inc., Public Interest Watch argues that "grants made by Greenpeace Fund, Inc. to Greenpeace, Inc., suggest that charitable funds are being spent for non-501(c)(3) purposes. The grants to Greenpeace International and other foreign Greenpeace organizations, which are known to frequently engage in aggressive advocacy efforts, also point to an abuse of charitable trust."

Public Interest Watch gives the following examples of exempt funds being used to support non-exempt advocacy and activism:

- Campaigning against genetically modified crops
- Blockading a naval base in protest of the war in Iraq
- Boarding an oil tanker for a "banner hang"
- Breaking into the central control building of a nuclear power station
- Padlocking the gates of a government research facility

Greenpeace reacted strongly and predictably to the accusations. "There really is no story there.... There's no merit to what they are accusing us of," a Greenpeace spokesperson told *National Review*'s Deroy Murdock. "Given the severity of these accusations by Public Interest Watch, Greenpeace USA is now considering its various legal options."

So did the IRS. According to the Public Interest Watch Web site, "After an intensive audit, the Internal Revenue Service found nine deficiencies in the management and practices of Greenpeace USA and warned that "Failure to ensure appropriateness of grant and gift funds could jeopardize the exempt status of [Greenpeace] fund." In fact Greenpeace USA's two arms, its 501(c)(3) Greenpeace Fund and its 501(c)(4) advocacy wing Greenpeace Inc., were told to change their practices "due to the illegal nature of their activities."

This should have been a huge moral blow to all those well-meaning people who have had "a minute for Greenpeace." It is not as if many who were there at the beginning, like Patrick Moore and Greenpeace Foundation, did not warn us.

Earth Day Is Pay Day

Of course, such saintly individuals need their gargantuan self-esteem to be backed up with gargantuan salaries. Back in 2004, Public Interest Watch decided to take a look at how the executives who had built up these massive empires were compensated. Its report, "Executives at Environmental Charities Go (For The) Green," carefully analyzed the earnings of top executives at four major environmental organizations—the Natural Resources Defense Council (NRDC), Environmental Defense, Inc., Greenpeace Fund, Inc., and the Sierra Club Foundation. The data are culled from the most recent IRS Forms 990 available (2001 or 2002), and are a matter of public record (see guidestar.org for online versions).

According to the report, NRDC employs nine people who each earn over $150,000 a year, including President John Adams, who was paid a whopping $368,342 in 2001 (he got even more in his final year, 2004—see below). These salaries include deferred contributions to employee-retirement funds, but even without these, eight of the nine still grossed salaries of over $140,000. Together, these nine employees were paid a total of $1,753,849 in 2001.

Yet even this figure is dwarfed by the huge amount paid to its principal employees by Environmental Defense, Inc., whose top thirteen employees received $2,120,980 in the same year. President Fred Krupp was compensated to the tune of $327,414, while Senior Vice President Diana Josephson and Vice President Marcia Aronoff each grossed over $200,000.

To put this into perspective, consider that Environmental Defense received just over $25 million in individual memberships and contributions in 2002, according to its own annual report. So 8.5 cents of every dollar donated goes to the bank accounts of just these thirteen people. Think about it like this: Las Vegas casinos will bank a "house take" of 9 percent from some rolls on a craps table.

Both NRDC and Environmental Defense are charitable organizations with certain restrictions, organized under section 501(c)(3) of the internal revenue code. Yet there are environmental organizations whose compensation packages do not appear to be unreasonable. According to its Form 990, People for the Ethical Treatment of Animals, an organization whose aims and tactics many Americans find objectionable, is at least reasonable in its payment structure. The top five executives there earned only $294,234 in 2001 with the president, Ingrid Newkirk, seemingly leading by example with a gross salary of just over $30,000.

Public Interest Watch also investigated the payments made by Greenpeace Fund, Inc., whose exact status raises the interesting questions we discussed above. This "shell corporation" paid nine employees $418,022 each in 2001, more than the Sierra Club Foundation did to its top officers. Moreover, as Public Interest Watch points out, some of these employees "received additional compensation from Greenpeace itself (Greenpeace, Inc.)."

The whole compensation issue belies the aggressive "grassroots" marketing campaigns these groups use to drag in the greenbacks. Greenpeace volunteers harass people on street corners with the words, "Have you got a minute for Greenpeace?" which eventually morphs into requests for money. Environmental Defense offers supporters t-shirts if they pass on the e-mail addresses of other likely donors.

As Public Interest Watch Executive Director Lewis Fein commented, "These groups literally beg for donations, giving the impression that they cannot accomplish their mission unless the average citizen pitches in. At the same time they are quietly paying their executives huge six-figure salaries."

Indeed they are. Here are the total compensation packages paid to the heads of the environmental groups we've talked about, as reported in the *National Journal*'s survey of interest group executives in February 2006, or otherwise culled from the IRS 990 forms:

CENTER FOR SCIENCE IN THE PUBLIC INTEREST: Michael Jacobson, secretary, $200,318

ENVIRONMENTAL DEFENSE: Fred Krupp, president, $357,057

ENVIRONMENTAL WORKING GROUP: Kenneth Cook, president, $160,122

FRIENDS OF THE EARTH: (U.S.) Brent Blackwelder, president, $125,975[3]

GREENPEACE: John Passacantando, executive director, $162,038

NATURAL RESOURCES DEFENSE COUNCIL: John Adams, president, $704,796

PETA: Ingrid Newkirk, president, $35,664

SIERRA CLUB, Carl Pope, executive director, $241,224

WORLD WILDLIFE FUND: Kathryn Fuller, president, $339,752

To those we can add the people who run the leading liberal environmentalist think tanks, Resources for the Future (Paul Portney, $317,476), the Rocky Mountain Institute (Amory Lovins, $189,163) and the World Resources Institute (Jonathan Lash, $302,186).

Now none of this would be problematic were it not for the notion of "sacrifice" on which the movement bases its moral righteousness.

There *is* sacrifice in the green lobby—at the bottom. Most of these organizations pay the majority of their employees very poorly. As environmentalism replaced Marxism as the central economic principle of the liberal left, the principle "from each according to his abilities; to each according to his needs" appears to have been jettisoned. Young, high-powered professionals in the overwhelmingly leftist public interest field are treated in a fashion that might once have been called exploitative. As the *Washington Post* reported in November 2007:[4]

> Numerous young Washingtonians bemoan the improvisational and protracted career track of the area's public interest profession. They say the high competition for comparatively low-paying jobs saps their sense of adulthood, forcing them to spend their 20s or early 30s moving from college to work to graduate school and back to work that might or might not be temporary.

Many of these youngsters aren't aware of the substantial sums earned by their bosses. The American Land Rights Association and the National Inholders Association ran a series of adverts around Earth Day one year in the early 90s using the slogan, "For some people, Earth Day is Pay Day." The advertisements drew attention to the high salaries of the top figures in the environmental movement. The organizers later learned that this simple act of transparency had an unexpected result; several low-paid environmentalists resigned in disgust.

Another question arises. Liberal environmentalists believe that consumption is a bad thing. So what exactly are all these people spending these vast sums on? It can't be green power and hybrid cars, can it, because they expect the rest of us to absorb those higher prices within our current salaries. It can't be private school—the head of Greenpeace USA's daughter Mollie became a minor celebrity after she and her friends spent recess marching round her Fairfax County, Virginia, public school bearing signs reading "Stop global warming. Save the polar bears" (evidently, history teaching at Fairfax County public schools needs strengthening).[5]

I sometimes wonder if the answer is a radical response to the problem of Status-Income Disequilibrium. In his wonderful book *Bobos In Paradise: The New Upper Class and How They Got There*, David Brooks outlines how the new intellectual class feels uncomfortable when confronted with their peers from college:

> In the 1950s, when intellectuals socialized mostly with each other, they did not feel the pain of their own middle-class income. The rich were remote. In those days an investment banker went to Andover and Princeton, while a newspaper person went to Central High and Rutgers. But now the financiers and the writers both are likely to have gone to Andover and Princeton. The student who graduated from Harvard cum laude makes $85,000 a year as a think tank fellow, while the schlump she wouldn't even talk to in gym class makes $34 million as a bond trader or TV producer. The loser who flunked out of Harvard and never showered is worth $2.4 billion in Silicon Valley. Pretty soon the successful intellectuals start to notice that while they have achieved social equality with these money types, financially they are inferior.

Carl Pope, executive director of the Sierra Club, graduated summa cum laude from Harvard in 1967, then went on to the Peace Corps and was later political director of Zero Population Growth (we'll get on to why that's only to be expected from an environmental leader later). Fred Krupp is a Yale graduate and a former partner in Connecticut private law firms. They certainly fit Brooks' description. Yet they seem to have come up with a radical answer to the status-income disequilibrium problem. They have massive budgets, so why not pay themselves enough to overcome the problem? If you're earning $300,000 a year, there is much less disequilibrium with your peers.

Big Brother Knows Best

The titans of the green lobby, then, are well-educated, well-compensated crusaders who, by the standard account, are fighting the good fight. Put them in a room with lawmakers looking to make a difference, and you've got breeding ground for hubris and elitism.

Armed with belief in their own intelligence, distrust of the masses, disdain of the markets, and certainty of their own intentions, there is no problem too big to tackle and no plan too big to pull off.

Today, the green lobby is behind many of the plans to save the planet. We've discussed the full-court press for that miracle-fuel ethanol. We've discussed the schizophrenic central planning that led to Yellowstone's devastation. In the following chapters, we'll look at some of the most disastrous effects of central planning.

Chapter Five

Cuyahoga Burning

How Progressives Set a River on Fire

Carol Browner is to the Environmental Protection Agency what Dan Rather is to CBS News. The former top aide to Senator Al Gore, Browner followed her boss into the Clinton administration, and went on to become the longest-serving administrator of the EPA.

She also played a larger role in the administration than any previous EPA chief. In a White House that tried hard to please the environmental Left, Browner was the hard-charging field marshal under Commander in Chief Gore. She imposed the most costly environmental regulations ever inflicted on the American economy. Unsurprisingly, that makes her a hero to liberal environmentalists; she possesses a list of awards as long as the list of her regulations.

When she finished her heady eight years atop the EPA in 2001, she penned a reflective piece in the *Harvard Law Review* describing her environmental awakening:

City after city, state after state, had essentially failed in their efforts to protect their air and their water, the land, the health of their citizens. By 1970, our city skylines were so polluted that in many places it was all but impossible to see from one city skyscraper to another.... We had rivers that were fouled with raw sewage and toxic chemicals. One actually caught on fire. There was a very famous photograph from my teenage years of the Cuyahoga River burning. In fact, it was memorialized in a song at the time.[1]

That song was by the perennial Oscar nominee Randy Newman:

> Cleveland, even now I can remember
> 'Cause the Cuyahoga River
> Goes smokin' through my dreams
> Burn on, big river, burn on.[2]

The image is evocative. In Cleveland, right in the industrial heart of the United States, man has turned nature so upside down that water and fire mix. Hell might as well be freezing over, pigs flying, dogs and cats living together.

The Cuyahoga River Fire that took place on June 22, 1969, is probably the first of those events that form the mythic cycle of liberal environmentalist legend. Mythic it certainly is, not only for the Pindaric nature of its content—water catching fire!—but also because the true happenings have been replaced by layer upon layer of interpretation and confusion.

The Cuyahoga fire is cited repeatedly as a terrible warning even today. It has a "never again" quality to its mentions. Conservative legal scholar Jonathan Adler, who has sifted through the stories about the fire and dug up a less black-and-white truth, puts it this way:

Today, the 1969 fire is regularly referenced in discussions of environmental quality. The image endures as a symbol of rampant environmental despoliation prior to the enactment of federal environmental laws. That fires no longer burn is an oft-cited sign of environmental progress, a factoid that is repeated with "numbing predictability" in speeches commemorating Earth Day or the passage of landmark environmental legislation. "The days of rivers bursting into flame and lakes dying are behind us," noted EPA Administrator Browner in recent congressional testimony. The comparison between oil-covered waters aflame and comparatively clean waterways in much of the nation is "dramatic," to say the least.[3]

Looking beyond the myth reveals that the oft-cited "facts" about the river are fire false. But more importantly, the common understanding of the fire's root causes is dead wrong.

Environmentalists, textbooks, and the media say that capitalism lit the fire, and the federal government cleaned the river. In truth, big government struck the proverbial match, and federal involvement came only after earnest cleanup efforts had begun. The real root cause of this mythic fire was not corporate greed, but a political philosophy called "progressivism."

The Cuyahoga was a victim not of the free market, but of a series of abuses in the name of the "greater good," something Friedrich Hayek called the "fatal conceit."

The Environment and Its Enemies

Environmentalism, I have mentioned, has become the guiding economic principle of modern liberalism. It's worth looking deeper into the thinking behind environmentalism. We will see that the fusion of discredited totalitarian ideals with a completely unrealistic new view of "the environment" has resurrected a philosophy that should have breathed its last in 1990.

Modern western history is mostly a story of the triumph of individual liberty, including the free enterprise system. American history, English history, and much of the history of Western Europe—especially in the Netherlands—have all shown us that where each individual freely interacts with his or her neighbors, good things follow. It is no accident that Britain and the United States, generally the freest countries, have also been the wealthiest, healthiest, most innovative, and safest countries in the world.

Societies in free countries develop in a manner unplanned, organic, and tremendously successful. Free enterprise has produced far more scientific and technological advances than the centrally planned dirigisme of the French empire. It eschewed the ultimately tragic militarism of the Prussian system and avoided the stagnation of the Islamic caliphate and Chinese empire. It also proved tremendously stable. The Dutch, English, and Americans have seen no further meaningful civil conflict that threatened the system since their founding revolutions in 1581, 1689, and 1776 respectively (although the Dutch suffered a French invasion masked as a revolution in 1795). The American Civil War can be seen as a struggle between two variants of the system—one agrarian, the other industrial—but both sides aggressively supported free enterprise. The free enterprise system pioneered by these three nations has been successful wherever it has been allowed to thrive.

In the mid-nineteenth century, however, a group of German philosophers built a new philosophical system based on a different definition of freedom that can be traced back to the ancient philosophers, Plato and Aristotle. To Hegel and his follower Karl Marx, the free enterprise system was anything but free. A working man had no choice when working for his employer, and

therefore freedom existed only in the absence of such subjuga-
tion. Workers must control their own factories and the means of
distribution and exchange of the goods produced required common ownership; without such conditions, freedom was illusory.

Common ownership in turn required a system of administration. This system became known as socialism or communism. It
embodied central direction or planning of the entire economy.
Enterprise was a political decision, not a free association between
two contracting parties. Employment itself was political, with
wages determined by government processes.

The idea was tremendously attractive and gained adherents all
over the world. It was implemented most fully in the communist
nations of Eastern Europe and Asia, but even the free enterprise
nations of Holland, Britain, and America adopted it to one
degree or another in the early mid-twentieth century.

Yet wherever it was tried, it failed. It did so for two reasons.
First, it embodied what Friederich Hayek called the "Fatal Conceit:" the belief that clever enough people can put their minds
together and come up with a plan that will direct an economy so
that there will be no losers.

Quite simply, this doesn't work, because however clever the
planners are, they never have enough knowledge to account for
all possibilities. This "knowledge problem" continually scuppers
their plans. As we saw in Soviet Russia, the planners were
increasingly forced to deny reality in an effort to insist their plans
were still on track.

Second, central planning failed because the free enterprise system actually delivered the goals of planning better than planning
did. For example, socialism promised access for all to the privileges of the wealthy. In actuality, it so depressed the economy that
those privileges ceased to exist for anyone except the corrupt.
Meanwhile, free enterprise extended those privileges relentlessly
as people worked hard to their mutual benefit.

No one has illustrated this better than the economist and philosopher Joseph Schumpeter, who said:

> ...the capitalist engine is first and last an engine of mass production which unavoidably means also production for the masses....
>
> There are no doubt some things available to the modern workman that Louis XIV himself would have been delighted to have—modern dentistry for instance. On the whole, however, a budget on that level had little that really mattered to gain from capitalist achievement. Even speed of traveling may be assumed to have been a minor consideration for so very dignified a gentleman. Electric lighting is no great boon to anyone who has enough money to buy a sufficient number of candles and to pay servants to attend them. It is the cheap cloth, the cheap cotton and rayon fabric, boots, motorcars and so on that are the typical achievements of capitalist production, and not as a rule improvements that would mean much to the rich man. Queen Elizabeth owned silk stockings. The capitalist achievement does not typically consist in providing more silk stockings for queens but in bringing them within reach of factory girls in return for steadily decreasing amounts of effort.[4]

So much for oppression. *Freedom*, in the Anglo-Dutch-American understanding of term, supplies far greater benefits than the *freedom* the German-Marxist-Communists sought. Marxism brought us the Gulags. The worst that most commentators can say about free enterprise these days is that it brought us McDonalds.

Marxism as a serious political system came crashing down with the Berlin Wall in 1990. Aspects of it certainly linger in European-style "social democracy" and in surviving elements of the New Deal in America. Every time you suffer an energy blackout, for instance, you are probably suffering from the Depression-era laws that led to a fragmented electricity transmission grid in the name of preserving jobs.

Yet the instinct to broadly and aggressively apply the tools of Marxism—central planning and government control—lives on. The instinct is the same as it was when Marx articulated it in the nineteenth century, but the old justification just doesn't fly. Free enterprise has proven itself not to oppress the working man, but to free him.

If the working man is no longer oppressed, the central tenet of Marxism no longer applies, but surely there must be another victim of capitalism to take its place? Women and minorities have advanced themselves under free enterprise just as surely as have the working man, and so they are not ideal candidates.

Luckily for the Left they have a victim ready on the shelf. This time it is one that will not exercise free choice in rejecting the ministrations of those who claim to speak for it. In the leftist's world view, the worker has been replaced by "the Environment."

The transition was seamless, because of a long history of cooperation between Marxists and environmentalists. Earth Day is held every year on April 22, a date deliberately chosen because it was Lenin's birthday. R.J. Smith, the veteran champion of free-market environmentalism and private conservation, told *Human Events*:

> "It is no accident it is on Lenin's birthday, April 22," he said. "It wasn't a coincidence. I knew some of the kids involved. They thought, 'What better day than Lenin's birthday because capitalism destroys the environment?' Most environmental ecologists believed the source of environmental degradation was the selfishness of capitalist owners. So we had to have a socialist system with a manager instead of an owner. Some of the constitutions of Communist states expressly forbid pollution. . . . "[5]

Those who advocate central planning in the name of the environment today don't usually declare wholesale war on the idea of a free economy. Instead, they use justify particular curtailments of free enterprise on the grounds of correcting for "externalities," as an economist would put it.

This is the idea that in every economic transaction, while most of the benefits are captured in the price, there are some other effects—mostly costs—that are not reflected. These costs are "external" to the market process. Thus, were I suddenly to decide to take up smoking and buy a packet of cigarettes, the price I pay would reflect both the costs incurred by the producer and the value I place on enjoying a puff of the noxious weed. It would not, however, cover the costs of the discomfort I place on others by discharging smoke in their faces. This, whether or not it causes cancer, is an example of an externality—a cost I impose on other people by my economic transactions.

To the Marxist, an externality is an example of "market failure" and the perfect excuse for the government to step in. The market cannot be trusted to bring about the best outcome, and so the government must fill the gap.

Can you spot that fatal conceit at work? There are all sorts of things the inventive centralist can do to correct the behavior that leads to the externality (remember, these are very clever people). They can ban a product or activity. They can impose taxes designed not just to capture the costs of the externality, but to punish those even thinking about indulging in the wrong behavior. They can issue or sell permits for the activity, which the inventive speculator can trade, creating a new, government-approved market.[6] They can subsidize alternative "good" behavior or products, or mandate them, or (as we've seen in the case of biofuels) both. The interventionist's toolkit is rich and varied.

When it comes to the environment, there seem to be all sorts of justification for intervention to correct externalities. Some activities might endanger rare species of wildlife or plants, for instance. Others might involve discharge of pollution into common resources, like water, land, or air, harming everyone who uses them. Yet others might pose theoretical risks of future catastrophe, like the potential for genetically modified organisms to spread beyond the intended beneficiaries.

Each of these is used to justify government control. In the case of global warming, where the external costs are said to be massive and emanate from the very use of energy fundamental to our economy, externalities are the final justification needed for the resurgence of central planning.

However, this is smoke and mirrors. Many years ago Nobel laureate economist Ronald Coase pointed out that the whole argument over externalities was illusory. He said it was simply an indication that property rights had not been properly defined.

This is a crucial point: yes, environmental problems often arise from problems related to markets and private property; but the answer is not abolishing markets and private property—it's more fully and accurately applying the principles of free enterprise. Conservative approaches can solve most of the current environmental problems, and we'll return to this later.

For the moment the thing to understand is that people do not spit on their own doorstep and that people who have their doorstop spat on by someone else get angry and seek redress. So proper definition of property rights—assigning the doorsteps to people rather than governments—is very important. Nor is there any reason to think government intervention should help the environment any more than it helped the working man.

More fundamentally, concentrating on externalities can gum up the works of even the most successful economy. British economist Arthur Seldon, an important influence on Margaret Thatcher, said the following on the subject in his *Everyman's Dictionary of Economics*:

Almost all economic activities, private or governmental, have external effects, and attempts to prevent, or calculate and compensate for them would probably make the economy seize up. In many instances, the effort to prevent or control for them may be more costly than their effects, and it may be better to tolerate some of them as unavoidable consequences of human fallibility.[7]

Far from being an excuse for massive bureaucracy, taxes, and regulation, externalities should be used only sparingly as a reason for government action. But haven't things gotten *so* bad that central planning is now needed?

Environmentalists base their calls for government controls on dire warnings and dark pictures of the current state of the environment. An honest assessment of the environment, then, is crucial to considering these arguments.

When you look closely at the true condition of the planet, the results are surprising.

The Real Environmental Indicators

To believe the massive publicity machines of the environmental groups, the Earth is on its last legs. Rivers are polluted, forests are dying, and species are going extinct even as you walk by them. The atmosphere is full of poisons, and the oceans are turning to green, bubbling acid. Our foodstuff is hopelessly compromised: fish is full of mercury that will rot your brain while crops are packed with engineered genes that will either wipe out all other plant life or create mutant superweeds when they inevitably escape. Once again, a compelling picture. Once again, a false one.

Every year since 1995, Steve Hayward of the Pacific Research Institute has issued a report, the "Index of Leading Environmental Indicators" that looks at how environmental quality is doing.

Surprisingly given all the doom-laden stories we are fed, he has consistently found that environmental quality, in America at least, is improving. As he puts it:

> Above all, this Index is designed to shine a spotlight on, and deepen our understanding of, environmental progress—the side of the environmental story that is seldom told. It does not shy away from the bad news or tell only the good news; however, the media and activist obsession with bad news skews our priorities and blinds us to ways of transferring our success to areas where there has been progress.[8]

This is an important point. If we continue to divert resources and effort to environmental issues where there has been significant, sustained progress, we are probably wasting our time and money. Yet, as we'll see, *success* is anathema to the liberal environmental movement. One concession, one moment of retreat, and their *raison d'être* evaporates. This is their last best hope to impose central planning on us. They can't let that slip away through inconvenient admissions of reality.

Take air quality, for example. On every indicator Hayward can find, air quality has been improving more or less relentlessly for thirty years.

Excess ozone is almost the definition of poor air quality. Yet 2005 was the second lowest year for ozone exceeding the Environmental Protection Agency's standards since monitoring began in the 1970s and the trend line is steeply downward (see the chart below).

The same story applies to emissions of real atmospheric pollutants like carbon monoxide and sulfur dioxide. Emissions in all cases are down substantially since the 1970s and have continued the trend in recent years. In 1970, for instance, we emitted 197 million tons of carbon monoxide (a poisonous gas, not to be confused with Al Gore's dread carbon dioxide). Despite the massive expansion in population and economic activity since then, the figure for 2005 was 89 million tons, a decrease of 55 percent. In 2000, we emitted 102 million tons, so the figure has declined 13 percent even since then. Emissions of particulate matter have decreased from 12 million tons in 1970 down to 2 million today, with a continued decline of 13 percent since 2000. Lead has been virtually eliminated, with 221,000 tons emitted in 1970 and just 3,000 today.

This is an inconvenient truth for the liberal environmentalists, and so it should come as no surprise that one of the many complaints issued about global warming is that it will reduce air quality. Steve and his colleague Joel Schwartz tested this during the heat wave of 2006. They looked at the ozone data for three major metropolitan areas—Dallas, Los Angeles, and Washington, D.C.—and compared ozone levels for the month of July 2005, which was cool by recent standards, and the heat-wave month of July 2006. The data showed an *improvement* in air quality in Los Angeles and Dallas from 2005 to 2006, despite the hotter weather. The results from Washington, D.C. were mixed. On the face of it, therefore, there is no reason to suppose that

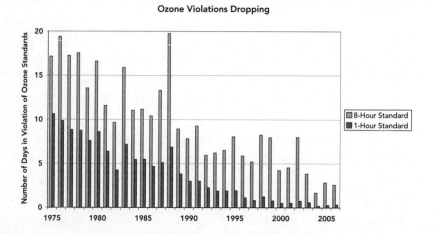

Ozone Violations Dropping

warmer summers would reverse our thirty years of improvement on air quality. Moreover, those improving years came at a time when global temperatures were increasing rapidly enough to start off the global warming scare.

Perhaps the best indicator of "pollution," as generally understood, is the amount of toxic chemicals released into the environment. Since 1988, the Environmental Protection Agency has compiled a Toxic Release Inventory. Sadly, its approach has not been consistent during its existence, meaning that it is often difficult to compare one year with another. For instance, in 1988 only three hundred chemical compounds were covered, but the inventory now examines more than 650. The number of facilities required to report their release of toxic chemicals has also grown significantly. It should also be noted that "release" includes the safe disposal of chemicals in specially designated areas and even recycling of some chemicals, not just the pumping of poisons into drinking water.

Even with these points borne in mind, the inventory's story is a good one. There has been a steady decline of over 60 percent since the 1988 baseline. Since 1998, there has been a 45 percent decline even though the inventory almost doubled in size during that time. The metal mining industry has seen a decline from over 3 billion tons of releases in 1998 to just over half a billion tons in 2004. All these indicators suggest that "pollution" is far less of a problem now than it was a decade or more ago.

What this all means is that the concept of environment has been radically redefined. If pollution isn't the problem it was when the Environmental Protection Agency was set up, what exactly is the point of all the regulation? Under the new definition, the environment is no longer simply the natural surroundings in which man interacts, but more radically nature in its pristine state—a hypothetical mankind-free world. This means that the point of the Agency and all the environmental laws today is not to ensure that mankind works within the environment without imposing irrevocable harm, but to work towards the eradication of mankind's presence in the environment. If that means the end of industrial civilization and a return to the cave, then so be it. Even the old Marxists would never have gone that far.

Progress Helps the Environment

How has America managed to clean up its act so much? Liberal environmentalists credit the tools of central control: regulation and punishment specifically. Government, they conclude without any hesitation, has forced evil polluters to stop valuing profit over the environment. Yet the truth is much more complicated. There are a variety of factors at play when it comes to environmental improvement, and the role of central government actually appears to be quite small.

Take, for example, the history of air quality in the United States. As we've seen, it has improved dramatically over the past thirty years. The liberal environmentalist habitually claims this as a victory for the Clean Air Act, introduced during the Nixon administration in 1970.[9] For example, the Sierra Club credits the Clean Air Act with enormous benefits:[10]

> The benefits of the Clean Air Act, the landmark environmental program enacted in 1970, have far outweighed its costs. According to the EPA, for every dollar spent on the Clean Air Act from 1970 to 1990, we received a $20 return on the investment. In fact, the EPA estimates Americans have realized benefits 70 times greater than the costs of implementing the program. In 1990 alone, tailpipe and smokestack controls saved an estimated 79,000 lives and resulted in an estimated 15 million fewer respiratory illnesses, including:

- 13 million cases of hypertension
- 18,000 heart attacks
- 10,000 strokes
- 146,000 cases of respiratory symptoms

Sounds like a good value doesn't it? Well, the truth isn't quite as simple. The Sierra Club bases its claims on the findings of the EPA. If we follow that lead, we're taking a government agency's word that its impositions on our lives make us better off. The Left doesn't buy that line from the Pentagon or the CIA, why should we buy it from the EPA?

Indeed, there is evidence the EPA has massively overstated its impact on the environment.

In examining this issue, four questions must be asked. How much pollution was there in the past? How much is there now? How much did regulation contribute to that change? And how much healthier are we, thanks to that change?

On almost every score, the EPA uses dubious methods, resulting—surprise, surprise—in a self-serving conclusion.

On the Clean Air Act, explains Susan Dudley of George Mason University,[11] the EPA takes credit for reducing the amount of particulate matter (soot) in the air, and goes on to credit soot reductions for the health benefits cited above. Dudley points, out, though:

> ...many commentators have questioned the methodology EPA uses to derive these high benefits. The fact that the benefits reported by OMB are so dominated by the questionable analytical approach used to value reductions in one pollutant illustrates the problem with relying uncritically on agency estimates.

The Agency, in other words, has given itself too much credit for reduction of soot, allowing it to conclude that its regulation has made the country much healthier. Without this questionable analysis, the Clean Air Act would seem much less important than liberal environmentalists and the Agency itself claim it to be.

Joel Schwartz of the American Enterprise Institute agrees. He told me:

> EPA attributed 90 percent of the benefits of all air pollution regulations through 1990 to reductions in particulate matter [PM] (and 8 percent to removing lead from gasoline), and 99 percent of the incremental benefits of the Clean Air Act Amendments of 1990 to PM reductions.
>
> But these are phantom benefits, because the air pollution deaths are phantom deaths. It's been a long time since U.S. air pollution was high enough to kill people. The true health benefits of the Clean Air Act are only a tiny fraction of what EPA self-servingly claims.[12]

In other words, even if the EPA and the Clean Air Act really *are* reducing soot in the air, the reductions aren't worth anything anymore. Soot used to be at dangerous levels in the air. Now it's not. Reducing it further doesn't help us. The air is clean and Americans are not going to let it get dirty again. So claiming benefits from the avoidance of deaths that would not happen even if the Act and Agency vanished overnight is a regulatory Three Card Monty.

That's not all, though. Michael Greenstone, an economist at MIT, has examined many of the claims made for the Clean Air Act and also found them overblown. When it comes to lives saved (remember, the Sierra Club claims 79,000 a year), he found the same problem Schwartz suggested: regulations can reduce soot, but they don't reduce mortality. Or, as he put it, "regulation-induced reduction in [soot] is not associated with improvements in adult mortality."[13]

So even if the Clean Air Act had been successful in reducing particulate matter to the clean levels we now have, that wasn't responsible for any reduction in mortality anyway. Not only are the supposed future benefits illusory, so are the ones we have already supposedly banked. The Clean Air Act didn't save anyone's life, never mind 79,000 a year.

Dr. Greenstone also examined the claim that it was the Clean Air Act that was responsible for the remarkable reduction in Sulfur Dioxide content in the air that we noted above. Once again, it appears that reports of the Act's efficacy have been greatly exaggerated. Yes, SO_2 concentrations dramatically fell over the last three decades, but the Clean Air Act—empowering the EPA to slap localities with a "nonattainment" label—had played a minor role.[14]

On the other hand, Greenstone also assessed the *cost* of the Clean Air Act on the economy. Liberal environmentalists tend to dismiss claims that the Act has had significant economic impact. Yet Greenstone's work identifies the true size of the burden placed on the economy:[15]

> I find that in the first 15 years after the Amendments became law (1972-1987), nonattainment counties (relative to attainment ones) lost approximately 590,000 jobs, $37 billion in capital stock, and $75 billion (1987$) of output in pollution intensive industries....Importantly these findings are robust across many specifications, and the effects are apparent across a wide range of polluting industries.

So half a million Americans lost their job as a result of the Clean Air Act. Given that there is a clear and demonstrated link between income and health—the wealthier you are, the healthier you tend to be—it is quite plausible that the Clean Air Act may have reduced the nation's overall health, not improved it.

The Clean Air Act just doesn't appear to have had the effects claimed for it—no improvement in future health, no improvement in past health, no obvious effect on emissions—and yet came at a high price. Precisely the reverse of the Sierra Club's claims.

What could have caused the dramatic improvements in air quality we have seen if it wasn't the Clean Air Act with all the powers it gave to the Environmental Protection Agency? Indur Goklany examined this question in great detail in the late 1990s.[16] He found that improvements began two decades before the Act, and that those trends continued at the same rate after the Act was passed.

Goklany's findings completely contradicted the line argued by liberal environmentalists in favor of their power grab. They argued that air quality was declining because state and local governments were engaged in a "race to the bottom," where each jurisdiction sacrificed the environment in favor of jobs and industry. The Clean Air Act was therefore necessary in order to nationalize protection of environmental quality.

As Goklany found, this wasn't the case. State and local governments were not engaged in a "race to the bottom" at all. In fact, they were engaged in a "race to the top." Goklany explains:

[S]tates are continually engaged in a "race to the top of the quality of life." At early stages of economic and technological development, such progress masquerades as a "race to the bottom" for environmental quality. That is because at those earlier stages society places a much higher priority on acquiring basic public health and other services such as sewage treatment, water supply, and electricity than on environmental quality, which initially worsens. But as the original priorities are met, environmental problems become higher priorities. More resources then are devoted to solving those problems. Environmental degradation is arrested and then reversed. And the race to the top of the quality of life looks more like a "race to the top" of environmental quality. In fact, there sometimes emerged the not-in-my-back-yard (NIMBY) situation, with states trying to avoid pollution whether the federal government is pushing them or not.

This finding is central to the whole environmental debate, and liberals hate it. It shows that environmental quality is not only best *achieved through*, but is actually *intrinsic to*, the economic development and rising standards of living that the free enterprise system has best delivered. If you're a capitalist, you are by your very nature an environmentalist. Your success will help deliver environmental improvement far more effectively than any number of laws, regulations, and targets.

This argument is also critical in the current debate over global warming and globalization. Much of the world is just beginning to industrialize. About 1.6 billion people have never flipped a light switch. Billions more do not own cars. Large segments of humanity will be industrializing for decades to come. Poor nations will need a lot more energy, and the most affordable kinds of energy. That means coal to generate electricity and gasoline to power cars and trucks. If we restrict affordable energy, the prospect of Africa freed at last from darkness will fade away before our eyes.

An industrialized Africa, however, will not necessarily mean an Africa of poisoned rivers and choking air. Evidence from all over the world suggests the presence of what those dismal scientists known as economists call an "environmental Kuznets curve." This is an expression of the phenomenon Goklany describes, whereby societies as they develop first concentrate on activities that may cause harm to the environment, but after a certain level environmental quality becomes important, and so harm to the environment drops.

A variety of research projects, including one by the United Nations Development Program, have found this same curve.

For different environmental improvements, the curves are different, which makes sense as some are more expensive than others. In general however, environmental improvements begin in earnest after per capita GDP reaches $8,000. Before that threshold, other needs take precedence. After it, environmental quality achieves its own value, a value that citizens are willing to purchase.

So progress and the environment go hand in hand. Golkany's work, and this curve, bothers liberal environmentalists for another reason. Goklany found that central planning is no substitute for important democratic institutions found in the free enterprise nations:

America was fortunate that its political and legal system supported the institutions that fostered economic growth and technological change. For the same reasons, many of the world's developed nations have gone through similar environmental transitions for various air pollutants over the last several years. Other nations, such as the erstwhile centrally planned economies, which lacked such institutions, have had the worst of all worlds—they are poorer and their environment is wretched. Their problems were further aggravated by the absence of democracy that provides a powerful incentive to decision makers to constantly monitor and improve the quality of the ordinary citizen's life.

The research on the Kuznets curve backs this up. Bruce Yandle of Clemson University and his colleagues have found[17] that mere economic progress is not enough to trigger what is termed the "environmental transition" that is seen at the top of the Kuznets curve. Other institutional factors are needed as well, and foremost among these is that bane of the Marxist and modern liberal environmentalist alike, private property:

[W]e should recognize that the movement along an Environmental Kuznets Curve can be thought of as movement through a set of property rights stations and their accompanying institutions. For example, in primitive societies managed by tradition or tribal rule, part of the resource base may be treated as a commons. The cost of defining and enforcing transferable private property rights is simply too large to do otherwise; the net gains are too small. With growing scarcity, however, a time comes when some aspects of the commons become defined as public or communal property.

As "propertyness" expands—and private property is the most incentive enriched form—individuals have a greater incentive to manage, to conserve, and to accumulate wealth that can be traded or passed on to future generations. Under such circumstances, what might be viewed as a waste stream affecting the commons, or no-man's-land, is seen as an invasion of property. Those who impose uninvited costs are held accountable. A similar response can occur in tribal settings where social pressures that punish or reward treatment of communal property are effective.

Eventually, when scarce aspects of the environment are defined as property—either public property managed by government or private property managed by individuals—the community moves rapidly in the race to improve environmental life.

In other words, the more people own free and clear title to their own property, the better they take care of it. As noted earlier, people do not spit on their own doorstep—a notion as important to wildlife as it is to air and water.

As an example, the founding document of Anglo-American political thought, Magna Carta, laid the basis for rights of access to river resources in 1215. It is precisely these rights that led

British anglers in the 1960s to sue companies that polluted rivers and therefore affected their private property in the shape of the right to fish. The courts found in their favor, and the companies that were polluting the rivers had to stop doing it.

And it's not limited to England conserving wildlife. Pre-Colombian Indians in Canada, for instance, had a very sophisticated set of property rules for conserving the animals on which their civilization depended. The Montagnais' property-based game conservation and similar stories involving wood ducks in the U.S. and leopards in Africa are discussed in more detail in Chapter 6.

Tradition, property, and conservation: these are the three strands that have repeatedly dictated environmental protection. They have cleaned up rivers and brought species back from the brink of disaster. As we will see later on, they protect forests from wildfire and provide the potential to restock the oceans.

The importance of this insight cannot be overstated. It provides the next step in understanding why conservative approaches to the environment succeed and liberal approaches fail. Environmental conservation is traditional, and therefore right.

How Progressives Set the Cuyahoga River on Fire

On June 22, 1969, the Cuyahoga River in Cleveland "caught fire." This fact is indispensible to central-planners and the enemies of industry. The "burning river" is one of the founding myths of big-government-environmentalism—particularly on the *federal* stage.

Thankfully, Jonathan Adler has done the work to reveal that, while the fire did happen, the story about how it came to be is largely myth:

The conventional narratives, of a river abandoned by its local community, of water pollution at its zenith, of conventional legal doctrines impotent in the face of environmental harms, and of a beneficent federal government rushing in to save the day, is misleading in many respects.... The river did catch fire in 1969—or, more properly, oil and debris floating on the river's surface caught fire—but this was not clearly due to state and local malfeasance or a failure of common law protections. And, while federal intervention likely did accelerate river cleanup in many parts of the country, there are still reasons to question the federal government's record with regard to the Cuyahoga, and river quality generally.[18]

The first thing we should know is that when people talk about remembering seeing the flames leaping out of the river, they are showing how faulty their memories are. No TV crews made it to the river to take those pictures before the fires were put out; they were under control within thirty minutes. The total cost of the damage inflicted by the fire was a mere $50,000. Beyond a brief mention on the front page, the full story of the fire was covered by the *Cleveland Plain Dealer* on page 11-C and merited only five paragraphs. Firefighters called the blaze "unremarkable" and said it "wasn't a big deal."[19]

So what did people remember? There is a photo of a fireboat fighting a river on fire that accompanies the *Time* story on the conflagration. It isn't of the 1969 fire, though. In fact, it was an archive picture of a river fire from 1952, a much more severe burn that caused much greater damage. The hidden truth is that the Cuyahoga had caught fire several times before, and that was not unusual for rivers in industrial towns in that age.

More important than the factual discrepancies is the myth about how the river got so polluted. The official explanation is that *laissez-faire* policies and negligent local governments polluted the river. Environmental writer Philip Shabecoff captured the standard sentiment when he wrote, "In 1881, the mayor of Cleveland called the Cuyahoga River 'an open sewer through the center of the city.' It remained so until passage of the Clean Water Act in 1972." The implication is clear: business abused the river while Cleveland stood by, and then Washington came in and saved the day.

The real story is more complex, and a good portion of the blame lies on the shoulders of big government—specifically on the "progressive" abolition of property rights in favor of "common" ownership. In short, one key problem was that nobody had property rights over the river. It was nobody's "doorstep," and so everybody was spitting on it.

We discussed above the presence of water rights in Magna Carta. In early American history, this principle of private ownership supported by common law was the model for waterways. As settlers moved into the drier areas of the country this principle changed, with the "progressive" notion of common ownership replacing it. With water belonging not to individuals, but to the state, the way was opened for pollution. The principle of common ownership contributed to environmental degradation in a way that the tradition of private property did not.

This meant that industrial areas tended to treat their commonly owned rivers as common dumping grounds, hence the mayor's description of the Cuyahoga as "an open sewer through the center of the city."[20] The industrialization of the city was viewed by city managers and residents alike as a desirable thing, and the side effects exhibited as the Cuyahoga changed color and odor were viewed as signs of progress. The city moved to take its domestic water from Lake Erie rather than clean up the river.

With oil, debris, and other effluent accepted as part of the river, fires were inevitable, and common. The river is believed to have caught fire in 1868, 1883, and 1887. A river fire in 1912 killed five men. The same spot ignited in 1922, and there was yet another fire in 1930. By 1936, concern was growing, but it concentrated on lack of appropriate fire control services rather than on the state of the river. Fires burst out again in 1936, 1941, and 1948. The 1952 fire was caused after a Standard Oil facility had spread a two-inch thick oil slick across the river, and the resultant blaze caused as much as $1.5 million worth of damage, destroying a shipyard and a bridge. There was no loss of life, if only because the fire started on a Saturday.

Other rivers caught fire in this period: the Buffalo River in New York State in the 1960s, the Rouge River in Dearborn, Michigan (repeatedly), the Schuykill River, and a river leading into Baltimore Harbor. The Cuyahoga was probably the worst offender, but it was by no means alone.

To hear the environmentalist myth, one would believe that the river's plight was caused by selfish local companies and that the river was saved only by federal intervention in the shape of the Clean Water Act of 1972. Yet cleanup of the Cuyahoga had started after the terrible fire of 1952. In 1959, fish reappeared, testimony to some remarkable progress. The leading businesses of the area formed the Cuyahoga River Basin Water Quality Committee in 1963. In 1968, voters approved by a two-to-one margin a bond issue totaling $100 million for the purposes of cleaning up and protecting the river. One commentator noted that before this:

> [T]he failure to provide adequate municipal sewage treatment is almost entirely due to a lack of community interest in abating its harmful waste discharges for there are no technological problems.[21]

The actions undertaken by the city reflected actions taken around the same time by the state of Ohio, and other cities and states around the nation, to control water pollution since the 1950s. When the Environmental Protection Agency undertook its first National Water Quality Inventory in 1973, it found that there had been "significant improvements" in water quality over the preceding decade.[22] What appears to have happened is that the American people in industrial areas had gone through the environmental transition (remember the Kuznets curves above) in and around the 1950s and 1960s. They were starting to value clean water for its own sake, rather than viewing the river as a common resource for industrial benefit. Things appeared to have been slowed by a conflict between state and city officials in the 1960s, but there was clear political will for an aggressive approach to cleaning up the river before the Federal action of 1972.

More importantly, however, the capacity for enforcing cleanup of the Cuyahoga was already in place in the shape of the Common Law. It is part of the mythology of the Cuyahoga fire that it demonstrated the failings of the Common Law in protecting against pollution, yet as Jonathan Adler says, the law "may have gotten something of a bum rap."[23]

Indeed, anyone looking for the culprit in the river's pollution would have to first turn to the government, which relied on "progressive" anti-traditional, anti-property-rights arguments to justify its actions.

By the 1960s, the state of Ohio had basically taken "ownership" of the river. That put the Cuyahoga's fate in the hands of bureaucrats in Columbus, the state capital, 120 miles from Cleveland, and nowhere near the Cuyahoga. They officially declared the river to be for "industrial use."

Nominally to reduce pollution, the state government issued pollution permits, allowing certain businesses to dump their waste into the river. These state-issued permits completely smashed the recourse the people of Cleveland would traditionally have: common law tort.

Adler suggests that one cause was the "state water pollution permitting system which insulated permitted facilities from public nuisance actions and generally inhibited local efforts to combat pollution."[24]

Cleveland's utilities director Ben S. Stefanski II explained after the fire that Columbus's permit system had made the city impotent. "We have no jurisdiction over what is dumped" in the river, he told the *Plain Dealer*. "The state licenses the industries and gives them legal authority to dump in the river. Actually, the state gives them a license to pollute."[25]

Far from the government standing by while business polluted the river, sometimes, the government stood in the way while business tried to clean up the river. In 1965, for example, a real estate company sued the city to stop allowing use of the river as an industrial dump. It won, but the verdict was overturned by the state supreme court, which found that state law trumped common law rights. In 1968, Arnold Reitze noted that "common law actions for water pollution abatement are not common and perhaps the protection afforded by the permit system is the reason."[26]

But long before the state of Ohio trampled on common law and property rights to pollute the Cuyahoga, the city of Cleveland was doing the same.

After the Cuyahoga had spent decades as an "open sewer," a paper manufacturer sued the municipality in 1936 to prevent the city dumping sewage into the river, harming the manufacturer's business. The city claimed it had a "prescriptive right" to use the river in that way.

Influenced by decades of "progressive" thought, the court agreed with the city—the city government got to determine what was done with the river, no matter how much it harmed others. However, as a legal doctrine known as strict liability gained currency, courts in the 1940s were holding that, "One may not obtain by prescription, or otherwise than by purchase, a right to

cast sewage upon the lands of another without his consent." It is
likely that the businesses and individuals so badly affected by the
city's attitude would soon have been able to use the courts to
force the city to end its practices and recognize the value of clean
water, had not the state launched its pollution permit system.

So if the city and state governments hadn't trumped the legal
system, what might have happened? We can construct an alternative history by looking at the court cases won by British anglers
that we mentioned earlier. As mentioned, thanks to a definition of
rights that stretches back to Magna Carta, British anglers enjoy
property rights in the form of rights to catch fish in rivers. In the
1940s, the Pride of Derby fishing club, named after a prize-win-
ning ram, realized that their rights were being impinged by local
companies and governments and decided to butt heads.

They took the Borough of Derby, British Celanese Limited, and
the British Electricity Authority to court, alleging that the three
defendants respectively discharged untreated sewage, industrial
waste, and superheated effluent into the river, killing fish and
thereby damaging the anglers' property rights. The Borough of
Derby took a line in court similar to the City of Cleveland, arguing that it had a statutory right to pollute. The court rejected this
argument, finding that the law forbade behavior that "shall be a
nuisance or injurious to the health or reasonable comfort of the
inhabitants [in the region]." Moreover, the court rejected an
attempt to substitute damages for an injunction on discharges into
the river. It held that, "In the present case, it is plain that damages
would be a wholly inadequate remedy for [the angling club], who
have not been incorporated in order to fish for monthly sums."
The court required the borough to redesign its sewage system,
Celanese to change how it discharged its waste, and the Authority to reduce its release of superheated water.[27]

If the Common Law had been allowed to operate in the case
of Cleveland when that paper manufacturer had first sued in

1936, it is probable that similar injunctions would have been delivered by the court. City and industry alike would have been told to stop their damaging practices. The build up of oil and debris that led to the fire would have been cleared long before the big fires of the 1950s, and the blaze of 1967 would certainly not have occurred. No songs would have been sung and Administrator Browner would have had to find another iconic myth on which to base her demands for more power.

As Adler comments, "common law may not have been the perfect tool with which to combat water pollution, but it may have been more effective had it been allowed to operate."[28]

After decades of abuse at the hands of the city and then the state governments, anti-pollution advocates, rather than seeking repeal of the laws and a return to the common law that had shown all willingness to protect them, turned instead to advocating federal law.

Here it needs to be noted that the federal government had shown no sign of being interested in water pollution up to this point. There had been largely symbolic legislation in 1948 and throughout the 1950s, but the amount of money appropriated to support the legislation was negligible—statutes from 1950 to 1952 authorized $83 million of expenditure but appropriators only took up $9 million. As Adler notes:

> Federal spending and loans for water purification and pollution control in 1968 totaled $190 million—not even double the amount approved by Cleveland voters that same year. Of that total, only approximately $6 million was slated for Ohio. Cleveland received nothing.[29]

After the founding of the Environmental Protection Agency, the new administrator William Rucklehaus singled out the City of Cleveland for attack. Mayor Stokes called this a "cheap political plot" and commented on "the outrageous failure of his federal government to put a dime into Cleveland's sewer program."[30]

It seems possible, perhaps probable, that the Cuyahoga would have been cleaned up in the 1950s or even earlier if it had not been for the regulation and bureaucracy introduced instead that had the effect of blocking cleanup efforts. The licensing process gave polluters an incentive to pollute that replaced the disincentive of legal challenge. The regulatory approach so beloved of liberals replaced the traditional approach favored by conservatives. Its failure in Ohio merely propelled them towards asking for bigger, more powerful regulations at the federal level. The Cuyahoga River fire should actually be viewed as a moment for conservatives to say "we told you so," not as a liberal vindication.

As Adler concludes, in the event of federal action not being forthcoming:

> [D]esire for greater environmental protection would have been channeled toward other ends, potentially resulting in greater state and local regulation, the removal of regulatory obstacles to public nuisance actions and greater local initiative, the evolution of common law doctrines to accommodate the needs of environmental litigation, or the adoption of measures designed to supplement and enhance traditional common law protections. There is no reason to believe that the adoption of federal command-and-control regulations was the only means of providing the level of environmental protection demanded by an ecologically awakened public.
>
> It is quite possible to conceive of alternative regulatory frameworks that could have been developed to complement and build upon common law environmental protections and those state and local programs which were more successful. The administrative state is not without its problems and there are many aspects of the common law framework that make it

well suited to address certain aspects of environmental problems. Measures to reinforce property rights, ensure the vitality
of private and public nuisance actions, and perhaps to provide
scientific, technical and financial support to state and local
agencies may have been a viable alternative. As the fables of
the Cuyahoga River fires illustrate, policymakers may have
been too quick to dismiss the potential of such alternatives.[31]

A river on fire makes for a great "meme," as they call them
these days. A river on fire caused by evil capitalists is an even better meme for a liberal mentality that hates the idea of industry
and profit. A river on fire caused by bureaucracy and political
buck-passing is less attractive. It is no wonder that the Cuyahoga
River fire swiftly became surrounded by myth and obfuscation.

We have allowed ourselves to be led astray from a sensible,
traditional path, by the ministrations of clever people who suffer
from a massive dose of fatal conceit. The solution is to ignore
those clever people, and to let decisions be taken at the level most
connected with the problem. Far from looking upwards, to the
federal government or transnational bodies like the European
Union or, Lord help us, the United Nations, we should seek to
solve environmental problems at local levels and via local institutions. We shall return to this idea in the final chapter, but
before that there are many more examples to discuss of how liberalism has brought disaster.

Chapter Six

Endangered Species Act

Shoot, Shovel, and Shut Up

Riverside County, California, 1993: late one evening, at around 11:30 pm, the wind knocked down a high-voltage power line. A fire sprang up that swiftly became a conflagration. Flames ripped through 25,000 acres and bore down on three hundred homes. Many of the homeowners stood helpless.

The traditional method for protecting their homes from fire—disking, or digging a firebreak by tractor—had been forbidden them because they lived in a "preserve study area" for the Stephen's kangaroo rat. In the end, twenty-nine houses were destroyed, nineteen of which had stood in the study areas.

However, one affected landowner, Michael Rowe, saw the flames coming at around one in the morning. He cut through his neighbors' fence, leaped onto his tractor, and disked a firebreak to save his property. His action worked. By defying the United States government, he avoided losing his land and his home. ABC News covered his valiant story.

Yet the very idea that violating the Endangered Species Act could have saved his home was anathema to the liberal environmentalist establishment. The Democratic Congress set the Government Accountability Office on him, which produced a report that claimed Rowe had acknowledged the disking had nothing to do with saving his home. The *Washington Post* ran a report on the incident saying, "Great story. But it turns out not to be true."

Michael Rowe had been the victim of an establishment frame-up. After the government report, Rowe told his tale to Ike Suggs of the Competitive Enterprise Institute:

> According to the GAO, Mr. Rowe "acknowledged that the wind direction shifted as the fire came close to his property and that the fire shifted its path and proceeded to destroy other homes." Mr. Rowe is outraged: "I never said that; the wind was blowing right at me." Mr. Rowe says that he had a garage full of ash, facing the direction from which the fire came to prove it. Indeed, the fire hit his firebreak, burned along the edge of it where there was something to burn, and then around the edge of the disked area.
>
> Yet the GAO went even further, claiming that Mr. Rowe actually "stated that the changing wind direction was likely as important in saving his home. Mr. Rowe cannot believe that a federal agency charged with the responsibility of ferreting out the truth could claim that he had actually made that statement. "I do not see how the GAO's mistake could have been an honest one," he says. Mr. Rowe's veracity has been corroborated by a witness to the conversation with the GAO investigator.[1]

Meanwhile, the Fish and Wildlife Service denied it had ever suggested that people not cut firebreaks, going so far as to tell that to John Stossel of ABC's *20/20*. After a host of threatening letters to homeowners and fire service officials made that claim untenable, it started blaming those local fire officials.[2]

Rowe, the Domenigonis next door (whose family had operated a ranch on the property for over a hundred years), and all their neighbors were victims of a callous bureaucracy. Moreover, they were then railroaded by those who had too much to lose if the truth became widely known. If ever there was a whitewash operation, this was it.

In 1990, the U.S. Fish and Wildlife Service had ordered the Domenigonis to stop cultivating all eight hundred of their tillable acres, stating this would constitute a "taking" of the rat, for which they would face impoundment of their farm equipment, a year in jail, and possibly a $50,000 fine for each and every taking of an individual rat. For three seasons their fields lay idle and they lost $84,000 in foregone crops each season. The land-friendly practices they had developed over a century were stopped.

In 1993, after the fire, a Fish and Wildlife Service biologist named John Bradley authorized the family to plow their fields, having determined that the kangaroo rat no longer lived in the area. However, Bradley said the rats had left before the fires because the brush and weeds had grown too thick for them.

Not only had the Endangered Species Act destroyed human habitat, it had driven away the animals it was designed to protect.

Once again, big-government environmentalism yielded exactly the negative effects that free enterprise and private ownership supposedly perpetrate. Once again, liberalism caused an environmental disaster that traditional notions of property and liberty could have prevented.

In previous chapters we saw how property rights help keep the American landscape healthy and how liberal environmentalist repugnance at the idea led to disaster. The same is true of wildlife, not just in America but across the globe. Rightly concerned at the number of species currently in danger of extinction, the liberal environmentalists have imposed an anti-property dogma aimed at saving them but which actually exacerbates the situation. Meanwhile, private approaches have helped species recover all over the world, at least until government intervenes again. Just like the rest of us, the last thing an endangered species wants to hear is, "I'm from the Government; I'm here to help."

Yet as the kangaroo rat story shows, the disastrous impact of the liberal environmentalist endangered species strategy is not just a problem for the impacted species, it's a problem for us humans as well. Over the years, the model has gained a momentum of its own that threatens to crush growth and development like a runaway boulder. The model is liberal managerialism at its worst. Bureaucrats check their boxes and make the rest of us pay for it. In the meantime, animals die.

The Reversal of Freedoms Act

Probably the best popular explanation of the liberal environmentalist model for endangered species came in an episode of that subversively conservative[3] animated television series *The Simpsons* broadcast in 2002. In "The Frying Game," Homer Simpson buys a Koi pond for his wife Marge. They discover that a horrendously loud and annoying insect called the screamapillar has started living in it. What happens next is obviously satirical, but familiar to all too many land owners:

LISA: What was that?

SCREAMAPILLAR: Argghh, arghhh!

HOMER: What the hell is that noise?

LISA: That caterpillar is screaming

HOMER: Aww, the poor thing's in pain. What he needs is a visit from kindly old Dr. Foot [rears back on one foot preparing to stomp the insect, only to be confronted by a man sliding out from behind a tree].

EPA OFFICIAL: Hold it right there Dr. Foot! You're about to kill an endangered species—the screamapillar [rubs screamapillar lovingly], which has chosen your yard as its home.

HOMER: Fine! I won't kill it ... [stage whispering to Lisa] finish the job.

EPA OFFICIAL [CLEARLY ANNOYED]: Mr. Simpson, allowing an endangered species to die is a federal offense, under the Reversal of Freedoms Act of 1994. You are now legally responsible for the safety and well-being of this screamapillar!

Forced to coddle the creature, Homer proceeds to read it bedtime stories in an effort to keep it from screaming all night long. When he accidentally squishes the "horrible bug" with the storybook, armed EPA agents descend from a black helicopter and he is arrested at gunpoint. Taken to court, Homer is found guilty of, erm, "attempted insecticide and aggravated buggery."

It's funny because it's true. The Endangered Species Act, passed at the request of President Nixon in 1973, has indeed become the Reversal of Freedoms Act. Landowners who happen to have threatened or endangered species on their lands or who simply have habitat that might be used by endangered species are routinely prevented from using their lands or property. They are stopped from undertaking such activities as harvesting their trees, planting their crops, grazing their cattle, irrigating their fields, clearing brush along fence lines, disking firebreaks around their homes and barns, or building new homes.

This reversal of freedoms provides a perverse incentive. The tale of a man named Benjamin Cone shows exactly why. Mr. Cone, a landowner of Greensboro, N.C., bought 8,000 acres of timberless, cutover land on the Black River. He and his son, Ben Cone, Jr., allowed the forest to grow back over many years and managed it for wildlife values. Their policy of environmentally and arboriculturally sound prescribed burns and selective thinning maintained a healthy forest and created ideal habitat for species and environmental amenities for many others. It also created a near ideal habitat for the red-cockaded woodpecker.

Because of that attraction of the endangered species to the new habitat he had created, Mr. Cone was denied any logging rights to 1,560 acres of his land. A real estate appraiser determined that the value of the land without the woodpeckers was $1.7 million; with the woodpeckers and the accompanying land-use controls, the value was a mere $260,000. Few people can afford million-dollar losses. So, to mitigate losses, Cone clear-cut all his land that was not yet inhabited by the bird. As he said:[4]

> I cannot afford to let those woodpeckers take over the rest of the property. I'm going to start massive clear-cutting. I'm going to a forty-year rotation instead of a seventy-five-to eighty-year rotation.

This isn't just the reaction of one idiosyncratic landowner. It's a rational and natural reaction, repeated all over the country. As the celebrity economists Stephen Dubner and Steven Levitt wrote in the *New York Times*:

> The economists Dean Lueck and Jeffrey Michael wanted to gauge the E.S.A.'s effect on the red-cockaded woodpecker, a protected bird that nests in old-growth pine trees in eastern

North Carolina. By examining the timber harvest activity of more than 1,000 privately owned forest plots, Lueck and Michael found a clear pattern: when a landowner felt that his property was turning into the sort of habitat that might attract a nesting pair of woodpeckers, he rushed in to cut down the trees. It didn't matter if timber prices were low.[5]

Other economists have found similar patterns for other species. Dubner and Levitt continue:

> In a new working paper that examines the plight of the cactus ferruginous pygmy owl, the economists John List, Michael Margolis and Daniel Osgood found that landowners near Tucson rushed to clear their property for development rather than risk having it declared a safe haven for the owl. The economists make the argument for "the distinct possibility that the Endangered Species Act is actually endangering, rather than protecting, species."

What message does the Endangered Species Act send to landowners? It tells them that a rare bird or insect on their property is a cost to them, not a benefit. As Sam Hamilton, former Fish and Wildlife administrator for the state of Texas has said:[6]

> The incentives are wrong here. If I have a rare metal on my property, its value goes up. But if a rare bird occupies the land, its value disappears. We've got to turn it around to make the landowner want the bird on his property.

Well, indeed, but that idea would be anathema to the liberal environmentalist. We have already seen how the concept of profiting from the environment is viewed with utter distaste by liberal environmentalists. It would be alien to their worldview to allow a landowner to accrue extra value because an endangered species "chooses their yard as its home."

The cost, of course, only appears when the feds show up. Better by far, then, if the federal government never knows about the presence of the species. In what is surely the most perverse incentive of all, the landowner is actually encouraged by the workings of the Endangered Species Act to erase its habitat or, at worst, kill off the animals. When you threaten landowners with uncompensated losses, you encourage them to get rid of wildlife habitat and sterilize their lands. It creates the "shoot, shovel, and shut up" syndrome whereby wildlife is viewed as a liability, not as an asset. There are surely many Homer Simpsons out there who have introduced their screamapillars to Dr. Foot.

That's certainly the view of some experts. Larry McKinney, director of resource protection for the Texas Parks and Wildlife Department, has said:[7]

> While I have no hard evidence to prove it, I am convinced that more habitat for the Black-capped Vireo, and especially the Golden-cheeked Warbler, has been lost in those areas of Texas since the listing of these birds than would have been lost without the ESA at all.

Moreover, the Act can lead to the destruction of habitat even when it is strictly complied with as we saw in the story of the kangaroo rat.

Now any conservative will accept that the world is rarely perfect and sometimes there might be trade-offs of benefits. In this case the price might be worth paying if the Act has helped species recover from the brink of extinction. To listen to liberal environmentalists you'd think this Act was one of the most successful pieces of legislation ever. Here are the over-the-top claims of some leading environmental groups:

THE SIERRA CLUB: Thanks to this landmark law, wild salmon still spawn in the rivers of the Pacific Northwest, wolves have returned to Yellowstone, and the bald eagle soars from coast to coast. The ESA has been successful in keeping over 99 percent of all the fish and wildlife under its care from going extinct, but the Bush administration is rushing to gut the law by changing regulations to make it easier for developers to pave and pollute the nation's wildlands and our special places.[8]

NATURAL RESOURCES DEFENSE COUNCIL: The Endangered Species Act has saved hundreds of species from extinction, including the bald eagle, grizzly bear, gray wolf and wild stocks of Pacific and Atlantic salmon. 98 percent of the species protected by the law have survived. Nearly 40 percent of species protected for at least 6 years are stable or improving; the longer a species is protected by the act, the more likely it is to be on the road to recovery.[9]

ENVIRONMENTAL DEFENSE: A strong Endangered Species Act (ESA) is essential to preserve our nation's unique natural heritage for future generations. The ESA was enacted on December 28, 1973 with the simple but ambitious goal of reversing the decades of neglect and abuse that have pushed many irreplaceable species of plants and animals to the brink of extinction. Now, more than a quarter century later, over a thousand animals are protected by this law which has been called the "crown jewel" of our country's environmental legislation. Endangered species success stories (species which have recovered or are recovering) are found in all 50 states.[10]

These are grandiose, sweeping claims, but the keen-eyed reader will note that the very nature of the claims suggests caution. Merely because a species was endangered, was placed on the endangered species list, and has since recovered does not mean that the Endangered Species Act was responsible. The common and useful phrase "correlation does not imply causation," seems to have been banned from the liberal environmentalists' workplaces.

There is very little evidence that the Endangered Species Act has had any positive effect in its almost quarter-century of existence. Under the Act, the federal government identifies endangered and threatened species, and puts them on "endangered" and "threatened" lists. At the end of 2006, there were 1,177 animals on the endangered/threatened species list and 747 plants.[11] In addition, the Fish and Wildlife Service is considering 280 candidates for such lists.[12] Of the nearly two thousand plants and animals that have graced the Endangered Species List, a mere forty-seven have been delisted.[13] Nine of these are extinct; seventeen were improperly listed; and twenty-one are counted as "recovered."

The Fish and Wildlife Service likes to credit the Act and their own actions under the Act for saving each and every one of the species it placed on the "recovered" list. As might be expected, on closer examination, it is highly dubious to credit the punitive elements of the Endangered Species Act with saving these species from extinction. More often than not, there are non-Act related explanations for each "recovery" and certainly all of the "recoveries" could have been achieved without the Act's punitive land use regulations.

Here's an example of how outrageous the Fish and Wildlife Service's claims are: three of the species listed as "recovered" are Australian kangaroos. The Endangered Species Act's land-use restrictions—having no authority in Australia—obviously played no role in their recovery. Two of the twenty-one species of the current "recovered" list were probably not as threatened as believed. The Fish and Wildlife Service admits that recovery might also be due to improper listing in the first place.[14] The gray whale recovered because the U.S. stopped whaling decades before the passage of the Endangered Species Act.

The American alligator recovered in part because it was probably improperly listed. Populations were higher than estimated at the time of listing and the animal may have been listed as a "charismatic megafauna" (remember them?) in order to help raise public support for the passage of the Act in the first place. There is no doubt that the animal had been under severe pressure, but it was recovering by the early 1970s because of conservation efforts that began before the ESA passed. For example, a University of Florida summary of information on alligator populations notes:[15]

> This act [the Lacey Act, which banned exports of the skins], combined with the reduced demand for alligator skins resulting from a decline in many traditional retail markets, virtually eliminated poaching. Although much has been said about the poaching of Florida's alligators during the 1960s, alligators remained abundant in remote and inaccessible areas. The rapid recovery of the reptiles throughout the 1970s, once they were effectively protected, suggests they endured poaching better than once thought.

Similarly, Randal O'Toole of the Thoreau Institute writes:[16]

> The American alligator recovered after being protected from hunting, but might have recovered in any case through state efforts; at the time of its listing in 1973 its populations were increasing or stable in most of its range.

More controversial, perhaps, are the reasons for the recovery of some of the larger birds, such as the peregrine falcon, the brown pelican, and the national bird of the United States, the

American bald eagle. Many, including the libertarian Reason Foundation, claim that the main reason for the recovery of these birds was not the Endangered Species Act, but the DDT ban we examined in Chapter 1. For instance, Brian Seasholes argues:[17]

> The banning of the pesticide DDT in 1972, not the passage of the ESA in 1973, is widely acknowledged as the paramount reason for the bald eagle's recovery. "Nearly everyone agrees that the key to the eagle's resurgence—even more so than the Endangered Species Act—was the banning of the use of the insecticide DDT in this country in 1972," admits the National Audubon Society. DDT, specifically its metabolite DDE, or the form into which it breaks down, caused widespread reproductive failures in raptors like the bald eagle as well as the brown pelican. DDT reduced the amount of calcium in eggshells, which resulted in thinshelled (sic) eggs susceptible to breaking or infertility. DDT came into widespread use after World War II. It proved very effective as a means to control mosquitoes as well as a wide range of insects problematic to the agricultural and forestry industries. The relationship between DDT and the bald eagle's decline and subsequent recovery has been very well established by an authoritative body of peer-reviewed literature.

As we've already seen, there are reasons to doubt DDT's effects on human health and on smaller birds, but Seasholes and his colleagues probably have a point that, if DDT had any harmful effects on avian life, it inflicted them on large predatory birds. Yet as we've also seen, DDT was being used inappropriately as a large-scale agricultural pesticide that reduced its effectiveness. The fact that the DDT ban may have helped populations of larger birds recover in no way invalidates the arguments for its use in the developing world, nor does it justify the self-serving preachings of the liberal environmentalists that it is uniquely evil.

DDT could still be re-introduced at appropriate levels into American use without having these effects.

Moreover, Brian goes on to list many other factors that give one pause in considering that the Endangered Species Act made any meaningful contribution to the bald eagle's recovery. To wit:[18]

> ...the bald eagle was never faced with extinction in the first place;...ESA-driven habitat conservation efforts often backfired; there was no ESA protection for 70 percent of bald eagles in the contiguous 48 states; state and private projects to reintroduce eagles to former habitat worked; other laws, the eagle's charisma, and a decline in shooting eagles made ESA protections less relevant; banning lead shot for hunting waterfowl that eagles eat was relatively unimportant; bald eagles met the criteria to be taken off the endangered species list in the mid-1990s but only now, in 2007, is the Fish and Wildlife Service doing so.

That first point is actually vital. There have always been plenty of bald eagles in the North American continent. About 50-75,000 birds have happily existed in Alaska and British Columbia without any problems befalling them. It was only in the lower forty-eight states that the bald eagle population fell to low numbers. The Canadian and Alaskan populations have always represented the bulk of the animal's numbers. Not that that stopped liberal environmentalists from misrepresenting the position. Roger Schlickheisen, president of Defenders of Wildlife, once wrote:[19]

> Picture an America without its greatest national symbol, the bald eagle. But for the Endangered Species Act, it would be extinct.

That isn't even hyperbole. It's an outright lie.

Also in 1997, the Yellowstone grizzly bear came off the endangered species list, having met all the criteria originally laid out in its "recovery plan" for no longer being regarded as endangered. The population had increased from about 250 in 1975 to around 600 in 2006, a number regarded as sufficient for the population to continue to thrive without extra protection. Most of the animal's turf is controlled by the Forest and National Parks Services. As we've already seen, however, that consideration and the so-called protection of the Endangered Species Act were no help against the Grant Village development destroying prime grizzly habitat. Environmentalists, meanwhile, alternately condemned the delisting and commended it as proving that the Endangered Species Act works. It should also be noted that there are around 40,000 grizzly bears in North America and the species as a whole is in no way threatened.

Similar considerations apply to the grey wolf, of which several sub-species were once listed. There may be as many as 60,000 grey wolves in North America, but because of a classification into dubious sub-species, several have been listed. In 1944, two biologists listed forty-four separate sub-species, but today the accepted number is only five. Even that classification can be doubted, as biologists have great difficulty telling them apart. The difference in the sub-species is more likely geographic than biological. R.J. Smith explains how these classifications really represent just guesswork:[20]

Subspecies do exist—at least for man's purposes to help explain a very plastic and constantly changing and evolving natural world. Until recently subspecies were largely in the eye of the beholder. Where some biologists thought they all looked the same, others saw scores of subspecies. A subspecies is simply an "isolated" geographic race or form of a widespread species. And over time as these races remain separate and don't

Chart of Species Regarded as Recovered Under the Endangered Species Act with Analysis of Real Reasons for Recovery

Listed	Delisted	Species	FWS Claim	More Likely Explanation
1967	1987	American Alligator	Recovered	Potential Data Error, market changes, and other non-ESA activities
1967	2001	Aleutian Canada Goose	Recovered	Data Error and other factors unrelated to the ESA[22]
1967	2003	Columbian White Tailed Douglas County Deer	Recovered	State and local efforts; species outside Douglas County still endangered
1967	2007	Eagle, Bald (lower 48 states)	Recovered	DDT ban and other factors
1970	1985	Palau Dove	Recovered	Data Error and other factors related to the ESA[23]
1970	1999	American Peregrine Falcon	Recovered	DDT ban
1970	1994	Arctic Peregrine Falcon	Recovered	DDT ban
1970	1985	Tinian Monarch	Recovered	Data Error and other factors unrelated to the ESA[24]
1970	2004	Palau Owl	Recovered	Data Error and other factors unrelated to the ESA[25]

**Chart of Species Regarded as Recovered Under the Endangered
Species Act with Analysis of Real Reasons for Recovery**

Listed	Delisted	Species	FWS Claim	More Likely Explanation
1970	1985	Palau Fantail Flycatcher	Recovered	Data Error and other factors unrelated to the ESA[26]
1970	1985	U.S. Atlantic Coast Brown Pelican	Recovered	DDT Ban
1970	1994	Gray Whale	Recovered	Market changes: Decline in Whaling
1974	1995	Eastern Gray Kangaroo	Recovered	Overseas, non-ESA related efforts
1974	1995	Red Kangaroo	Recovered	Overseas, non-ESA related efforts
1974	1995	Western Gray Kangaroo	Recovered	Overseas, non-ESA related efforts
1975	2007	Bear, grizzly Yellow-stone DPS	Recovered	Park service efforts and other non-ESA protections; population as a whole never endangered
1978	2007	Wolf, gray MN	Recovered	Dubious sub-species; population as a whole not endangered
1980	2002	Robbins' Cinquefoil	Recovered	Voluntary private efforts and FWS cooperation that did not require ESA[27]

Chart of Species Regarded as Recovered Under the Endangered Species Act with Analysis of Real Reasons for Recovery

Listed	Delisted	Species	FWS Claim	More Likely Explanation
1992	2007	Idaho Springsnail	Recovered & Original data in error (New information discovered)	Data error as essentially admitted by the FWS
2003	2003	Hoovers Wooly Star	Recovered & Original data in error (New information discovered)	Data error as essentially admitted by the FWS
2006	2007	Wolf, gray, western Great Lakes DPS	Recovered	Dubious sub-species; population as a whole not endangered
1990	2003	Eggert Sunflower	Recovered & Original data in error (New information discovered)	Data error as essentially admitted by the FWS

easily mix, they develop more and more differences—both morphological (this one is greyer, this one has larger ears, etc) as well as genetic differences which are more telling. As sufficient differences develop over time they reach a point where they can no longer interbreed, or at least easily and regularly interbreed, and become essentially separate species. But that is hard to test—because if they are widely separated geographically how do you know that a southern bald eagle will not interbreed with a northern bald eagle. Since their ranges don't overlap there is no physical test.

Slowly morphological differences for determining subspecies are giving way to genetic tests, like DNA tests. But even there you have man's relative choices. How much genetic difference between population A and population B must there be for them to be separate subspecies or separate species? There are no natural rules out there. The biologists make the guesses, the determination. Again it represents their views. Their efforts to make nature and evolution understandable by trying to squeeze a very plastic Mother Nature into a grid of concrete pigeon holes, like a mail box—where they won't really fit.

Man needs labels and names to deal with the natural word. Nature doesn't care and just does whatever she wants.

This isn't the biased justification of an ESA opponent. It's basically a paraphrase of Charles Darwin, who wrote in *The Origin of Species*:[21]

I look at the term species as one arbitrarily given for the sake of convenience to a set of individuals closely resembling each other...it does not essentially differ from the term variety, which is given to less distinct and more fluctuating forms. The term variety, again in comparison with mere individual difference, is also applied arbitrarily, and for mere convenience sake.

If you're a federal bureaucrat looking for more control, convenience dictates you multiply the number of subspecies. The more subspecies you define, the more endangered species listings you can make. Be careful—the Fish and Wildlife Service biologists might one day find a subspecies perfectly adapted to life in your backyard.

To sum up, the Endangered Species Act has been bad for humans and animals and hasn't really helped any species recover. Yet its real potential is for the destruction of the American economy. Liberal environmentalists have that plan well in hand.

How Four Drowned Polar Bears Could Destroy the U.S. Economy

We mentioned before how the polar bear (ursus maritimus, to give it its scientific title) has replaced the panda bear as the iconic animal of the environmental movement. This is because, while it is hard to blame the continued threatened state of the cuddly panda on global warming, current arctic conditions make it all too easy to say that the attractive but ferocious[28] polar bear is threatened by America's carbon emissions.

We can see this by turning to the pronouncements of the Goracle once again. In *An Inconvenient Truth* he says:[29]

> A new scientific study shows that, for the first time, polar bears have been drowning in significant numbers.

Well, if that's true, it's something to pay attention to. But of course, it isn't. My colleague Marlo Lewis tracked down the study.[30] This is what he found:[31]

> The study in question reports that in September 2004, "4 dead bears were seen floating far offshore," apparently

drowned by "an abrupt wind storm." So the study may have uncovered an unusual case, related to a specific storm, rather than a trend, and the "significant numbers" turn out to be four.

Meanwhile, newspapers around the world have made famous a photograph that apparently shows a family of polar bears stranded on a swiftly melting iceberg, ninety miles off the coast in the Barrow Sea.

Once again, the truth is not what it seems. As Rob Lyons of the British web magazine *Spiked* found out when he talked to the photographer:[32]

> The student who took the photograph, however, gives a slightly different account: "They were on the ice when we found them and on the ice when we left. They were healthy, fat and seemed comfortable on their iceberg."
>
>   Amanda Byrd, an Australian graduate student at the University of Alaska Fairbanks (UAF), says she took the picture around three years ago—in the summer. The photograph was not "taken by environmentalists" but as part of a field trip with the university.

So much of the concern surrounding these animals is hyperbole and exaggeration. Yet the hysteria is now driving an attempt to declare the polar bear endangered under the Endangered Species Act. This will have enormous consequences.

The Fish and Wildlife Service is considering listing the animal for a variety of reasons, but the case may be summarized as follows:

1   Loss of polar sea ice in recent decades is due to global warming from rising greenhouse gas levels.

2 Therefore, Arctic ice will continue to shrink as greenhouse gas levels rise, producing ice-free or nearly ice-free conditions in the summer months by the end of the twenty-first century or sooner, possibly as early as 2040.

3 Polar bears depend on sea ice as a platform for hunting prey, for mating, for transport from areas of low prey availability to areas of higher prey availability, and for transport from hunting areas to maternal denning areas and vice versa.

4 Therefore, projected losses in Arctic ice are likely to push the polar bear to the brink of extinction within its habitat in the foreseeable future (roughly forty-five years).

As might be expected, given the state of alarmism surrounding global warming, arguments (1) and (2) are questionable, which means that the conclusion (4) is as well. We actually know very little about the natural variability of the Arctic climate, and indeed about how polar bears respond to such variability. What we do know is that massive ice melt is nothing new. On November 2, 1922, the *Washington Post* ran a story from the Associated Press headlined, "Arctic Ocean Getting Warm; Seals Vanish and Icebergs Melt." It went on:

> Reports from fishermen, seal hunters and explorers . . . all point to a radical change in climatic conditions and hitherto unheard-of temperatures in the arctic zone. Exploration expeditions report that scarcely any ice has been met with as far north as 81 degrees 20 minutes.

We also know that the 1930s was a very warm in the arctic, warmer than today in fact.[33] Yet the great buildup in greenhouse gases did not occur until after that time. Moreover, NASA itself has published research that suggests that the current ice melt has more to do with changing wind patterns than global warming:[34]

> [Lead researcher Son] Nghiem said the rapid decline in winter perennial ice the past two years was caused by unusual winds. "Unusual atmospheric conditions set up wind patterns that compressed the sea ice, loaded it into the Transpolar Drift Stream and then sped its flow out of the Arctic," he said. When that sea ice reached lower latitudes, it rapidly melted in the warmer waters.
>
> "The winds causing this trend in ice reduction were set up by an unusual pattern of atmospheric pressure that began at the beginning of this century," Nghiem said.

The attempts to link greenhouse gases to the loss of polar bear habitat are somewhat shaky, but the habitat does appear to be shrinking (although in winter 2008, the Canadian Ice Service has reported increased ice thickness of four to eight inches). Setting aside the causes for now, we should also ask ourselves what effect the shrinkage is having on the bears.

The answer appears to be "not much." When the Great Bear Scare began in 2002, University of Virginia climatologist Patrick Michaels asked the obvious question: is there any correlation between the status of various polar bear populations and the changing temperatures in those regions? The data suggest something surprising. There are only two populations that appear to be declining; these declines are occurring in areas where the temperatures actually *cooled* from 1950 to 1995.

Even now, five years later, despite all the hype, the polar bears seem to be getting by swimmingly (except during storms, of course). Northern Canada has a vast autonomous Inuit area called Nunavut. The chief polar bear biologist for the government of Nunavut is Dr. Mitchell Taylor. He has publicly called for an end to the hyperbole surrounding polar bears, writing:[35]

Climate change is having an effect on the West Hudson population of polar bears, but really, there is no need to panic. Of the
13 populations of polar bears in Canada, 11 are stable or
increasing in number. They are not going extinct, or even
appear to be affected at present. It is noteworthy that the neighboring population of southern Hudson Bay does not appear to
have declined, and another southern population (Davis Strait)
may actually be over-abundant.

Of course polar bears are bound to adapt their behavior if sea
ice decreases, as it has, but this simply means that the bears spend
more time on land. There have therefore been more human
encounters with polar bears over recent years, and many of those
were not pleasant. When natural history filmmaker Nigel Marven recently made a trip to Churchill, Manitoba, to cover the
supposed plight of the polar bear, his guide related a the story of
a typical event:[36]

> To explain what might have happened [had Marven's bear
> encounter gone worse], he recounts the chilling story of a
> female researcher in her 20s who was savaged near here.
>   The only predator that will actively stalk a human, the polar
> bear had hidden in wait behind the huge tyres of a tundra
> buggy and pounced as the woman disembarked from a heli-
> copter and dashed to the vehicle.
>   "She had four huge puncture wounds in her back, and
> would have died if a guy hadn't jumped out of the buggy and
> hit the bear with a long pole," Dennis says.
>   "Those bears seem to love the scent after people drink cof-
> fee, and I'd hate to have to shoot one."

Marven himself spent eighty days recording the ways of the
polar bear for his documentary. Naturally he formed a view as to
whether the polar bear is currently threatened or not:[37]

After almost three months of working with those who know the Arctic best—among them Inuit Indians, who are appalled at the way an animal they have lived beside for centuries has become a poster species for "misinformed" Greens—Nigel Marven finds himself in broad agreement.

"I think climate change is happening, but as far as the polar bear disappearing is concerned, I have never been more convinced that this is just scaremongering.

"People are deliberately seeking out skinny bears and filming them to show they are dying out. That's not right.

"Of course, in thirty years, if there's no ice over the North Pole, then the bear will be in trouble.

"But I've seen enough to know that polar bears are not yet on the brink of extinction."

There is one final question we should ask here: Have polar bears ever experienced warmer conditions before and survived? The answer to that is an unqualified yes. During the last interglacial period, summer temperatures were 7–9 degrees Fahrenheit above present temperatures, yet polar bears survived. This was a time when hippopotami swam in the rivers of Britain and birch forests reached the shores of the Arctic Ocean. We have actual physical evidence that the polar bears survived this period, in the shape of the oldest known polar bear bone, which is some 110 million to 130 million years old. The discoverer of the bone, Professor Olafur Ingolfsson of the University of Iceland, told the BBC:[38]

We have this specimen that confirms the polar bear was a morphologically distinct species at least 100,000 years ago, and this basically means that the polar bear has already survived one interglacial period. This is telling us that despite the ongoing warming in the Arctic today, maybe we don't have to be quite so worried about the polar bear. That would be very encouraging.

Indeed it would, but will it be enough to stop the Endangered Species Act?

A question that leaps to mind, but which the Fish and Wildlife Service never addresses, is: what additional legal and regulatory actions would the proposed polar bear listing obligate or allow U.S. policymakers to take?

Regulations under the Endangered Species Act often operate as prohibitions on economic activities believed to destroy, modify, or curtail species habitat. In this case, the Service claims that CO_2 emissions are destroying polar bear habitat. Thus, it would seem, for the Endangered Species Act is to have any effect for polar bears, the Act must somehow be stretched to prohibit CO_2-emitting activities.

The problem, of course, is that CO_2 is the intended byproduct of energy use. Energy use, in turn, is both a necessary consequence, and a crucial component, of economic activity. There is hardly any economic activity in the modern world that does not directly or indirectly cause or contribute to CO_2 emissions. The soccer mom produces CO_2 emissions each time she takes her kids to school, cooks their dinner, pays the household electric bill, earns a paycheck, or brings another child into the world.

It is easy to imagine a scenario in which liberal environmentalists take legal action to prohibit builders, developers, utilities, manufacturers, banks, and so on from going about their otherwise lawful pursuits on the grounds that the associated emissions endanger polar bear habitat.

There seem to be two possibilities. Either: (a) the proposed listing is a purely symbolic gesture with no practical relevance to any of the firms and households that cause or contribute to the CO_2 emissions allegedly destroying polar bear habitat; or (b) the proposed listing is a regulatory Pandora's Box that will empower litigants and regulators to harass, impede, and penalize those who create jobs, provide for their families, and grow the economy.

Neither conclusion can be ruled out. The history of liberal "concern" for the environment is littered with empty gestures (recall our earlier discussion of eco-Lutheranism: "not by works, but by faith alone"). Yet it is also strewn with attempts, some successful, to thwart economic progress and the expressed desires of the American people.

Liberal lawmakers are unlikely to legislate their constituents out of a job in the name of wildlife, but if bureaucrats' regulations can do the job for them, that should satisfy their friends in the environmental church. If the same occurrence adds significantly to the welfare rolls, they will be able to distribute largesse in the form of taxpayer-funded benefits—at least until the productive economy finally collapses under the twin strains of regulation and welfare. That's why it is quite plausible that this use of the Endangered Species Act could destroy the American economy.

So once again we see how the liberal principle of legislative centralization combines with environmentalist fervor to create a situation that hurts the American citizen while doing nothing for the environment. Yet it's not just Americans who are harmed by this combination. The problem is global.

Elephants and Tigers, Oh My!

There is no direct international equivalent of the Endangered Species Act. Instead, there is something called CITES, the Convention on International Trade in Endangered Species. The Convention says nothing at all about habitat preservation or domestic protection of endangered species; it simply prohibits or significantly restricts international *trade* in them. Yet the Convention has been just as bad as the Endangered Species Act, for like the Act it creates perverse incentives by perversely valuing wildlife.

The main threat to wildlife around the world is human encroachment on their habitats. This is quite simply another manifestation of the Tragedy of the Commons that we examined in the last chapter. There is no reason why one person should not cut down a bit of forest for fuel or construction materials if someone else is going to do it anyway. This means that, in the poorest countries, wildlife is under threat primarily because of a lack of clear and enforceable property rights.

In the case of endangered species, many of them have become endangered for an additional reason: because people find aspects of them valuable. Elephants have become endangered because of their ivory, crocodilians because of their skin, and tigers because of their use in traditional Chinese medicines. The trade ban enshrined in CITES was supposed to put a stop to that. In fact, in combination with the Tragedy of the Commons, it has made matters worse.

There is actually a huge black market in endangered species around the world. The poorest of the world see in the destruction of the animals' habitat not just an opportunity to take usable resources, but also a jackpot in the form of the animal parts with very high retail value. Yet as with all black markets, it is the dealer who consumes the lion's share (sorry) of the profits.

Supporters of bans on anything point out that they raise the costs of criminal activity. At the same time, by restricting supply they raise the price the successful criminal can receive.

A ban will be effective—it will deter trade in the contraband— if the new costs exceed the new price. In the case of endangered species, the activity is evidently profitable, because by all accounts demand has not slowed down at all.

This is illustrated by the current trade in tiger parts. As a *New Statesman* investigation found in 2005, the dealers make a huge amount of money while the poachers that work for them get small amounts, although they still pocket an impressive haul by local standards:[39]

> China's insatiable appetite for tiger products for use in traditional medicines has created a huge incentive for Indian poachers to disregard the law and kill tigers for their claws, teeth, brains, eyeballs, whiskers, tails and penises because they supposedly cure sleeplessness, fever, laziness, malaria, epilepsy and toothache, as well as giving courage and enhancing virility. In October 2003, police stopped a truck heading for Lhasa and made an astonishing haul of 31 tigerskins. A dead tiger fetches £23,500 ($47,000); villagers work for poachers for £30 ($60), capturing tigers with iron traps or electric cables.

According to the World Bank, the average income for each Indian is just $620 a year.[40]

This demonstrates that the Convention doesn't understand the incentives that lead to trade in endangered species. As South African conservation biologist Michael 't Sas Rolfes writes:[41]

> CITES...fails to create mechanisms to control the supply of wildlife products or any direct means to influence consumer demand....Implicit in its existing structure is an assumption that all trade is somehow bad for conservation unless proven otherwise. Measures taken under CITES therefore tend to emphasize limitations on trade rather than ways to facilitate trade that may ultimately enhance the status of wild species.

In other words, the Convention imposes a negative incentive. Perhaps worse, it also fails to recognize that trade can be a positive incentive. By placing a tradable value on an endangered species within a legal framework, it can be a positive incentive to conservation. The presence of the negative incentive and the lack of the positive one come together to produce a perverse result: dead animals are more valuable than live ones.

As we will see below, various governments in southern Africa have instituted property rights regarding elephants, rhinos, and other endangered species that also produce goods people find desirable (ivory, rhino horn for more traditional medicines, and so on). They have lobbied time and again for the right to be able to trade these goods. The thinking—surely correct—is that the more demand there is for these goods, the more the proceeds will be reinvested in animal conservation by the rights holders and, in the end, the more animals there will be to satisfy the demand. India and Kenya, on the other hand, which have no such property schemes, oppose the idea.

Barun Mitra, who runs the Liberty Institute in New Delhi, India, goes even further. He argues that the only way to save the tiger is to farm it. In a *New York Times* opinion piece in October 2006, he argued his case:[42]

> [L]ike forests, animals are renewable resources. If you think of tigers as products, it becomes clear that demand provides opportunity, rather than posing a threat. For instance, there are perhaps 1.5 billion head of cattle and buffalo and 2 billion goats and sheep in the world today. These are among the most exploited of animals, yet they are not in danger of dying out; there is incentive, in these instances, for humans to conserve.
>
> So it can be for the tiger. In pragmatic terms, this is an extremely valuable animal. Given the growing popularity of traditional Chinese medicines, which make use of everything from tiger claws (to treat insomnia) to tiger fat (leprosy and rheumatism), and the prices this kind of harvesting can bring (as much as $20 for claws, and $20,000 for a skin), the tiger can in effect pay for its own survival. A single farmed specimen

might fetch as much as $40,000; the retail value of all the tiger products might be three to five times that amount.

He contrasts this idea with the ineffectiveness of the expensive anti-commercial schemes of the past thirty years:

> Yet for the last 30 or so years, the tiger has been priced at zero, while millions of dollars have been spent to protect it and prohibit trade that might in fact help save the species. Despite the growing environmental bureaucracy and budgets, and despite the proliferation of conservationists and conferences, the tiger is as close to extinction as it has been since Project Tiger, a conservation project backed in part by the World Wildlife Fund, was launched in 1972 and adopted by the government of India a year later.

The reaction to Barun's piece from liberal environmentalists was incredulous. *New Scientist* published a reaction that showed exactly how much the liberals have invested in opposition to commerce and profit:[43]

> Conservation of wild species and landscapes should be looked at in the same way as public health or primary education—as bringing long-term intangible benefits to society—and not as "commerce" as you report Barun Mitra to be suggesting. Proposed solutions must be not only pragmatic but also socially and culturally acceptable, and they need to be based on understanding of their long-term impacts.

The argument here is that the tiger is only worth saving if we can do it in a "socially and culturally acceptable" manner, and nothing is more socially and culturally unacceptable than profitable use of nature's resources. Their priorities are clear. Tigers going extinct: bad; capitalism: worse.

It is funny how the accusation, "you understand the price of everything but the value of nothing," is always thrown at conservatives by liberals. Yet it is they who misunderstand that price and value are correlatives. If you price something at zero, as the tiger has been priced for all law-abiding people, you send the signal that it has no value. Indeed, if you are willing to be a criminal or an accomplice, the tiger has great value if you kill it. For everyone else, it has zero value dead or alive.

If a farmed tiger can bring $40,000–$50,000 a skin, not only is that one less wild tiger slain, but it also represents a value that can be reinvested in genuine, effective tiger conservation. A tiger farmer will likely sell the skin after his tiger is done breeding. A tiger poacher has no such incentive because, in all likelihood, he will not get the benefit of the tiger's litter.

Commerce attaches incentives to "sustainable practices" (a favorite term among environmentalists, and a noble concept). That the liberal environmentalist cannot understand this is exactly why CITES and the Endangered Species Act have done so little to help species and so much to harm them.

With tigers, we can only hope for reform so that the world can see the conservation values of enterprise. Elsewhere, thankfully, we have empirical evidence of why conservative ideas of property and enterprise trump liberal notions of regulation and common ownership.

Tradition and Hunters Save the Environment

Any review of the history of environmental conservation has to acknowledge the importance of private property. This is why so many "environmental" organizations don't really do history, which tells you all you need to know about their collectivist dogma.

Recall from Chapter 5 the Anglo-anglers who sued the British companies polluting their fishing turf. The same idea was on display among the American Indians in Canada who, before the days of Columbus, used property rights to ensure sustainable deer hunting.

R.J. Smith explains:[44]

An especially illustrative example of private property rights in wildlife appears in the Montagnais Indians of Quebec and Labrador. The Montagnais dwelled in the forests of the Labrador Peninsula, hunting such furbearing animals as caribou, deer, and beaver. They treated wildlife as a common property resource, with everyone sharing in the bounty of the hunt. Because game was plentiful and the Indian population was relatively low, the common property resource system was able to work.

However, with the arrival of the French fur traders in the 1600s, the demand for beaver began to rise rapidly. As the value of the furs rose, there was a corresponding increase in beaver exploitation. But unlike the buffalo, virtually condemned to extinction as an unowned resource, the beaver were protected by the evolution of private property rights among the hunters. By the early to mid 18th century, the transition to private hunting grounds was almost complete and the Montagnais were managing the beaver on a sustained-yield basis.

It was a highly sophisticated system. The Montagnais blazed trees with their family crests to delineate their hunting grounds, practiced retaliation against poachers and trespassers, developed a seasonal allotment system, and marked beaver houses. Animal resources were husbanded. Each year the family hunted in a different quarter in rotation, leaving a tract in the center as a sort of bank, not to be hunted over unless forced to do so by a shortage in the regular tract.

This remarkably advanced system lasted for over a century and certainly served to prevent the extinction of the beaver. Unfortunately, more whites entered the region and began to treat the beaver as a common resource, trapping beavers themselves rather than trading with the Indians, and the beaver began to disappear. Finally, the Indians were forced to abandon their private property system and joined the whites in a rapid overexploitation of the beaver.

This is an excellent example of how traditional respect for private property protects wildlife, while the collectivization so beloved by liberals destroys it. We see it all over the world. In England, since medieval times certain rare species such as swans and whales have been regarded as "royal birds" and "royal fish," the personal property of the monarch, which has helped protect them. When tradition protects the environment, it is foolish to abandon it in the name of modernization.

In Zimbabwe, back when Robert Mugabe was still constrained by the rule of law, the black rhinoceros was saved from extinction by being moved from common land to privately owned land. Poaching on government land had been responsible for the catastrophic decline of the black rhino in response to demand from East Asia for rhino horn, a traditional aphrodisiac. After private land owners took responsibility for guarding the rhinos, the poaching dried up, with not one case in the two major conservancies between 1990 and 1997. The major conservancies helped finance their protection efforts through trophy hunting, not of the rhinos, but of other species on their lands, such as leopards. As Michael DeAlessi notes:[45] "While it may seem gruesome to some, there is no doubt that trophy hunting provides huge incentives to protect wildlife throughout Africa."

Do liberal environmentalists acknowledge this? Of course not. It goes against every collectivizing, government-centered, anti-property bone in their bodies. DeAlessi comments:

> Even the World Wide Fund for Nature, whose program office in Zimbabwe played a major role in both the movement of the rhinos onto private lands and the creation of the conservancies, hardly acknowledges the success of the conservancies. WWF International's website has a page entitled "What WWF is Doing to Save the Rhino," which has no mention of any private conservation activities. Another page, entitled "What Needs to be Done," highlights the fact that "rhino habitat needs to be protected from fragmentation and degradation so that viable rhino populations can survive." That is, of course, exactly what the conservancies have already done, but WWF fails to mention that and only goes on to call for "government management authorities [to] allocate more resources into rhino conservation."

The connection between private ownership of wildlife and hunting is important here in America, too. The wood duck has been saved from extinction largely by the efforts of private hunters, who installed over 100,000 artificial nests and raised ducks in captivity to see their numbers rebound. As Brian Seasholes found:[46]

> Private efforts helped the wood duck specifically in two ways: by creating artificial nesting habitat and propagating them in captivity. The wood duck is a cavity-nesting species, and the older trees containing suitable cavities have become increasingly scarce. As its habitat was destroyed, the wood duck suffered. In response, private citizens installed nest boxes across the country. Nest boxes played a key role in restoring the wood

duck to marginal habitat from which it had been largely extir-
pated and to core habitat where populations had declined.
There were also significant efforts to raise wood ducks cap-
tively and then release them to the wild. The wood duck is now
the second most common species of waterfowl in hunter's bags
east of the Mississippi River. Private efforts to conserve the
wood duck are evidence of the strong tradition of American
conservation.

This is certainly one of those ideas many liberal environmentalists would dub "socially unacceptable:" people taking care of
ducks in order to shoot them.

Tradition, property, and conservation: these are the three
strands that have repeatedly dictated environmental protection.
As well as they have worked on every continent, they can work
in the oceans.

How to Save the Oceans

It's probably the greatest environmental tragedy in the world
today, but chances are you've heard little about it. It's the near
total collapse of many of the world's fisheries. Almost one in
three currently fished marine species are at a "collapsed" level,
with catches below 10 percent of the maximum recorded catch.
The trend appears to be accelerating. Yet one of the main reasons
for this is governments subsidizing fishing fleets that would not
operate otherwise.

One example of what is going on might be useful. If you don't
remember Chilean sea bass being on the menu of your local
seafood restaurant a few years back, that's because it wasn't
called that until recently. After tasty Southern Hemisphere fish
such as the austral hake and the golden kingklip were fished into
memory, the large-scale industrial fishing fleets that had caused

the collapse of those stocks turned to a relatively inaccessible bottom-dwelling fish called the Patagonian toothfish. To make its name more palatable, and associating it with delicious Chilean wine, it was marketed in the U.S. and Japan under the label of Chilean sea bass. Now the toothfish is following its unfortunate predecessors. In 1986, there were 60,000 metric tons of the fish in the Southern Ocean. By 1999, that number had declined to 25,000 tons.

This story is being repeated all over the world, with all sorts of fish. Little wonder—fish is the primary source of protein for over a billion people worldwide and a substantial portion for a further 1.6 billion. What has happened is a classic example of the Tragedy of the Commons. Governments have all sorts of rules and regulations attempting to avert such tragedies in their waters, but in the deep, international waters those are very hard to enforce.

Yet what makes the tragedy of the deep oceans doubly tragic is that most of the fishing that goes on there would not be done without subsidies from governments. Internationally, governments underwrite fishing fleets to the tune of $30 billion to $34 billion a year. The worst offenders are Japan and the European Union (whose Common Fisheries Program has been a disaster for both British fish and British fishermen), but the problem is worldwide in scope. Yet wherever it appears, the problem is one of liberal interventionism designed to interfere with the free market, prop up failing industries, and divert resources from where they would be to centrally determined targets.

The pretexts vary. Subsidies are given supposedly to support traditional industries, to modernize boats and equipment, to compensate fishermen in an attempt to prevent them catching certain kinds of fish, or for research and safety. But the effect is the same: to make uneconomic fishing economic. A safety subsidy, for instance, would allow fishermen to stay out longer and catch more fish where previously bad weather would have forced them back to port.

On the other hand, Cornish fishermen in the UK have reported Spanish vessels, subsidized to the tune of €600,000 for two month's research into the fishing of "non-pressure" stocks like anchovies, involved in ripping the nets of their British rivals. The combined effect of the subsidies is to produce a global fishing fleet that is 250 percent larger than is needed to catch the number of fish that the oceans can replenish. While the problem of the Tragedy of the Commons means that, in the absence of genuine oceanic property rights, there will always be more fishermen than the oceans can supply sustainably, the inflation of the problem by governments is unforgivable.

Deep-sea fishing subsidies are particularly perverse. The deep-sea fishing industry receives subsidies worth more than $152 million a year, with most of the subsidies and fleets coming from Japan, Russia, South Korea, and Spain. Without its subsidies, the global industry would operate at an annual loss of $50 million because it uses such huge quantities of fuel to operate.[47] In other words, either the industry would not exist, or prices would go up, demand would go down, and the impact of deep-sea fishing would dramatically decrease—and it is in the deep seas that the effect of overfishing has been most keenly felt.

Getting rid of subsidies would be just the first step in an effort to stop the tragedy of the oceans. With typical approaches to regulation like the EU's Common Fisheries Policy having contributed to the problem, more and more observers are being drawn to the idea that effective solutions must be based on property rights. In the words of Charles Clover, the urbane author of *The End of the Line: How Overfishing Is Changing the World and What We Eat*, we need "to make the law of the sea more like the law of the land." It may be that the oceans provide the best example of how the free market and environmental protection can go hand in hand, for which we would all be grateful.

The first step, however, must be the elimination of those government subsidies that are encouraging nothing less than mass extinctions. That would, however, entail liberal politicians admitting that their favored tools of subsidy and regulation can have disastrous results.

Chapter Seven

Communism's Environmental Record

The Death of the Aral Sea

Should fortune ever bring you to the city of Aralsk in Kazakhstan, you will see a unique monument to Communism. Looking like some absurdist art installation, large ships lie rusting on an arid desert plain, with camels passing by.

One of these steel husks is a dredging ship, and it lies on its side near the channel it tried to carve in the dying days of the sea that once was here. The ships' corpses nearby are obvious evidence that this desperate effort failed.

In another former waterfront village in Kazakhstan, an old fisherman named Satykul Ubaidulaev told a magazine writer last year: "That was a beautiful bay down there when I was a young man. . . . We had sea breezes and plenty of fish and a nice life. Then the tide went out."[1]

The near loss of the Aral Sea is a gripping image. It's no wonder, then, that Al Gore invoked this disaster in *An Inconvenient Truth*. For Gore, it's a lesson in what awaits us if we continue to emit carbon dioxide. In truth, it's the bitter fruit of central planning and totalitarianism.

The Aral Sea's disappearance provides a telling example of how intellectually bankrupt Gore can be in his effort to blame all the world's problems on greenhouse gases. It is a great case study in how easy it is to gerrymander evidence to prove your point once science has become a tool of politics.

Gore doesn't actually blame the disappearance of the sea on global warming, although many people have left the movie theater with that impression. Yet he seems oblivious to the fact that his solution to what he regards as the global warming problem—massive control of the world's economy to ensure his favored targets are hit—is exactly what destroyed the Aral Sea.

The true story—and this is not even open to interpretation among honest men—is that irrigation carried out by totalitarian and communist governments has dried up the sea. Without the water there to cool the desert air, the region has warmed. Gore uses an environmental crime committed by government and central planning as an argument to restrict industry and capitalism. His argument is so far beyond rational that the light from rational takes an hour and a half to reach it.

Indeed, the free enterprise system in America and the United Kingdom has proved resilient. It has recovered from vast national outbreaks of "fatal conceititis" like the New Deal, the Carter-era energy policy, or the massive nationalizations in Britain after the Second World War.

Other nations have not been so lucky. Russia and the people of Central Asia have never really known free enterprise. In parts of the Middle East and Africa the British introduced it but were not there long enough for it to be established.

However damaging liberals' policies have been in the United States, the real destructive power of central planning has shown itself most clearly in the countries that have taken it to its logical extreme. Communists, socialists, and Ba'athists are the true believers in central planning, and their rule has yielded the world's worst environmental catastrophes, ones fully deserving of the name.

We start with what might be the greatest of many indictments against the Soviet Union: the loss of an entire sea. This is a continuing and growing problem, and the single greatest cause is the rigid obsession with targets set by a totalitarian government.

The Sacrifice of the Aral Sea

Aral Tengi, as it is known in the Kazakh language, was the "Sea of Islands." Occupying a drainage basin on the borders between modern day Kazakhstan and Uzbekistan, in 1960 it measured 26,250 square miles in area, larger than Lake Michigan, and was the fourth-largest inland sea or lake in the world. It was principally fed by two great rivers that flowed through desert: in the south, the Amu Darya, known to Alexander the Great as the Oxus (it took him five days to ferry his army across it); in the north, the Syr Darya (known to Alexander as the Jaxartes).

Throughout history, locals have used these rivers as sources of irrigation. As one history notes,[2] the sixth-century land of Sogdiana owed its wealth to the practice:

> At that period Sogdiana was a rather prosperous country. Agriculture, artificial irrigation farming in particular, held the key position in the country's economy. It should be noted that Sogdian people considerably succeeded in building irrigational structures. Thus, the inner part of Samarkand, shakhristan, was supplied with water by a special pipe aqueduct coming from the main city's canal named Chakardiza. In historical sources the canal is mentioned as "Jui-Arziz," or "Leaden canal," as water was fed into the city through lead-covered aqueduct supported by arched trestle. The whole year

round specially appointed supervisors guarded this unique hydro-engineering structure, built of baked bricks. Suffice it to say that this "Leaden canal" rivaled the famous Roman aqueducts.

By the sixteenth century, however, the system had begun to strain. In a foretaste of what was to come, English traveler Anthony Jenkinson noted in 1571:[3]

[T]he water that serveth all that country is drawn by ditches out of the river Oxus, unto the great destruction of the said river, for which cause it falleth not into the Caspian Sea as it hath done in times past, and in short time all that land is like to be destroyed, and to become a wilderness for want of water, when the river of Oxus shall fail.

In the mid-nineteenth century, the Russian czars swiftly conquered the Islamic lands of central Asia, the area of the Aral Sea and its water courses among them. Coincidentally, at the same time the cotton trade was being disrupted by the American Civil War. In these central Asian lands, with their great watercourses, they saw potential, and introduced cotton to the region. To this day—although the market conditions no longer warrant it—cotton remains the mainstay of the local economies, and it is the source of the Aral Sea's problems.

When the Bolshevik Revolution steered the Communists to power in Russia and led to the foundation of the Union of Soviet Socialist Republics, the era of central economic planning began. As we well know, Soviet industry was controlled by layers and layers of planning and bureaucracy, focused on meeting goals set by the bureaucrats. The cotton industry was a prime example. Moscow planners decided that national progress would be well served by the Soviet Union becoming a net exporter of cotton, or "white gold" as they termed it. The target was first achieved in 1937.

To water the thirsty cotton plants, however, would require massive irrigation. Despite Anthony Jenkinson's worries, the traditional agricultural techniques had kept the rivers flowing. What small traditional farmers could only threaten, the juggernaut of the Communist state could utterly destroy.

Traditional farming was swept aside by the Soviets' introduction of collective farms. These collectives required massively more water to meet their centrally dictated targets, and the Soviet engineers were under no illusions about what this would mean. They realized that the Aral Sea would be drained, but called the body of water "Nature's error" and hoped that it would "die in a beautiful manner." In 1968, one engineer said bluntly, "It is obvious to everyone that the evaporation of the Aral Sea is inevitable."[4]

The engineering proceeded in the full knowledge of this inevitability. In the 1950s, central Asian agriculture was expanded as a result of mechanization (this was the era when children would be named "Traktor"). In 1956, the Kara Kum canal was completed, diverting huge amounts of water from the Amu Darya into what is now Turkmenistan to the south. Millions more acres of land were opened up to irrigation during the 1960s. Cotton production doubled between 1960 and 2000.

This was the beginning of the end for the Aral Sea. In 1965, the sea was still receiving 50 cubic kilometers of water a year from its sources. By the early 1980s this was reduced to zero. The Communists had made this a sea with no access to water.

The Aral began to shrink rapidly, its sea level dropping by 20 centimeters per year in the 1960s, then accelerating to 50–60 centimeters per year in the 1970s and 80–90 centimeters annually in the 1980s. The result was that the sea more than halved in size by the mid 1990s, and splitting essentially into two smaller bodies of water. During this time, the sea's salt concentration increased, with disastrous results for the fish.

Historically there had been over seventy species of fish in the sea, and the fishermen who caught them had become national heroes in the 1920s, saving the Soviet Union from famine. Of course, as might be expected there had been a tragedy of the commons, and the Aral suffered from over-fishing. By 1977, the catch had decreased by 75 percent. The over-fishing combined with the increasingly hostile saltiness of the water eliminated the last commercially useful fish in the sea in the early 1980s, and the sea's twenty-four native species of fish had disappeared. An industry that had employed 60,000 people was shut down. Their fishing fleets were left in the docks. Today, they float on seas of sand.

Targeting Disaster

The collapse of the sea has had other effects. With the cooling sink of the sea gone, the local climate had become much hotter, with temperatures reaching to the 120s regularly.

The very local disappearance of the sea—not global warming—is the main cause of the region's climate change. Draining the sea set off a vicious cycle. To begin with, there is no water to absorb the heat, making the air get warmer. The lack of water also kills off vegetation around the sea, leaving desert behind. Heat energy that had been absorbed by plants is now reflected by sand. Without plants and sea giving off moisture, precipitation decreases, which further warms and further dries the region.

Meanwhile, 43 million tons of the salt and industrial chemicals that had increased in volume in the sea were now deposited on almost 11,000 square miles of dry land, where the desert wind whipped them up into the atmosphere. Respiratory and other health problems in the area abound and the dust storms have reached as far as the Arctic and Pakistan. This is what a true environmental catastrophe looks like.

The Soviets realized in the late 1980s, during Mikhail Gorbachev's time at the helm, what they had done. Of course, the Soviets could not resist a grand scheme, and so they planned to return water to the sea by diverting the Siberian River Ob. This plan fell victim to *glasnost* and the collapse of the Soviet Union. We should be thankful that it did.

Yet the collapse of the Soviet Union did not mean the end of the centrally dictated economy. In Uzbekistan, the head of the local Politburo, Islam Karimov, seized control and has wielded power there ever since, now under the banner of the Liberal Democratic Party. Karimov has continued to base his country's economy upon the cotton industry, and the environmental degradation has continued.

Craig Murray, the former British ambassador to Uzbekistan, describes the problems this causes:[5]

> The Uzbek cotton industry is a disastrous aberration created by Soviet central planning. Over 80 percent of the loss of water from the Aral Sea is due to irrigation for the Uzbek cotton industry, so it is responsible for one of the World's greatest environmental disasters. On most agricultural land in Uzbekistan, cotton has been grown as a monoculture for fifty years, with no rotation. This of course exhausts the soil and encourages pests. As a result the cotton industry employs massive quantities of pesticide and fertilizer....Uzbek farm workers are tied to the farm. They need a propusk (visa) to move away—which they won't get. The state farm worker normally gets two dollars a month. Their living and nutritional standards would improve greatly if, rather than grow cotton, they had a little area to grow subsistence crops.

President Karimov uses the cotton workers as virtual slave labor to enrich himself and his cronies. *New Scientist* journalist Fred Pearce gives us a further eyewitness account:[6]

> Today in Uzbekistan, the biggest producer, the government is still the only purchaser, and meeting cotton production targets remains a national obsession. During the harvest season, cotton employs a staggering 40 percent of Uzbekistan's workforce, including hundreds of thousands of schoolchildren. Every province, every canal network and every farm has its production target. Even as the old collective farms are privatized, the targets persist, and farmers and officials can lose their land and jobs for failing to meet them. And cotton still consumes most of the region's water.
>
> During October 2004, during my visit, the government declared that Uzbek cotton production had exceeded 3 million [metric] tonnes for the first time in several years. Ministers were interviewed on the TV standing in cotton fields brimming with pride. Officials that had seemed uptight and nervous suddenly relaxed. The bottles of vodka came out. Nobody cared that in the process the ratchet on the Aral Sea had been given one more turn.

As Pearce suggests, Karimov's supposed privatization of the collective farms is nothing but a sham. The state maintains its monopoly on agricultural inputs and remains the sole buyer of "strategic" commodities like cotton, purchasing the crop for a fraction of the market value. This is "market socialism" at its worst. The only way for the farmers to make ends meet is to employ child labor and slave wages.

Yet the Uzbeks think they are working for the good of the state. In the tear-jerking report by the Environmental Justice Foundation, "White Gold: The True Cost of Cotton,"[7] there are illustrative quotations from farmers and exploited children: "We serve the state when we pick cotton" (a ten-year-old girl from Namangan region), "Cotton is our national wealth and we are serving our fatherland.... Cotton is our white gold" (a fifteen-year-old girl from Tashkent).

This is what happens when the State is put above the individual. At least some Uzbeks recognize the problem. One cotton farmer quoted in the report says, "Being a cotton farmer here is like hanging between life and death. The government controls our lives very tightly. If we don't obey, we'll end up in trouble. All we want is freedom. And the State is punishing us for wanting freedom."

The situation is all the more tragic when you consider that so much of the water drained from the Amu Darya never even reaches the cotton fields. In 2001, a World Bank study estimated that 60 percent of the water leaked out of the 17,000 miles of aging and dilapidated irrigation structures before reaching the cotton land.[8] That amounts to about 3,000 cubic miles of water wasted. To put it in perspective, that's the volume of Lake Superior.

Meanwhile, the land itself has become more salty, making growing conditions difficult. How do the cotton farmers tackle this problem? By increasing the amount of water they take, in an attempt to flush away the excess salt. Salt, meanwhile, degrades cotton fiber quality. In the end, the demand for water may destroy the already dubious viability of the Uzbek cotton industry. If that happens, the country will become a humanitarian disaster as well as environmental disaster.

President Karimov has been supported by the United States because of his crackdowns on Islamic extremist organizations that have threatened his rule. Yet it is hard to see him surviving the collapse of his only source of revenue. The Islamists will be ready to pounce. Uzbekistan could yet become another Afghanistan. It is in the West's interests not to help Karimov prop up his disastrous Soviet-era economic policies, but to insist on genuine market reform, reform that will help the Uzbek poor, quiet the Islamic threat and do something to stop the environmental devastation.

Conservatives should be leading this demand, but so far they have been too quiet. In fact, when the aforementioned British ambassador Craig Murray made a nuisance of himself in pointing out Karimov's depravities, the Bush administration asked Tony Blair's government to sack him, which they duly did. As British columnist Simon Jenkins asks, "[H]ave the neo-cons turned yak-eating surrender llamas in the steppes of middle Asia?"[9] With his predilection for boiling opponents alive, Karimov is rapidly turning from another Soviet into another Saddam. That should be more than enough reason to do something, never mind the environmental benefits.

I mentioned above that the Aral Sea was now, for all intents and purposes, two separate bodies of water. The Uzbek branch, the South Aral, looks indeed to be doomed given the political situation. There is, however, hope for the North Aral. A comparatively small amount of investment in infrastructure has yielded significant returns. In the 1990s, the government of Kazakhstan built two makeshift dykes—levees, if you will—between the North and South Aral Seas, separating them. They both failed, but the second one proved that such a dyke, properly constructed, would raise the level of the North Aral.

Accordingly, the World Bank helped the Kazakh government to invest $86 million in building a sturdy, eight-mile-long dyke, together with other levees along the Syr Darya. Within eighteen months, the North Aral had swelled from a mere 888 square miles of water to 1,250 square miles. The scientists and engineers had expected it to take twice as long. A dozen species of fish have returned to the sea.

Unlike in Uzbekistan, there is optimism for the Aral in Kazakhstan. As Martin Fletcher of the *Times* of London reported in 2007:[10]

The northern Aral has since grown by 1,000 sq km. Its fish and fishermen are returning. The climate is improving. People are healthier. "Good News—The Sea is Coming Back," proclaims a billboard outside Aralsk. For the first time in a generation people in that rundown port dare to believe that ships will once again sail into their dried-up harbour. "This project has shown it's been possible to reverse one of the world's worst man-made environment disasters and bring back to life a sea that almost everyone thought was beyond saving," said Joop Stoutjesdijk, the World Bank water expert who helped to rescue the northern Aral from communism's ultimate triumph over nature.

Given the success of the first dyke, plans are afoot to build a second, longer dyke that would raise the sea level by a further thirteen feet. A series of canals would help bring water back to the vanished harbor of Aralsk. The benefits are already being seen, as Fletcher relates:

This second phase is expected to start in 2009, but the first phase alone is revitalizing Aralsk. Fishermen are returning. A large new fish processing plant is working at full capacity. A new fish hatchery will release 15 million fingerlings into the northern Aral this year, and reintroduce sturgeon this autumn. Another new factory is building fiberglass fishing boats. Aralsk processed 2,000 tonnes of fish last year—enough to export some to Georgia, Russia and Ukraine.

With clean drinking water now piped in from 120 km away, and fish back in their diet, people's health has begun to improve. Even the climate is changing for the better. "It's true. In April, May and June we now have rain," exclaims Nazhmedin Musabaev, Aralsk's jovial Mayor. There is more grass for livestock. Summers are a little cooler. Dust storms are

fewer. Swans, duck and geese are returning. Satykul Ubaidulaev yearns to see his young daughter swimming in the sea.
Babacha Kozhaeva will die happy if the water returns to
Aralsk. The Mayor looks forward to drinking beer with visitors around a refilled harbor.

This demonstrates that even the worst environmental catastrophe man has caused can be rectified quickly, affordably, and to
great economic and humanitarian benefit.

Indeed, the South Aral itself could yet be saved if the political
situation improves. A new reservoir in the old Adzhibay Gulf,
together with a series of dykes and canals could stabilize the
South Aral and allow it to recover ecologically.[11] It would likely
be much more expensive than the North Aral project, but it is
feasible. Above all, however, the Aral Sea's best hope lies in an
end to the policies of collectivism that have ruined the economy
and ecology of central Asia and allowed despots to thrive.

Saddam and the Marshes

It can be argued that the policies of the Soviets and their successors were not deliberately evil, but mistakes. The same cannot be
said of what has been called "the greatest environmental crime of
the century"— the destruction of the wetlands of Southern Iraq
by Saddam Hussein.

After the first Gulf War in 1990, Saddam Hussein faced a
series of internal rebellions, urged on by President George H.W.
Bush and the other victors in the liberation of Kuwait. The most
severe came from the South, where the Shiite Marsh Arabs rose
against him. The Marsh Arabs, or Ma'dan, are an indigenous
people who claim descent from the ancient Sumerians and Baby-
lonians. They build reed houses on artificial floating islands,
again made from reeds, travel by boat, and base their economy

on selling reed mats while raising fish, water buffalo, and rice. When the rebellion failed after it became apparent that the victors of Kuwait would send no material help beyond maintaining a no-fly zone, Saddam resolved to destroy the Marsh Arabs. He realized that their culture was dependent on the marshes. No marshes, no Marsh Arabs.

There had actually been plans to drain the marshes for fifty years. British colonial officials, suffering from the same degree of fatal conceit as their Soviet contemporaries in Central Asia, had decided that the marshes were an inefficient waste of water that could be used for irrigation purposes. They had therefore drawn up plans for a large drainage canal—a "Third River" besides the Tigris and Euphrates for which Mesopotamia had been named.

There had been fitful progress on this from the original 1953 start, but in 1991 Saddam turned all his resources to completing it as a political weapon against his opponents. Over 4,500 workers labored round the clock for a year to finish the canal in December 1992, and a dam on the Euphrates diverted all of its water from the marshes to the canal. The Tigris was blocked from the marshes by a series of other works, most of its water ending up in the Euphrates and thence the Third River. The tyrant would begin engineering works by clearing the area with a round of artillery fire. Troops would then move in to secure the area and, once completed, the works would be protected with land mines.[12]

The effect was devastating. Watercourses became mud, destroying the Marsh Arab's means of getting around. After a while, the mud itself dried out, to become arid, salty desert. The Marsh Arabs could do nothing but flee. Some went to refugee camps in Iran, others gave up and moved to the cities. In the 1950s, there were half a million Marsh Arabs; by 2004, there were just 80,000 still living in what once were their marshes.[13]

For the flora and fauna of the marshes, however, there was to
be no refuge. The marshes had been an important spawning
ground for the fish of the upper Persian Gulf, and a winter nesting ground for birdlife that ranked as probably the most important in Southern Asia. Sixty percent of all the fish consumed in
Iraq came from the marshes. With only 7 percent of the marshes
remaining by the time Saddam was removed from power, several
species had suffered extremely badly. The salt-tolerant vegetation
disappeared, along with fifty-two native fish species, the wild
boar, the red fox, and the river otter. Forty species of birds were
endangered, including the Dalmatian pelican, the pygmy cor-
morant, and the white-tailed eagle.

It did not take long after the fall of Saddam for the damage to
begin to be reversed. Remaining and returning Marsh Arabs
destroyed engineering works where they could. By 2004, 40 percent of the old marshes had been re-inundated. Scientists established that the restored marshes were similar in quality to the
marshes that had survived Saddam's depredations.[14] The rapid
progress has been aided by greater than normal snowpack melt
in the headwaters of the two great rivers, which reduced the
salinity (who said ice melting is always bad?).

To continue their progress, the marshes will need to keep
receiving good flows of water from the Tigris and Euphrates. A
potential confounder here is that the headwaters of the rivers are
actually in Turkey, which has made noises about using the rivers
to exert political pressure on both Iraq and Syria. Yet here there
is a great example of how free-market economics provides the
answer that benefits both sides. Azzer Alwash, director of Iraq's
Restore Eden project, explains:[15]

Let's be honest. The water Turkey is holding behind their dams
has nothing to do with irrigation. They want to exchange
water for oil. However, no Iraqi government will be able to

survive if they ever sell the historic right of Iraq—as documented by clay tablets from 3,000 B.C.—to the water of the Tigris and the Euphrates. Therefore, we're going to have to achieve a win-win solution by thinking outside the box. If Iraq and Turkey get into negotiating positions that lock them into their God-given rights, we will have a situation similar to that between the Palestinians and Israelis. Fifty years from now, Iraq will be dying of thirst, Turkey will be dying of a failed economy, and we'll still be negotiating. What I suggest is this. Iraq needs electricity. We suffer in Baghdad 10 hours of cut-off electricity each day in the summer, and God help you if you don't have a generator at 2 o'clock in the afternoon in July. Iraq's generating capacity at this point is about 5,600 megawatts. The need is for about 12,000, and that's without accounting for a potential increase in demand. We will have to buy electricity. I suggest to you that if Iraq buys electricity from Turkey, the by-product of that is that Turkey will have to release some water to do hydroelectric power generation. Water comes Iraq's way, and we bypass this hot potato. We did not sell our water rights, ladies and gentlemen, we actually bought electricity.

Once again, the forces of energy use, free-market economics, and exchangeable property rights are seen to contribute to environmental improvement, not work against it. That is something the Ba'ath Arab Socialist Saddam Hussein never understood.

Hanging Chad

In the center of North Africa lies Lake Chad. It has been shrinking almost as fast as the Aral Sea. Now Al Gore was traumatized by chads in Florida in 2000, and so it stands to reason he would try to associate Lake Chad's problems with global warming. As with the Aral Sea, the real culprit is not industrial growth and carbon dioxide, but a combination of socialist-inspired economic policies and, in this case, natural factors.

In *An Inconvenient Truth*, Gore places the blame for the undoubted disappearance of Lake Chad on global warming. In turn, the lake's diminution contributed to famine and genocide in the region. He sermonizes: Lake Chad's "fate is sadly emblematic of a part of the world where climate change can be measured not just in temperature increases but in lives lost." The "more we understand about climate change, the more it looks as if we [the United States, which emits a quarter of the world's greenhouse gases] may be the real culprit." He concludes: "It is time to take a hard honest look at our role in this escalating disaster. We helped manufacture the suffering in Africa, and we have a moral obligation to try to fix it."[16]

Yes, indeed, let's take a hard, *honest* look at our role in this "escalating disaster." Two responses are in order here, one regarding Africa generally, the other specific to Lake Chad. Since 1950 southern Africa and the Sahel region have experienced significant reductions in rainfall, drying the soil and causing the desert to expand—the process known as "desertification." Liberal environmentalists often blame desertification on carbon dioxide-induced global warming. However, a careful review of the recent science challenges this conventional wisdom.

Meteorologist Martin Hoerling of the National Oceanic and Atmospheric Administration compared in 2006 actual precipitation data with the UN's assumptions as to how greenhouse gases would affect precipitation. The UN's Intergovernmental Panel on Climate Change, in its Fourth Assessment Report, ran eighteen simulations of what greenhouse-gas-caused warming would do to precipitation levels. The Center for the Study of Carbon Dioxide and Global Change summarizes the Hoerling team's findings:[17]

In the words of the four researchers, "the ensemble of green-house-gas-forced experiments, conducted as part of the Fourth Assessment Report of the Intergovernmental Panel on Climate Change, fails to simulate the pattern or amplitude of the twentieth century African drying, indicating that the drought conditions were likely of natural origin." In fact, they say that for both of the regions studied, "the observed trend amplitude exceeded that of the greenhouse gas signal by an order of magnitude," and they state once again that they "therefore concluded that greenhouse gas forcing played little or no role in the 1950-99 observed African drying trends." What is more, they say there is "considerable spread" among the 18 model projections, making their mean trend so small that they suggest that "natural variability will continue to be the primary driver of [Africa's] low-frequency rainfall variations during the next century."

In short, the Center concludes, "there is absolutely no evidence that the twentieth-century drying of much of Africa was in any way related to CO_2-induced global warming, nor is there any model-based reason for supposing it will be so related over the next century." By the way, the analysis also provides further evidence that the computer models relied on so heavily by global warming alarmists have no useful predictive skill.

Turning now to the specific case of Lake Chad, a study by Jonathan Foley and Michael Coe of the University of Wisconsin concluded that lake's decline probably has nothing to do with global warming. The two scientists based their findings on computer models and satellite imagery made available by NASA. They attribute the lake's condition to a combination of regional climate variability and societal factors such as population increase and overgrazing. *National Geographic* interviewed the researchers and summarized their study:[18]

Historically, Lake Chad received most of its water from the
monsoon rains that fell annually from June to August. But
beginning in the late 1960s, the region experienced a series of
devastating droughts. As the rains increasingly failed to come,
the region began undergoing desertification. At the same time,
local people became more and more dependent on the lake as
a source of water to replace the water they had previously
obtained from the monsoons.

Note that the change from a wet to a dry climate began in the
late 1960s, when global climate was still in a cooling trend. The
article continues:

Overgrazing of the savanna is one of the biggest factors in the
shrinking of the lake, according to Coe and Foley. "As the climate became drier, the vegetation that supported grazing livestock began to disappear. Vegetation has a big influence,
especially in semiarid regions, in determining weather patterns," said Foley. "The loss of vegetation in itself contributed
to a drier climate." The situation is a "domino effect," the
researchers say. Overgrazing reduces vegetation, which in turn
reduces the ecosystem's ability to recycle moisture back into
the atmosphere. That contributes to the retreat of the monsoons. The consequent drought conditions have triggered a
huge increase in the use of lake water for irrigation, while the
Sahara has gradually edged southward.

In short, the Lake Chad disaster was one part local climate variation, one part local tragedy of the commons caused by lack of
property rights in the lake or savanna. Yet Gore blames the United
States of America. In the words of my colleague, Marlo Lewis:[19]

He calls global warming a "moral issue," but for him it is actually a moralizing issue. Global warming allows Gore to discover

moral agency and guilt in the workings of inanimate nature. It allows him to "blame America first" for misfortunes around the world that may be entirely due to local actions and/or climatic factors beyond human control.

Indeed, global warming propagandists blame humanitarian disasters all over the world on environmental crises caused by global warming, which in turn is caused by Americans driving SUVs. United Nations secretary general Ban Ki Moon is a great example, blaming the systematic massacre of Christians and animists in Darfur by the Islamic government of Sudan on global warming:[20]

> Two decades ago, the rains in southern Sudan began to fail. According to U.N. statistics, average precipitation has declined some 40 percent since the early 1980s. Scientists at first considered this to be an unfortunate quirk of nature. But subsequent investigation found that it coincided with a rise in temperatures of the Indian Ocean, disrupting seasonal monsoons. This suggests that the drying of sub-Saharan Africa derives, to some degree, from man-made global warming.
>
> It is no accident that the violence in Darfur erupted during the drought. Until then, Arab nomadic herders had lived amicably with settled farmers. A recent Atlantic Monthly article by Stephan Faris describes how black farmers would welcome herders as they crisscrossed the land, grazing their camels and sharing wells. But once the rains stopped, farmers fenced their land for fear it would be ruined by the passing herds. For the first time in memory, there was no longer enough food and water for all. Fighting broke out. By 2003, it evolved into the full-fledged tragedy we witness today.

As well as implicitly blaming American SUV owners, incredibly, Ban Ki Moon attempts to blame farmers seeking to protect their property for their own victimization. Perhaps if the herders had attempted to recompense the farmers for the loss of their property when it became scarcer, rather than killing them and stealing their property, things might have been a little bit different. The lessons of the marketplace are hard-learned in some areas.

In addition to being dubious on its face, Secretary-General Moon's assertion has not stood up to empirical testing. Helga Malmin Binningsbø, Indra de Soysa, and Nils Petter Gleditsch, from the Norwegian University of Science and Technology's Department of Sociology and Political Science recently set out to show the connection between environmental degradation and armed conflict. They actually found the reverse:[21]

> [L]ands where resources are heavily exploited show a clear connection to a lack of armed conflict. Or alternatively, nations troubled by war during the research period had lower exploitation rates of their natural resources. The findings give researchers solid empirical support for stating that environmental scarcity is not the reason behind violent conflict.
>
> A higher Ecological Footprint is negatively correlated with conflict onset, controlling for income effects and other factors, the researchers say in their article, published in the peer-reviewed journal Population and Environment. "Of course people fight over resources, that's not our argument. We believe, rather, that we have a strong scientific case against the Neomalthusian model," says Binningsbø.

In other words, "overconsumption" of resources doesn't start conflicts. In fact, some historians have known this for a long time. The historian Arnold Toynbee, who developed an early version of the arguments presented in Samuel Huntington's thesis of the "clash of civilizations," showed with example after example in *A Study of History* that environmental collapse was almost always a *product* of a society's breakdown and not a *cause*. It is the happy and successful civilization that lives in harmony with the environment and the resources it utilizes. Only when a society starts to collapse does the environment suffer. The Soviet/ Uzbek destruction of the Aral Sea and Saddam's draining of the marshes fit in perfectly well with this model.

We can glean further insight from Toynbee's great work. He posits the idea that a society collapses when the "creative minority," the entrepreneurs and intellectuals who give a society the impetus to progress, loses its creativity and becomes a "dominant minority." This new minority simply demands obedience rather than earns it. It resorts to fixation on romantic views of the past and of the civilization's potential to meet its challenges. On occasion it will enter a "transcendent" state where it seeks to meet the challenges of decay through quasi-religious insight. If this description reminds you of any elements of our own society, congratulations on paying attention throughout this work!

Happily, however, our society retains a creative minority even as its uncreative elements attempt to assert their dominance. In the final chapter we will look at how the ideas of this creative class can address the world's environmental concerns without destroying our American way of life.

Conclusion

The Promise of Stewardship

The Conservative Answer for the Environment

A s I said at the beginning of this book, way back in the preface, the world around us is a wonderful place, and possesses a meaning and value by virtue of its existence. Environmental disasters are tragic whoever causes them; whether they are the liberal environmentalists we've looked at in this book, short-sighted businesses, or careless governments. Liberal environmentalism, with its focus on box-checking rules, preference for word over substance, and its obsession with punishment of the guilty, has on too many occasions failed to prevent environmental damage, and in the meantime has harmed the economy and the humans whose well-being the economy represents.

It is no wonder that the word "environmentalist" conjures up an image of someone divorced from reality, even if the counterculture image is increasingly inaccurate with more and more environmentalists receiving handsome salaries and driving expensive (hybrid) cars. The word is simply not useful any more.

Yet there must be a word to describe the actions of the ordinary man—the man who is interested in preserving his property for his children, who wants them to grow up enjoying clean air, eating fish, and visiting forests, but who still wants to drive a car powerful enough to tow a trailer and who wants to be able to afford lighting his house at night, warming it in the winter, and cooling it in the summer. The word "conservationist," for many, sets the right tone; to me, however, that word provides only half the picture. In these days of high energy prices, we may all be in favor of energy conservation, but we generally recognize there are times when it is necessary to use lots of energy: in an icestorm, for instance, or attending a funeral across country.

Therefore, we need a word that encompasses two aspects of possession of natural resources: the value stored in conserving them, but also the value released in utilizing them. The balance between the two is what we all seek. The word that summarizes that view is *stewardship*.

Traditional Stewardship

The derivation of the word *steward* signifies its humble origins. It is a conflation of sty (as in pig sty) and ward (meaning guard). Yet the high stewards of England possessed considerable authority and power: the high steward managed the domestic affairs of the Royal Court. There is sometimes an association with food and drink, which is why flight attendants used to be called stewards and stewardesses. In the labor union movement, the shop steward is an important figure, representing the working men to their bosses, at least theoretically. Yet the common thread through these different uses is that of management—the idea of juggling many different demands and resources. The good steward makes best use and most appropriate use of his resources at the time. Thus it is a perfectly appropriate word to use of someone who manages the environment.

There is another defining aspect of stewardship, however, that a steward exercises his considerable authority on behalf of someone else. Given the importance I have attached to property rights throughout this book, some might raise an eyebrow here. Yet property rights do not disappear with the owner's death; part of their definition is that they are transferable. They are indeed an embodiment of the continuance of society and the rule of law, what Edmund Burke described as:[1]

> ...a partnership not only between those who are living, but between those who are living, those who are dead, and those who are to be born. Each contract of each particular state is but a clause in the great primeval contract of eternal society.

Indeed, later in the same work, Burke described what could be a definition of environmental stewardship:[2]

> [O]ne of the first and most leading principles on which the commonwealth and the laws are consecrated is [that] the temporary possessors and life-renters in it [should be mindful] of what is due to their posterity...[and] should not think it among their rights to cut off the entail or commit waste on the inheritance by destroying at their pleasure the whole original fabric of society, hazarding to leave to those who come after them a ruin instead of a habitation.

Note that Burke uses the language of building. While he disapproves of leaving the inheritance a ruin, he would be just as condemnatory of those who left posterity an untouched field. It is the habitation that is important.

This view is also reflected in the words of Theodore Roosevelt. A titan in the history of American conservation, Theodore Roosevelt is also regarded as a useful tool against conservatives by liberal environmentalists, because of his contribution to the nationalization of so much of the West into public lands and parks. Yet Roosevelt had a distinctly Burkean view of their purpose:

> We look upon these resources as a heritage to be made use of in establishing and promoting the comfort, prosperity and happiness of the American people, but not to be wasted, deteriorated or needlessly destroyed.[3]

In fact, Roosevelt appointed as head of the Forest Service Gifford Pinchot, a man whose views of the public forest were positively utilitarian:

> The object of our forest policy is not to preserve the forests because they are beautiful ... or because they are refuges for the wild creatures of the wilderness ... but for the making of prosperous homes. Every other consideration comes as secondary.[4]

It is hard to see Pinchot passing Senate confirmation with those views today, but they are informed by a traditional view of natural resources as to be used appropriately by the present generation while preserved for the benefit of the next.

So it is with stewardship. A steward must use his judgment about how best to use environmental resources, bearing in mind the traditional uses to which the resource has been put in the past (it would not do to knock down Mount Vernon to create the George Washington Wetland Nature Reserve, for instance) and the interests of the future holders of the property right. Failure to do so results in a breach of the steward's duty of care.

Yet this duty of care is not a recipe for inactivity. Anyone who simply preserves his property like a mounted butterfly is just as dilatory in his duty as someone who ruins it.[5] Judgment is essential, and so moral and economic principles must help inform that judgment.

The Cornwall Alliance for the Stewardship of Creation is a prominent evangelical Christian group that promotes the stewardship ideal. In its founding document, it outlines the following confusions that impede sound judgment on environmental stewardship:

1. Many people mistakenly view humans as principally consumers and polluters rather than producers and stewards. Consequently, they ignore our potential, as bearers of God's image, to add to the earth's abundance. The increasing realization of this potential has enabled people in societies blessed with an advanced economy not only to reduce pollution, while producing more of the goods and services responsible for the great improvements in the human condition, but also to alleviate the negative effects of much past pollution. A clean environment is a costly good; consequently, growing affluence, technological innovation, and the application of human and material capital are integral to environmental improvement. The tendency among some to oppose economic progress in the name of environmental stewardship is often sadly self-defeating.

2. Many people believe that "nature knows best," or that the earth—untouched by human hands—is the ideal. Such romanticism leads some to deify nature or oppose human dominion over creation. Our position, informed by revelation and confirmed by reason and experience, views human stewardship that unlocks the potential in creation for all the earth's inhabitants as good. Humanity alone of all the created order is capable of developing other resources and can thus enrich creation,

so it can properly be said that the human person is the most valuable resource on earth. Human life, therefore, must be cherished and allowed to flourish. The alternative—denying the possibility of beneficial human management of the earth—removes all rationale for environmental stewardship.

3. While some environmental concerns are well founded and serious, others are without foundation or greatly exaggerated. Some well-founded concerns focus on human health problems in the developing world arising from inadequate sanitation, widespread use of primitive biomass fuels like wood and dung, and primitive agricultural, industrial, and commercial practices; distorted resource consumption patterns driven by perverse economic incentives; and improper disposal of nuclear and other hazardous wastes in nations lacking adequate regulatory and legal safeguards. Some unfounded or undue concerns include fears of destructive manmade global warming, overpopulation, and rampant species loss.

There is little to dispute here. Throughout this book it has been shown how the anti-growth, anti-human, foolish and/or disingenuous ideas of the liberal environmentalist complex have led to problems, disasters and even catastrophes. Basing a polity's resource-use policies on these foundations is asking for trouble.

Instead, the Cornwall Alliance proposes a more nuanced, calmly judged series of aspirations:

1. We aspire to a world in which human beings care wisely and humbly for all creatures, first and foremost for their fellow human beings, recognizing their proper place in the created order.

2. We aspire to a world in which objective moral principles—not personal prejudices—guide moral action.

3. We aspire to a world in which right reason (including sound theology and the careful use of scientific methods) guides the stewardship of human and ecological relationships.

4. We aspire to a world in which liberty as a condition of moral action is preferred over government-initiated management of the environment as a means to common goals.

5. We aspire to a world in which the relationships between stewardship and private property are fully appreciated, allowing people's natural incentive to care for their own property to reduce the need for collective ownership and control of resources and enterprises, and in which collective action, when deemed necessary, takes place at the most local level possible.

6. We aspire to a world in which widespread economic freedom—which is integral to private, market economies—makes sound ecological stewardship available to ever greater numbers.

7. We aspire to a world in which advancements in agriculture, industry, and commerce not only minimize pollution and transform most waste products into efficiently used resources but also improve the material conditions of life for people everywhere.

This declaration has so far been signed by over 1,500 clergy, theologians, policy experts, and other people of faith, including such well-known leaders as Dr. Charles Colson, Dr. James Dobson, Rabbi Jacob Neusner, Dr. R.C. Sproul, Fr. Richard John Neuhaus, and Rev. Dr. D. James Kennedy, among others. If environmental policy had been based for the past hundred or so years on these aspirations, many of the disasters we have seen would likely never have occurred.

As the aspirations suggest, alongside the moral principles that guide stewardship should go the objective analysis techniques of economics. In particular, that branch known as the "new resource economics" that has now become better known as "free-market environmentalism."

Free-Market Environmentalism

Liberal aspirations for the environment—founded on the ideas that humanity is bad for nature, that there is some pristine state that must be preserved at all costs, and that apocalyptic visions of the future must restrain us in the present—are certainly confused. The tools by which they want to realize their aspirations, however, are fatally flawed. We have seen throughout this book how legislation, regulation, and targets have imposed perverse incentives and unusual punishments. We have seen how bans aimed at protecting bird life are killing human children, how biofuel mandates are clearing the rainforest and endangering the orangutan, how sacred cows are polluting rivers, how nationalizing land lets fires run wild, how well-meaning laws and regulations burned a river, how laws to protect endangered species put them in peril, and how grand visions of communal national greatness dried up an entire sea.

As John Baden, who started the Foundation for Research on Economics and the Environment, put it, "the experiment of public sector ownership, management, and control has been an unambiguous failure in terms of environmental quality, productivity, and economic efficiency." Yet Baden also counsels that it is wrong to regard the people who administer these laws and regulations as incompetent or immoral (although for some, like those who misrepresented Michael Rowe, we may need to make an exception). Instead, like all human beings, in general they are responding to information, signals and incentives. The problem is that the laws and regulations generate the wrong information, signals, and incentives.

This problem is not confined to the environment. Free-market economists such as the Nobel Laureates F.A. Hayek, Ronald

Coase, and James Buchanan realized that an over-regulated society was not a desirable thing. Buchanan, for example, pointed out that political decisions are made within the economy, not outside it. Thus, government officials are not Olympian judges, but they make decisions based on their own economic needs. I now recognize that the decisions I took when I was a British civil servant were very much based on what was good for me. I didn't think so at the time; I very much believed I was doing the right thing—but that was Hayek's fatal conceit in action. Coase, meanwhile, recognized that, although people respond to tax and regulatory incentives, this was often a very inefficient and wasteful way of achieving desirable outcomes, and that the market generally did it better.

Hayek, Buchanan, and Coase were inspirational to the founding fathers of what they called the "new resource economics." These were men like Baden, Terry Anderson, Donald Leal of the Political Economy Research Center (later renamed the Property and Environment Research Center) in Bozeman, Montana, and Bruce Yandle of Clemson University. They applied their thinking to environmental policy and they found that—on the score of protecting environmental quality—environmental regulation proved less efficient than private measures, because government officials are not punished for inefficiency and waste. Michael Copeland wrote: "Wasting a resource does not result in a loss or a reduced profit. Bureaucrats also tend to favor programs with visible benefits and invisible costs."[6] Private individuals, groups, or companies, on the other hand know that invisible costs are as bad as visible ones.

In the private sector, profit and loss provide very clear price signals about how people behave, and when the signals are obscured, as happened in the subprime loan crisis, failure invariably follows. Bureaucrats, on the other hand, operate in an informational vacuum. As a result, predicting the impact of regulations is very difficult, because there is little or no information as to how people will react, and the information that exists is of poor quality.[7]

Liberal environmentalists tend to talk of "market failure" in protecting the environment. The "new resource economics" demonstrated that "government failure" is even more likely. Moreover, government regulation of the environment carries other costs as well, in the shape of an increasingly powerful and arrogant bureaucracy. As my boss, Fred Smith, has put it, "the disastrous road to serfdom can be just as easily paved with green bricks as with red ones."[8]

Free-market environmentalism follows the thoughts of Ronald Coase in theorizing that the environmental "costs" represented by pollution, overuse, and habitat loss are in fact imposed because of a lack of property rights. With well-defined property rights, the owners whose assets are damaged have a right and incentive to get those who are damaging them to stop. This can be by common law action, bargaining, or in many cases self-restraint, because in many cases the appropriate property right holder would be the one inflicting the damage.

Jonathan Adler explains how such property rights work:[9]

For incentives to work, the property right to a resource must be definable, defendable, and divestible. Owners must be free to transfer their property rights to others at will. Even someone indifferent or hostile to environmental protection has an incentive to take environmental concerns into account, because despoiling the resource may reduce its value in the eyes of potential buyers. The role of government is to protect property rights for environmental resources and secure the voluntary agreements property owners contract to carry out. Moreover, FME [free-market environmentalism] advocates insist on the application of common law liability rules to environmental harms, such as polluting a neighbor's property, to protect property rights and to provide additional incentives for good stewardship. To harm someone's property by polluting it is no more acceptable than vandalizing it.

Or, as Fred Smith puts it, "rather than the silly slogan of some environmentalists, that 'trees should have [legal] standing,' our argument is that behind every tree should stand an owner who can act as its protector."[10]

One example of how free-market environmentalism has worked in practice comes from Montana, where the re-introduction of the wolf was opposed by ranchers worried about the effect of the "new" predators on their flocks and herds. The early theorists of free-market environmentalism suggested their concerns would be addressed if the people who want wolves back in the wild arranged some form of compensation whenever a beast was taken.[11] That way, the wolf supporters would take on a form of property right in the wolf and compensate ranchers for "vandalism" by their property. Ranchers, in turn, would respect the property right by not having an incentive to kill the wolf to reduce future losses.

Remarkably, the environmental group Defenders of Wildlife agreed. As the wolf was reintroduced, the group established a Wolf Compensation Fund. "What we're trying to do is devise a system whereby all those people who care about endangered species restoration actually pay some of the bills," explained Defenders of Wildlife staffer Hank Fischer on National Public Radio. "What this solution attempts to do is utilize economic forces—in other words, to make it desirable to have wolves."[12] As might be expected, the fund has paid out more and more as the wolves have been reestablished, paying out $231,597 in 2007 for attacks on 224 cattle and 309 sheep (compared to $26,000 just ten years ago). In all, the fund has paid out almost a million dollars in compensation over its twenty years of existence. The fund is completely financed by private donors. Ranchers have declared themselves happy with the unbureaucratic nature of the scheme. It is a fine example of what an environmental group can do when it does not resort to laws and regulation.[13]

That is a rare example, though. For the most part the liberal environmentalist establishment is wedded to the punishment of businesses, landowners, and taxpayers for their role in "harming the environment" by taxes and regulations, abiding by the liberal dogma that markets are exploitative. Rather than spend the money directly on conservation efforts—as in the Wolf Compensation Fund, they spend their money on lobbyists in Washington or in state capitals. As liberal economist Thomas Michael Power and *Sierra* magazine associate editor Paul Rauber put it: "Markets are not neutral, technological devices. They are social institutions whose use has profound consequences. All societies purposely limit the extent of the market in order to protect basic values."[14]

Yet that's paradoxical thinking. Even the most passionate of liberals recognize rhetorically that the free market is a basic value for Americans. When he was president, Bill Clinton acknowledged the importance of developing a "market-based environmental-protection strategy," noting that "Adam Smith's invisible hand can have a green thumb."[15] More recently, John Kerry and Hillary Clinton have both argued that the market must have a role in environmental protection. When you get to the details, though, it is clear that their definition of a free market is one that is only able to operate within strict government guidelines. To them, the invisible hand has to wear a motion sensor.

Kerry, for instance, debated Newt Gingrich on environmental issues in 2007. After Newt had explained that regulation and targets were not going to solve the global warming problem, Kerry responded with his version of free-market environmentalism:[16]

Kerry agreed that the marketplace will play a key role, but he said an "economy-wide" cap on carbon emissions is vital because climate change is such a pressing crisis.

"You can't just sit there and say, 'Oh, let the market respond,'" Kerry said. "That's like saying, 'Barry Bonds, go investigate steroids.' Or like saying, 'Enron, you take over the pensions for America.' Not going to happen."

A cap, he said, would provide the structure businesses would need to craft a response.

Yes, just like being told you can only drive ten miles per week would "provide the structure" to which you would respond. Notice also the direct assertion that businesses behave like criminals. That's, one might think, an attitude that has profound consequences.

The "market-based mechanisms" that so many liberal environmentalists are proud to propose are nothing of the sort. They are "market-like," in the words of Terry Anderson. He says of these proposals:[17]

Free-Market Environmentalism has come a long way in showing how markets can provide environmental goods, but regulations aimed at global warming suggest that there is much farther to go. Dressing centralized regulations in Market-Like Environmentalism clothing doesn't make them Free-Market Environmentalism. Secure private property rights that hold people accountable and markets that communicate human values and opportunity costs are the core of Free-Market Environmentalism, and they are as applicable to global warming as they are to land and water conservation.

Fred Smith goes further and calls them "market socialism." Their similarity to the methods by which the Soviets set targets for industrial production, and by which the Uzbeks have set the ruinous cotton policies we discussed earlier, should be fair warning as to their true effectiveness. He also points out that the beloved liberal policies of targets and regulations aimed at hitting those targets ignore half the potential of the market:[18]

[T]he efficiency gains of market systems occur not only in production, but in allocation as well. This means that markets are
as effective at determining what is to be done as they are at
determining how it should be accomplished.

In other words, the market determines what the appropriate
quantity of any good is just as it determines the price. If production harms property rights, that will be factored into the equation just as surely as any tax increase. The market response will,
however, be more accurate than a tax rise, as that would be set
by the guesswork of a bunch of academics, filtered through the
political dealings of the now smoke-free back rooms of Congress
or Statehouses. The market response is instead set by the individual reactions of myriad producers and consumers. It therefore
contains far more information.

Unfortunately, it seems that market-like measures look suffi-
ciently like free-market measures to fool the electorate. Caps on
carbon emissions are likely over the next couple of years. Once
again, the continent of Europe contains a horrible warning to us
about what happens when such systems are put in place. The European Union put in place a cap on carbon emissions a few years ago.
As the British think tank Open Europe found, it was a playground
for politics and people who were able to game the system:[19]

> The first phase of the European Union's Emissions Trading
> Scheme (ETS), which runs from 2005 to 2007 was a failure.
> Huge over-allocation of permits to pollute led to a collapse in
> the price of carbon from 33 to just 0.20 per [metric] tonne,
> meaning that the system did not reduce emissions at all.
>
>   Worse still, since some countries (such as the UK) had set
> tough quotas on emissions, and others set lax targets, the sys-
> tem acted as a wealth transfer mechanism, effectively subsidiz-
> ing polluters in states which were making little effort by taxing

states with more stringent allocations. Overall there are about 6 percent more permits than pollution. However the UK has to buy about 22 million tonnes worth of permits a year, while firms in France and Germany could sell off a surplus of around 28 and 23 million tonnes respectively.

Finally, the ETS in phase one was not a real market—instead of auctioning off permits to pollute, member states allocated them free of charge to companies based on how many the government believed they needed. This created severe distortions. Large companies which lobbied for more permits than they needed were able to sell them on at a profit. Other institutions—particularly smaller institutions like hospital trusts—proved less effective at lobbying. They got too few permits and therefore had to pay into the system.

The supporters of this sort of cap program in America insist that we will learn from Europe's mistakes. Yet not only is Europe continuing to make more, entirely predictable, mistakes, the original European system is exactly the model that is being discussed.

The punitive, regulation- and tax-based approach to environmental protection has comprehensively failed. Market-like mechanisms are also failing. What is interesting is that even some in the environmental establishment are beginning to wake up to this.

A Breakthrough in Environmentalism

Ted Nordhaus and Michael Shellenberger are lifelong members of the environmental establishment. Ted Nordhaus' résumé, for instance, includes stints at the U.S. Public Interest Research Group, the Sierra Club, and Environmental Defense. In 2004, however, they took on the environmental establishment in spectacular fashion, releasing a monograph entitled *The Death of Environmentalism*.

Shellenberger and Nordhaus are concerned that politicians have been unable to do anything about global warming. Yet this misplaced concern allowed them great insight. In analyzing why liberal politicians and their allies in the conservative movement like John McCain had been unable to pass any legislation on global warming during the presidencies of both Bill Clinton and George W. Bush, they realized that environmentalism had become a special interest:

> We believe that the environmental movement's foundational concepts, its method for framing legislative proposals, and its very institutions are outmoded. Today environmentalism is just another special interest. Evidence for this can be found in its concepts, its proposals, and its reasoning. What stands out is how arbitrary environmental leaders are about what gets counted and what doesn't as "environmental." Most of the movement's leading thinkers, funders and advocates do not question their most basic assumptions about who we are, what we stand for, and what it is that we should be doing.[20]

They are correct to identify and criticize this objectivization of "the environment" as something separate from the rest of human life. Not only do they recognize that, but they also realize that the liberal environmentalist movement has become an establishment:

> The institutions that define what environmentalism means boast large professional staffs and receive tens of millions of dollars every year from foundations and individuals. Given these rewards, it's no surprise that most environmental leaders neither craft nor support proposals that could be tagged "non-environmental." Doing otherwise would do more than threaten their status; it would undermine their brand.[21]

These are excellent insights. Shellenberger and Nordhaus went on to write a full-length book, *Break Through: From the Death of Environmentalism to the Politics of Possibility*, that further critiqued the environmental movement. It contains one perceptive comment after another, such as their words on the failure of liberal environmentalists to understand the value of progress:

> [E]nvironmentalism has also saddled us with the albatross we call the politics of limits, which seeks to constrain human ambition, aspiration and power rather than unleash and direct them. In focusing attention so exclusively on the nonhuman worlds that have been lost rather than also on the astonishing human world that has been created, environmentalists have felt more resentment than gratitude for the efforts of those who came before us. And the "rational" environmentalist focus on just fixing what's wrong with the present narrows our vision at a time when we desperately need to expand it.[22]

That's almost Burkean in its recognition of the role of the past and the future in the present. They even seek to condemn Saint Rachel Carson and High Priest Al Gore:

> There was nothing in the movie [*An Inconvenient Truth*] or the accompanying book aimed at helping viewers or readers imagine a brighter future for themselves and their families.... Instead, Gore spoke almost entirely of nightmares.[23]
>
> Silent Spring set the template for nearly a half century of environmental writing: wrap the latest scientific research about an ecological calamity in a tragic narrative that conjures nostalgia for Nature while prophesying ever worse disasters to come, unless human societies repent for their sins against Nature and work for a return to a harmonious relationship with the natural world.... The tragic narrative ... appeared to

be responsible for motivating action on the pollution problems of the 1960s and 1970s. As we have seen, the less obvious but far more powerful drivers...were growing postmaterial desires, rising prosperity and postwar optimism. In primarily crediting books like *Silent Spring*...environmentalists continue to preach terrifying stories of eco-apocalypse, expecting them to result in the change we need.[24]

Shellenberger and Nordhaus diagnose the problem with liberal environmentalism perfectly, even going so far as to acknowledge the value of conservative research into what really caused the Cuyahoga river fires. To them, as to us, human prosperity and innovation are the solutions to environmental problems.

Yet while they correctly describe the symptoms and the likely general cure, they fail to prescribe the right course of treatment. They advocate a liberal approach to improving human welfare, condemning those who worship at "the altar of the market." They have failed to realize that liberal economics fail for precisely the same reason that liberal environmentalism fails—they are both defined by the politics of limits. Liberal redistribution of wealth is predicated on the idea of making the rich pay for the poor, whether it is achieved by internal taxation or international aid. The free enterprise system, on the other hand, sees the rich and the poor rise together to mutual benefit. Similarly, the great institutions in which Shellenberger and Nordhaus place so much trust—the World Trade Organization, the World Bank, and the International Monetary Fund—are as vulnerable to the delusions of self-interested public choice and what Hayek called the "knowledge problem" as any Soviet central planner.

In the end, Shellenberger and Nordhaus need to reconsider that the environmentalism they lament, in driving its economic policies and providing its religious justification, is already at the heart of contemporary liberalism. Discarding the politics of limits means also discarding the remnants of Marxism. Demystifying the environment and casting down the objective Gaia will leave liberalism without a spiritual core.

Having said that, Shellenberger and Nordhaus represent a hope for the general discourse on the environment. By recognizing the pathological syndrome of current liberal environmentalism, they have laid open the possibility that others might follow them. The Church of Environmentalism may yet have a Reformation.

Because in truth, rejecting the politics of limits means rejecting liberalism. It is only the free enterprise system that truly sets aside the failed model. It is only the free enterprise system, guided by the principles of stewardship, that can provide both prosperity and environmental protection.

A prime example exists in the best approaches to the problem with which we began this discussion, global warming, and the current crusade of Al Gore. We can see how Gore and the liberal establishment are determined to repeat the mistakes of the past, and how conservatives can help avoid another disaster.

The Conservative Solution to Global Warming

The year 2007, at first glance, appears to be the seventh-warmest year on record. It is also the coolest year of the millennium so far. The temperature record shows no significant increase since 1998. The last ten years have seen global temperatures stabilize. The last three years have even seen a slight cooling trend, which even the alarmist scientists of Britain's Meteorological Office say will continue in 2008.[25] It is therefore appropriate to ask whether the centrally dictated emissions targets proposed as global warming mitigation policies are justified. Any dispassionate analysis will suggest that they are not. Instead, the fatal conceit appears to be at work again.

In over ten years of analyzing public policy issues, I have come to see that the affordable energy provided by fossil fuels is a blessing. Energy use leads to prosperity, which leads to improved living conditions. Where energy is abundant and affordable, people are better educated, live longer, and are freed from back-breaking labor. Women in particular are emancipated from the tyranny of domestic tasks and can devote their time to more rewarding activities. We are now able to see the prospect of these advances spreading to developing countries. A healthy, wealthy world is within our grasp.

During the twentieth century, global economic output increased by a phenomenal 1,800 percent, meaning that world GDP today is about eighteen times bigger than it was in the year 1900. This unprecedented economic growth produced many beneficial consequences. Average human life expectancy doubled. Per capita food supply increased even while global population nearly quadrupled. Literacy, leisure, medical care, and personal mobility ceased to be elite privileges and became widely available. Even the air and water got cleaner, at least in countries achieving the most rapid economic progress. Fossil fuels were the main energy source for this phenomenal improvement in human welfare.

It has sometimes been suggested that fossil-fuel-based energy use is immoral. This is wrong-headed. Fossil-fuel-based energy use has literally been the engine of the greatest improvement in human welfare ever seen.

Yet policies favored by the climate doomsayers will slow, halt, or even reverse this progress. Indeed, the more aggressive climate policies, such as Mr. Gore's proposal to cut carbon dioxide emissions by 90 percent, could not be accomplished without wrecking the economy of the developed world. Even much milder restrictions on energy use can chill job creation, and the burden of higher energy costs always falls most heavily on the poor. Gore's plan will represent yet another humanitarian disaster inspired by the liberal environmentalist movement.

Already, the global warming crusade has diverted public attention, political will, and billions of dollars in resources and expertise from more urgent, yet more solvable, threats to people in
developing countries—perils like HIV/AIDS, malnutrition,
malaria, and water-borne disease. In short, misguided global
warming policies hurt working families and the poor.

Al Gore declares that the time for discussion is over, and the
time for action is now. Just what does he mean by "action?" He
means a centrally dictated target for overall deep reduction in
greenhouse gas emissions in the medium term. Who dictates this
is an interesting question—at the very least it will be a national
government, more likely an international treaty but plausibly
even a world governing body (former French president Jacques
Chirac called the Kyoto treaty the first example of "an authentic
global governance").

We know the scale of the humanitarian disaster this will bring
about. My organization, The Competitive Enterprise Institute,
asked Canadian economist and professor Ross McKitrick to ana-
lyze various proposals for emissions reduction being considered
by the U.S Congress. Professor McKitrick explained to us that an
economy's total emissions can be thought of as the product of
three factors: population, per capita economic output, and emissions intensity.

Mathematically, it looks like this:

$$\text{Emissions} = \text{Population} \times \text{Per Capita Economic}$$
$$\text{Output} \times \text{Emissions Intensity}$$

This last factor requires some explanation. Emissions intensity
is the average quantity of greenhouse gas emitted per dollar of
economic output. This mathematical expression is complete.
Only the three factors on the right side of the equation contribute
to the emissions on the left side.[26]

If you want to reduce emissions, you must reduce one of these
three factors. There is no other way.

In the U.S., emissions intensity declined a massive 54 percent from 1960 to 2005. Industry had cleaned up its act, homes became more efficient, cars poured less out through the exhaust pipe. Yet overall emissions doubled. Why? Because, in a triumph for the free enterprise system, the U.S. population grew substantially and per capita GDP increased by a massive 169 percent.

This leads us to an inevitable conclusion. If emissions intensity continues to improve at the same rapid pace and population also keeps its upward trend (both reasonable assumptions), the U.S. has only one way to reduce emissions dramatically: make everyone poorer.

If we are to cut by about 70 percent by 2060, as proposed in various bills before Congress, real per capita GDP will have to decrease by 50 to 75 percent instead of rising by 200 percent as trends would suggest. High levels of unemployment will be institutionalized. Those who are worried about the current effect of the subprime crunch in the U.S. should consider what effect that level of economic downturn will have on the rest of the world. We should also consider the effect this will have on our valuation of the environment. Such reduced standards of living will force us back along the environmental Kuznets curve, not forward. When we have less money to spend on the environment, it will almost certainly suffer in some ways.

Environmentalists, however, will argue that government action can influence the third factor—emissions intensity—and not harm per capita GDP. They say Washington (or the UN) should set a price on greenhouse gas emissions, which will lead people to demand, and industry to deliver new technologies, thus rapidly decreasing emissions intensity.

It's a nice theory, but we have empirical evidence that it doesn't work. The evidence is called Europe. Gasoline taxes are large in Europe compared to the U.S. Even if the price paid at the petrol pump is not inflated for the specific reason of greenhouse gas abatement, there is still a de facto penalty, and therefore a disincentive, for greenhouse gas use. In fact, the general level of European and British taxation is equivalent to a carbon dioxide price of \$200 to \$300 a ton. What has been the result of this massive deterrent to CO_2 emission (which is far above what most economists consider a reasonable reflection of the costs of CO_2)? No miracle fuels to replace petroleum. No zero-emissions vehicles. Europe does have a lot of small, unsafe cars, but it has nevertheless seen an increase in overall transportation emissions in the EU of about 25 percent since 1990, the baseline year for Kyoto.

Even if this pricing did work to spur technological development, and emissions intensity doubled its rate of decline, U.S. real GDP would at best see no real increase between now and 2060; at worst, we would see a real decline of 50 percent. That would represent half a century of stagnation, not just for the U.S., but for the world. In fact, the only economies that have successfully cut emissions significantly since 1990 are those of Eastern Europe. Economic collapse, it seems, is the only proven way to guarantee emissions reduction.

There is one other way to achieve the emissions reduction targets without sacrificing living standards. That is massive social engineering to achieve a significant reduction in population. To meet the 70 percent reduction, we could cull our ranks from 300 million plus today to 167 million in 2060, less than the population in 1960. Given their support for immigration, it is hard to see how even the liberal environmental establishment could advocate that.

The only way to meet the targets, therefore, is to find a way of significantly reducing emissions intensity over and beyond the current pace of reduction. Can we do that by ramping up things like clean coal technology? Possibly, but sequestering large amounts of CO_2 underground is unproven on an economy-wide scale and comes with risks of its own. Moreover, it will increase the cost of generating electricity which will in turn have adverse effects on the poor. One study from Johns Hopkins University found that replacing three-quarters of U.S. coal-fired electricity with higher priced alternatives like clean coal or renewable energy would lead to an extra 150,000 premature deaths a year. Another study from Penn State calculated that replacing two-thirds of U.S. coal with higher priced alternatives would cost three million to four million jobs. These are illustrations of what really happens when governments move to cap emissions without thinking of the consequences. Making energy more expensive affects the poor severely. Not only do they spend a higher portion of their income on energy than the middle and upper classes, but their other purchases are highly sensitive to the price of energy. The poor can't buy iPhones even when the price goes down, but they do buy food whose price is raised by biofuel mandates.

None of the other potential miracle technologies is yet up to the task. Wind is ineffective as a source of base-load power, especially land-based wind. It needs back-up conventional sources. Denmark, which invested heavily in wind power, is cutting back as it has experienced severe intermittency problems. Turning to solar power, economic large-scale or even house-size solar installations remain as elusive as ever. In 1978, there was a headline in the *Wall Street Journal*, "Solar Power Seen Meeting 20 Percent of Needs by 2000; Carter May Seek Outlay Boost." Indeed, President Carter's environmental council actually predicted 25 percent. Needless to say, this never materialized. Affordable, reliable, large-scale solar power remains an aspiration rather than a reality.

Nuclear power is certainly a source of carbon-free emissions, but is opposed by environmental groups the world over for other reasons. The British government has announced that it will build a new fleet of nuclear reactors. Finland and the Baltic States are also turning to nuclear. France has relied on nuclear for most of its electricity for many years. Despite nuclear's resurgence in the rest of the world, however, the prospects for new substantial new nuclear generation in the U.S.A. are slim.

Setting targets for CO_2 emissions and for the price of carbon are excellent examples of how the fatal conceit works. We have no proof either that the emissions reductions proposed are either feasible (evidence seems to suggest they are not) or will have any real effect on the climate in the long-run. Yet big government politicians all over the world have jumped on them as an example of how government can save the world. Perhaps the fact that their ineffectiveness will not be demonstrated until well after the politicians leave office has something do with that. Governor Schwarzenegger won't be back when the targets he has set California come due.

So the liberal environmentalists are once more pump-priming a disaster: a massive, unnecessary, unprecedented recession that will cause poverty, hardship, and social unrest, none of which have ever been proven to be good for the environment. Bearing in mind the premises of this book, we should ask what approach can be taken that can avoid the disastrous effects of emissions reduction?

A Conservative Solution

I propose a three-pronged approach: technology, resiliency, and adaptation.

First, we should look to the ultimate resource. It would be prudent to increase the amount of money we are spending on technological answers to the emissions intensity problem. This does not mean increased federal government spending. There are ways to do this without government picking winners or directing private investment decisions. A series of prizes for achieving certain targets would remove the interference of politicians seeking to direct money towards their favored technologies or constituents. Private sources can also provide useful incentives in this way: Sir Richard Branson's billion dollar prize for a less-emitting jet fuel is an example that more philanthropists should emulate.

Second, we should recognize the value of wealth and property, and strengthen societies to be more resilient. By that, I mean changes in institutions to make people wealthier and less vulnerable to the big hit. As Bjorn Lomborg relates, when Hurricane Katrina hit, one insurance firm found that the places that had implemented hurricane-loss prevention methods experienced one-eighth the losses of those that had not done so. By spending $2.5 million, these communities avoided $500 million in damage. With Kyoto, the world would spend $180 billion annually to reduce hurricane damage by about half of one percent. At a fraction of the cost, proven hurricane protection methods and reforms in government insurance and disaster relief policies could reduce hurricane damage by 50 percent.

In Mexico last year, we saw the value of resiliency in another way. Fifty years ago, Hurricane Janet slammed into the Yucatan Peninsula in Mexico and killed six hundred people. In 2007, Hurricane Dean hit the Yucatan and killed no one. The hurricanes were identical in speed, intensity and ferocity. What was different was that Mexico was richer. Even if storms like Dean become more frequent in the future, people will adapt and survive if they have the financial resources. It does indeed seem silly to take those resources away in futile attempts to "stop global warming"—which no one even knows how to do—when they could save lives by allowing people to adapt to our ever-changing climate.

As Hernando de Soto and others have shown, the quickest way to such resiliency is to reform the institutions of property so that people have easy access to the capital represented by the land they own. From small investments in aiding developing world governments to reform or create land registries, massive amounts of capital can be freed up to propel the developing world out of poverty and into a resilient state. Global warming—if it develops as the alarmists say it will—won't be nearly as much of a problem.

Adaptation—responses to specific threats enabled by resiliency—is the third leg of the strategy. It combines the ultimate resource with the resilient society. We are often told that global warming will make malaria much worse, for instance. This is not true, by the way, as climate is a very minor factor in the spread of malaria. But even assuming it is, which makes more sense: fighting malaria directly now or trying to change the composition of the atmosphere to make the temperature slightly less warm in fifty years time? To ask the question is to answer it. And fighting malaria directly costs vastly less than atmospheric tinkering.

According to Indur Goklany, author of *The Improving State of the World*, even if we could somehow stabilize atmospheric carbon dioxide concentrations, this would at best reduce the number of people at risk of hunger by 2 percent and malaria by 3.2 percent. Even coastal flooding would be reduced by just 20 percent. All this would be at an annual cost of over $180 billion. Yet according to the UN, we could reduce hunger, malaria, and coastal flooding by half to three-quarters each at an annual cost of only $22 billion.

In short, we can avoid the latest disaster of liberal environmentalist policies and thrive even if the world turns out warmer. The approach of emissions reduction is a badly-aimed sledgehammer intended to crack what really is a very small nut in global warming. Instead, we should seek to open that nut and feast on it if we can by following policies aimed at reducing the costs of global warming via a three-pronged strategy of technological development, resiliency and adaptation. Even if global warming turns out not to be a problem, this program will greatly aid global development and the fight against poverty, something that emissions reduction would actually hinder. As global warming alarmists like to say, our children will thank us for it.

American Values: The Environment's Last Best Hope

Throughout this tour of the disaster zones of liberal environmentalism we have seen two things confirmed time and time again: that American values like property, enterprise, and freedom work well to protect the environment; and that the environment suffers when these values are replaced by contrary values like nationalization, central planning, and control.

It is indeed illuminating to realize that virtually all the programs and problems date from those times when traditional American values have been in retreat—during the Progressive Era when vast tracts of the West were nationalized, during the New Deal when the seeds were sown for the burning of the Cuyahoga, and during the Nixon-Carter eras when the Environmental Protection Agency was founded and a series of useless or dangerous environmental laws were passed.

In our current era when American self-confidence seems to be retreating following the problems in Iraq and the fiscal excesses of a once conservative Congress, American values are under threat once more. It is likely that our legislators, administrators, and courts will impose more restrictions on what people can do with their property, burden businesses and individuals with more taxes and rules, and seek to control what people can do everywhere except in the bedroom. It also seems likely that one of the prime pretexts for such control will be the need to "do something" about global warming.

Thus not only are American values the best defense we have for the environment, rejecting the liberal environmental argument is a great defense of American values. If we stand up for freedom, prosperity, and private property we will stand up for the majesty of God's creation around us. If we let them fall, not only will we have insulted the memory of the men of Lexington and Concord, but we will reap the whirlwind of environmental destruction. The fishermen of the Aral Sea could tell you that.

Acknowledgments

Thanks to all those without whom this would be impossible: Fred Smith, Wayne Crews, Myron Ebell, Chris Horner, Marlo Lewis, Sam Kazman, Eli Lehrer, John Berlau, Greg Conko, Angela Logomasini, Julian Morris, and all the FME Roundtable. Particular thanks to R.J. Smith for blazing the way (and providing much of this book), Courtney Helfrecht for the long but civil arguments, Tim Carney for editing above and beyond the call of duty, Louise Bagshawe for setting a benchmark, and, above all, my wife for her tireless devotion, proof-reading and encouragement while I was writing this book.

Notes

Part I: Al Gore Is Bad for the Planet

Introduction: **Al Gore: Savior of the Planet?**

1. "Keeping America competitive requires affordable energy. And here we have a serious problem: America is addicted to oil, which is often imported from unstable parts of the world."—President Bush, State of the Union Address, January 31, 2006. Http://www.whitehouse.gov/news/releases/2006/01/20060131-10.html. In fact, much of America's oil comes from Canada and Mexico. The Middle East supplies less than 20 percent of our oil.
2. Richard Lindzen, Alfred P. Sloan Professor of Meteorology at the Massachusetts Institute of Technology regularly characterizes the "scientific consensus" on global warming as consisting three "relatively trivial points"—see, for example, http://www.geocraft.com/WVFossils/Reference_Docs/Lindzen_2005_Climate_Claims.pdf.
3. Although it sounds crazy, the British government is seriously investigating the feasibility of instituting personal carbon rations.
4. Committee on the Science of Climate Change [Cicerone et al.], "Climate Change Science: An Analysis of Some Key Questions," National Research Council, 2001.
5. Arthur B. Robinson, Noah E. Robinson, and Willie Soon, "Environmental Effects of Increased Atmospheric Carbon Dioxide," *Journal of American*

Physicians and Surgeons (2007) 12, 79-90, http://www.oism.org/pproject/s33p36.htm.

6. When scientists dismiss these concerns, they generally do so by citing their "expert judgment." In other words, "Trust us, we're very clever."

7. See Marlo's three papers, "Al Gore's Science Fiction," "A Skeptic's Primer on Al Gore's *An Inconvenient Truth*," and "Some Convenient Distortions," all published by the Competitive Enterprise Institute in 2007. They are available, together with video presentations, at http://www.cei.org/gencon/030,05821.cfm.

8. For full discussion, see Lewis, "Al Gore's Science Fiction," 37 ff. Http://www.cei.org/pdf/5820.pdf.

9. Ibid.

10. Ibid.

11. "Intergovernmental Panel on Climate Change, Fourth Assessment Report 2007," Working Group I Report, The Physical Science Basis, 820. The liberal environmentalist movement has dismissed these figures, claiming that they underestimate the effects of sea level rise because they do not include any likelihood of massively increased ice melt that might result from global warming. However, the Panel report says clearly: "Abrupt climate changes, such as the collapse of the West Antarctic Ice Sheet, the rapid loss of the Greenland Ice Sheet or largescale [sic] changes of ocean circulation systems, are not considered likely to occur in the 21st century, based on currently available model results," 818.

12. William Nordhaus, "The Challenge of Global Warming: Economic Models and Environmental Policy in the DICE-2007 Model," July 24, 2007. For cost figures, see p.84. Available at: http://nordhaus.econ.yale.edu/dice_mss_072407_all.pdf.

13. Al Gore, *An Inconvenient Truth*.

14. Ibid.

15. "Al Gore's Personal Energy Use Is His Own 'Inconvenient Truth,'" Press Release, February 26, 2007, http://www.tennesseepolicy.org/main/article.php?article_id=367.

16. Data from the U.S. Department of Agriculture's Economic Research Service, http://www.ers.usda.gov/Data/Unemployment/RDList2.asp?ST=TN.

17. Adam Stein, TerraPass Customer Survey Results, TerraPass Blog, August 21 2007. http://www.terrapass.com/blog/posts/terrapass-custo. Bizarrely, Mr Stein uses the survey results to argue that carbon offsets are not indulgences, as if someone being a committed environmentalist cannot feel guilty about their sin.

18. Drew Johnson, "Carbon Credits Aren't All They're Cracked Up to Be," September 1 2007, http://www.tennesseepolicy.org/main/article.php?article_id=548.

19. Those with a strong stomach can read some of the choicest samples of abuse and bile here: http://www.tennesseepolicy.org/files/pdf/e-mails.pdf.

20. "Al Gore, $100,000 Man," http://www.thesmokinggun.com/archive/years/2007/0717071gore1.html.

21. Robert Frank, "Living Large While Being Green," *Wall Street Journal*, August 24, 2007.

22. Ibid.

23. Joel Gibson, "$50 for beer? Sydney's Livid Earth," *Sydney Morning Herald*, July 9, 2007.

24. "Johannesburg Live Earth Concert Kicks Off in Half-Empty Venue," Deutsche Press Agentur, July 7, 2007.

25. See: http://www.intelligentgiving.com/the_buzz/the_blog/what_on_live_earth_is_going_on.

26. See the Alliance's IRS Form 990 from 2006 at www.guidestar.org.

27. "Nineteen million tune in to Live Earth concerts," Associated Press, July 9, 2007.

28. Paul Driessen, *Eco-Imperialism: Green Power, Black Death* (Bellevue, Washington: The Free Enterprise Press), 2002.

Chapter One: **Malaria: The Plague of Environmentalists**

1. Michael Finkel, "Malaria: Bedlam in the Blood," *National Geographic*, July 2007.

2. Or "vector," hence malaria is often called a "vector-borne disease."

3. See Isaac Rosenberg's 1918 poem, "The Immortals," for a good illustration: "Then in my agony I turned/ And made my hands red in their gore./ In vain-for faster than I slew/ They rose more cruel than before." He is talking about lice.

4. This is a publication of Lyndon LaRouche, but the questionable venue should not detract from the arguments, which are sound.

5. Available online at: http://www.21stcenturysciencetech.com/articles/summ02/Carson.html.

6. Albert Schweitzer, *Out of My Life and Thought: An Autobiography. (Aus meinem Leben und Denken: Leipzig*, Felix Meiner, 1931.) Translated by C.T. Campion. (New York: Henry Holt, 1933, 1949), 262.

7. Strangely, liberal environmentalists do not object to this particular example of what they have termed, "The Republican War on Science."

8. Roger Bate, "The Rise, Fall, Rise and Imminent Fall of DDT," AEI Health Policy Outlook No. 14, American Enterprise Institute, November 2007.

9. "African Health Ministers to Discuss DDT," Gerald Businge, AND Network, June 18, 2006. Available online at: http://www.fightingmalaria.org/news.aspx?id=583.

10. Http://www.polianna.com/2005/06/29.DDT.Africa.shtml.
11. Http://timpanogos.wordpress.com/2007/10/03/carnival-of-ddt/#comment-40452.
12. John Kerry and Teresa Heinz Kerry, *This Moment on Earth: Today's New Environmentalists and Their Vision for the Future*, (New York: PublicAffairs, 2007).
13. Http://www.culturekitchen.com/lorraine/blog/blogtour_awe_and_the_environment, April 23 2007.
14. John Berlau, *Eco-Freaks: Environmentalism Is Hazardous To Your Health*, (Nashville: Thomas Nelson, 2006) 28.
15. Joan Goldstein, *Demanding Clean Food and Water: The Fight for a Basic Human Right*, (New York: Plenum Press, 1990).
16. Richard J. Campana, *Arboriculture: History and Development in North America* (East Lansing: Michigan State University Press, 1999).
17. I am indebted to Rich Burlew's *Order of the Stick* cartoon series for this vivid analogy.

Chapter Two: Ethanol: Save the Planet, Starve the World

1. Albert Gore, *Earth in the Balance* (New York: Plume, 1992), 326.
2. Bob Woodward, *Plan of Attack* (New York: Simon and Schuster, 2004).
3. Energy Information Agency, "Annual Energy Outlook, 2007," U.S. Department of Energy, February 2007, 59.
4. Some researchers allege this is optimistic, and that ethanol production may actually consume more energy than is produced. If this is true, ethanol production is an inherently losing proposition.
5. Dennis Avery, "Biofuels: Food or Wildlife? The Massive Land Costs of U.S. Ethanol," *Competitive Enterprise Institute Issue Analysis*, September 21, 2006.
6. *Good Morning America*, ABC, June 27, 2007. See "How More Ethanol Means Pricier Pizza," http://abcnews.go.com/GMA/Consumer/story?id=3321005.
7. Http://www.nass.usda.gov/QuickStats/index2.jsp.
8. Allen Baker and Steven Zahniser, "Ethanol Reshapes the Corn Market," *Amber Waves*, Vol. 4, Issue 2 (April 2006), updated May 2007. Http://www.ers.usda.gov/AmberWaves/May07SpecialIssue/Features/Ethanol.htm.
9. International Monetary Fund, *World Economic Outlook 2007*, April 2007, 44.
10. U.S. Department of Agriculture, Economic Research Service, "Livestock, Poultry, and Dairy Outlook," April 18, 2007, 5.
11. See "Commonly Accepted Fallacious Statistics," Stats.org, December 2002. Http://www.stats.org/stories/2002/commonly_dec13_06.htm.

12. Http://www.secondharvest.org/news_room/2007_press_releases/103007. html.
13. Javier Blas, Chris Giles and Hal Weitzman, "World food price rises to hit consumers," *Financial Times*, December 16, 2007.
14. Manuel Roig-Franzia, "A Culinary and Cultural Staple in Crisis," *Washington Post*, January 27, 2007.
15. Keith Bradsher, "Rise in China's Pork Prices Signals End to Cheap Output," *New York Times*, June 9, 2007.
16. Javier Blas and Jenny Wiggins, "Surge in biofuels pushes up food prices" and "UN warns it cannot afford to feed the worl," *Financial Times*, July 15, 2007.
17. Http://www.actionagainsthunger.org/resources/hunger-faqs.
18. "Nissan Qashqai 2.0 Tekna (4x4)," *The Times*, April 29 2007.
19. "The Oil for Ape Scandal: How Palm Oil is Threatening the Orangutan," Friends of the Earth UK, http://www.foe.co.uk/resource/reports/oil_for_ape_summary.pdf.
20. Ian Mackinnon, "Palm oil: the biofuel of the future driving an ecological disaster now," *The Guardian*, April 4, 2007.
21. Chris Brummitt, "Palm oil boom threatens Orangutan, jungle," Associated Press, September 1, 2007.
22. Kevin Bullis, "Will Cellulosic Ethanol Take Off? Fuel from grass and wood chips could be big in the next 10 years—if the government helps," *Technology Review*, February 26, 2007. Http://www.technologyreview.com/Energy/18227/.
23. *The Economic Feasibility of Ethanol from Sugar in the U.S.*, U.S. Department of Agriculture, 2006.
24. Figures from the Bioenergy Feedstock Information Network, http://bioenergy.ornl.gov/papers/misc/energy_conv.html.
25. "Cornell ecologist's study finds that producing ethanol and biodiesel from corn and other crops is not worth the energy," Cornell press release, July 5, 2005. Http://www.news.cornell.edu/stories/July05/ethanol.toocostly.ssl.html.
26. Marcelo E. Dias De Oliveira et al, "Ethanol as Fuel: Energy, Carbon Dioxide Balances, and Ecological Footprint," *BioScience*, Vol. 55, Issue 7, July 2005, 593-602.
27. Righelato, R. and D. V. Spracklen (2007), "Carbon Mitigation by Biofuels or by Saving and Restoring Forests?" *Science* 317(5840), 902.
28. "Conservation more effective than biofuels for fighting global warming," August 15 2007, http://news.mongabay.com/2007/0816-biofuels.html.
29. Thomas Searchinger et al., "Use of U.S. Croplands for Biofuels Increases Greenhouse Gases Through Emissions from Land Use Change," *Science* Express, February 7, 2008.

30. Available online at: http://www.foeeurope.org/publications/2007/OECD_
    Biofuels_Cure_Worse_Than_Disease_Sept07.pdf.
31. Martin Evans, "As candidates look to Iowa, ethanol becomes top issue,"
    Newsday, July 22, 2007.

Part II: Blind Faith in the Green God

Introduction: EcoPaganism

1. "The 2004 Political Landscape: Evenly Divided and Increasingly Polar-
    ized," Chapter 8: Religion in America, http://people-press.org/reports/dis-
    play.php3?PageID=757.
2. The whole speech, at http://www.michaelcrichton.com/speech-environmen-
    talismaseligion.html, is well worth reading.
3. See, for instance, "Al Gore, Rock Star: Oscar Hopeful May Be America's
    Coolest Ex-Vice President Ever," William Booth, *Washington Post*, Febru-
    ary 25, 2007.
4. S.A. Miller, "Scientists Doubt Climate Change," *Washington Times*,
    December 21, 2007.
5. Http://www.desmogblog.com/400-prominent-scientists-dispute-global-
    warming-bunk.
6. Http://gristmill.grist.org/story/2007/12/21/112933/48.
7. Http://www.prospect.org/csnc/blogs/tapped_archive?month=12&year=
    2007&base_name=stuck_in_denial_mode.
8. Http://www.nanowerk.com/news/newsid=3812.php.
9. Christopher C. Horner, *The Politically Incorrect Guide*(TM) *to Global
    Warming and Environmentalism*, (Washington, D.C.: Regnery, 2007), 288.
10. Http://gristmill.grist.org/story/2005/8/9/183352/2738.
11. The French philosopher Blaise Pascal argued that it was better to believe in
    God than not, because the rewards of true belief—everlasting life—were
    infinitely better than the rewards of not believing, whether the rewards of
    belief existed or not.
12. Golding's scientific expertise can be deduced from his writings arguing for
    the existence of the Loch Ness Monster. I have been unable to locate Prof.
    Lovelock's views on Nessie.
13. James Lovelock, *Gaia: A New Look at Life on Earth*, (New York: Oxford
    University Press, 1979). Criticisms mentioned at http://en.wikipedia.
    org/wiki/Gaia_hypothesis.
14. James Lovelock, "The Living Earth," *Nature*, Vol 426, 18/25 December
    2003, 769-770.
15. James Lovelock, *The Revenge of Gaia* (London, UK: Allen Lane, 2006).

16. He argues repeatedly that the current interglacial warm period in which humanity has thrived is a "physiological system failure."

17. *The Revenge of Gaia*, op. cit.

18. Stephen B. Scharper, "The Gaia Hypothesis: Implications for a Christian Political Theology of the Environment," *Cross Currents*, Vol 44, Issue 2, 1994, 15.

19. Http://www.sierraclub.org/compass/2006/08/dr-gaias-bitter-pill.asp.

20. See http://www.gaiafestival.com/community.html; for the description see http://www.gaiafestival.com/about.html.

21. I'm not making this up: see http://gaiaselene.com/ where you can click on Gaia and get lectured by animated Earth Mother.

22. Gore, as is his wont, chooses to illustrate his point with reference to technology—a hologram in this case, which uses a "resistance pattern" to display its image.

23. Http://www.arcworld.org/faiths.asp?pageID=99.

24. Http://www.grist.org/news/maindish/2005/10/05/cizik/.

25. See: http://scripturetext.com/genesis/2-15.htm.

26. Available at: http://www.vatican.va/holy_father/benedict_xvi/messages/peace/documents/hf_ben-xvi_mes_20071208_xli-world-day-peace_en.html.

27. Http://news.bbc.co.uk/2/hi/science/nature/4584572.stm, January 6, 2006.

28. A treatise arguing that human ingenuity is the ultimate resource, which deserves to be as famous as *The Population Bomb*.

29. Donald G. Macneil Jr., "The World-Subtract Billions; Demographic 'Bomb' May Only Go 'Pop!'," *New York Times*, August 29, 2004.

30. Mark Tapscott, "A Leftie Golden Oldie-Zero Population Growth," Examiner.com, November 10, 2007.

31. Anne Kornblut, "In His Wife's Campaign, Bill Clinton Is a Free Agent," *Washington Post*, October 30, 2007.

32. The CIA World Factbook, see https://www.cia.gov/library/publications/the-world-factbook/rankorder/2127rank.html.

33. Jan Kelly, "Baby Tax Needed to Save Planet, Claims Expert," *The Advertiser*, December 10, 2007.

34. Fred L. Smith, Jr., "Review of Robert Nelson's Economics as Religion," Competitive Enterprise Institute, 2002, http://www.cei.org/pdf/5462.pdf.

35. Mark Steyn, "Nothing to Fear but the Climate Change Alarmists," *Chicago Sun Times*, April 23, 2006.

36. Roy Beck and Leon Kolankiewicz, "The Environmental Movement's Retreat From Advocating U.S. Population Stabilization (1970-1998): A First Draft of History," June 2001, available at Minnesotans for Sustainability: http://www.mnforsustain.org/beck_environmental_movement's_retreat_long_intro.htm.

37. Susan Jacoby, "Anti-Immigration Campaign Begun." *Washington Post,* May 8, 1977.

Chapter Three: **The Pill as Pollutant: When Safety Doesn't Matter**

1. Filby, AL, T Neuparth, KL Thorpe, R Owen, TS Galloway and CR Tyler. "Health impacts of estrogens in the environment, considering complex mixture effects." *Environmental Health Perspectives,* in press at the time of this writing.
2. Quotation from summary at Environmental Health News, September 5, 2007: http://www.environmentalhealthnews.org/newscience/2007/2007-0905philbyetal.html.
3. See, for example, Kidd KA, PJ Blanchfield, KH Mills, VP Palace, RE Evans, JM Lazorchak et al. 2007. Collapse of a fish population after exposure to a synthetic estrogen. Proceedings of the National Academy of Sciences 104(21):8897-8901. Liney KE, S Jobling, JA Shears, P Simpson and CR Tyler. 2005. Assessing the sensitivity of different life stages for sexual disruption in roach (Rutilus rutilus) exposed to effluents of wastewater treatment works. Environmental Health Perspectives 113:1299-1307. Martinovic D, WT Hogarth, RE Jones and PW Sorensen. 2007. Environmental estrogens suppress hormones, behavior and reproductive fitness in male fathead minnows. *Environmental Toxicology and Chemistry* 26(2): 271-278.
4. Nash et al., "Long-Term Exposure to Environmental Concentrations of the Pharmaceutical Ethynylestradiol Causes Reproductive Failure in Fish," *Environmental Health Perspectives* Volume 112, Number 17, December 2004
5. Nash et al, op. cit.
6. Wayne Laugesen, "Contracepting the Environment: Environmentalists Mum on Poisoned Streams," *National Catholic Register,* July 15-21, 2007.
7. Quoted in "A cause without a disease," Holger Breithaupt, EMBO Rep. 2004 January; 5(1): 16-18, European Molecular Biology Organization.
8. Michelle Allsopp, David Santillo and Paul Johnston, "Poisoning The Future: Impacts of Endocrine-Disrupting Chemicals on Wildlife and Human Health," Greenpeace Research Laboratories, October, 1997.
9. Stephen H. Safe, "Endocrine Disrupters: New Toxic Menace?" in *Earth Report 2000,* ed. Ronald Bailey (New York: McGraw-Hill, 2000), 192.
10. American Council on Science and Health, "Endocrine Disrupters: A Scientific Perspective," 14-15.
11. Op. cit.
12. A. Brake and W. Krause, "Decreasing Quality of Semen; Letter: Comment," *British Medical Journal* 305 no. 6867 (12 December 1992): 1498.

13. Stuart Irvine et al., "Evidence of Deteriorating Semen Quality in the United Kingdom: Birth Cohort Study in 577 Men in Scotland Over 11 Years," *British Medical Journal* 312, no. 7029 (24 February 1996): 467. L. Bujan et al., "Time Series Analysis of Sperm Concentration in Fertile Men in Toulouse, France Between 1977 and 1992," *British Medical Journal* 312, no. 7029 (24 February 1996): 417; Geary W. Olsen et al., "Have Sperm Counts Been Reduced 50 Percent in 50 years? A Statistical Model Revisited," *Fertility and Sterility* 63, no. 4 (April 1995): 887-93.

14. Marianne Barriaux, "L'Oreal au naturel," *Guardian*, April 9, 2007.

15. Mary S. Wolff et al., "Blood Residues of Organochlorine Residues and Risk of Breast Cancer," *Journal of the National Cancer Institute* 85 (21 April 1993): 648-52.

16. Stephen S. Sternberg, "DDT and Breast Cancer, Correspondence," *Journal of the National Cancer Institute* 86 (20 July 1994): 1094-96.

17. John F. Acquavella, Belinda K. Ireland, and Jonathan M. Ramlow, "Organochlorines and Breast Cancer, Correspondence," *Journal of the National Cancer Institute* 85 (17 November 1993): 1872-75.

18. National Research Council, "Hormonally Active Agents in the Environment," 250.

19. For an overview of many key studies see Stephen H. Safe, "Endocrine Disrupters and Human Health—Is There a Problem? An Update," *Environmental Health Perspectives* 108, no. 6 (June 2000): 487-93.

20. David J. Hunter et al., "Plasma Organochlorine Levels and the Risk of Breast Cancer, *New England Journal of Medicine* 337, no. 18 (30 October 1997): 1253-58.

21. L. Lopez-Carrillo et al., "Dichiorodiphenyltrichloroethane Serum Levels and Breast Cancer Risk: A Case-Control Study from Mexico," *Cancer Research* 57 no. 17 (1997): 3728-32.

22. Jonathan Tolman, *Nature's Hormone Factory: Endocrine Disrupters in the Natural Environment* (Competitive Enterprise Institute, March 1996), http://www.cei.org/MonoReader.asp?ID=478.

23. Tolman, op. cit.

24. Steven Safe, "Environmental and Dietary Estrogens and Human Health: Is There a Problem?", *Environmental Health Perspectives*, Vol 103, No 4, April 1995.

25. Earthbeat, January 17 2004: http://www.abc.net.au/rn/science/earth/stories/s1005677.htm.

26. Http://www.direct.gov.uk/en/Environmentandgreenerliving/Greenerlivinga quickguide/Oureffectontheplanet/DG_064397.

27. Http://www.wwf.org.uk/oneplanet/audio_0000003942.asp.

28. Http://www.environmentaldefense.org/documents/166_Nov96.pdf.

29. Http://www.earth-policy.org/Updates/Update18.htm.

30. *Guttmacher Policy Review*, Winter 2006, Volume 9, Number 1.

31. Http://www.mariestopes.org.uk/ShowContent.aspx?id=118.

32. Http://www.plannedparenthood.org/news-articles-press/politics-policy-issues/international-issues/environment-13118.htm.

33. Iain Murray, "Recent Research Suggests..." United Press International, March 7, 2003. Http://www.upi.com/NewsTrack/Business/2003/03/07/recent_research_suggests_/6621/.

34. Jesse Le, "Berkeley Lab Researchers Examine the Safety of SUVs: Contentious Study Challenges Conventional Wisdom," Wednesday, August 28, 2002.

35. See, e.g., "Energy Choices for the Next President," by ACEEE board chairman Carl Blumstein, *San Francisco Chronicle*, November 5 2000.

36. January/February 2003 issue.

37. Http://www.sierraclub.org/globalwarming/SUVreport/.

38. U.S. Department of Transportation, National Highway Traffic Safety Administration, "An Analysis of Motor Vehicle Rollover Crashes and Injury Outcomes," March 2007.

39. For more on this, see Iain Murray, "Statistical Traffic Wreck," TCSDaily.com, April 23, 2003, http://www.tcsdaily.com/article.aspx?id=042803E.

40. "Be Safer in the '90s: New Warnings from Ralph Nader," *Woman's Day*, October 24, 1989, 32.

41. Ralph Nader's introduction to "Small—On Safety: The Designed-In Dangers of the Volkswagen" (Center for Auto Safety, 1972), xiv.

42. You can see a copy of the book's cover and title page at http://www.cei.org/pdf/2353.pdf in case you were applying proper skepticism to Sam's claim.

43. See http://www.cei.org/pdf/2407.pdf, based on J. DeFalco, "The Deadly Effects of Fuel Economy Standards: CAFE's Lethal Impact on Auto Safety" (CEI, 1999).

44. Http://www.suvoa.com/pdfs/Barry_McCahill_Testimony_EPW_COMM.pdf.

Chapter Four: Yellowstone in Flames

1. Cass Petersen and T.R. Reid, "Flames and Images of War Swirl Through Yellowstone; Fires Destroy Buildings Near Old Faithful," *Washington Post*, September 8, 1988.

2. James F. Kieley, "A Brief History of the National Parks Service," United States Department of the Interior, 1940, available at http://www.nps.gov/history/history/online_books/kieley/index.htm.

3. Magoc notes how Langford's evocative language utilized "confounding, occasionally ludicrous evocations of order and chaos, power and beauty, and unsavory, diabolical, hellishness."

4. Langford, "The Wonders of the Yellowstone: Second Article," *Scribners Monthly*, June 1871, 128.
5. "Montana," *The Magazine of Western History*, Vol 53, No. 1, Spring 2003, 2.
6. Cited in Jonathan Adler's review of the book *Fire in Paradise* in *Reason*, January 1994.
7. In an amazing display of insensitivity, former Black Panthers tried to trademark the phrase in 2005, to help market a new brand of hot sauce.
8. See http://transcripts.cnn.com/TRANSCRIPTS/0707/10/gb.01.html for the whole fascinating interview.
9. Sean Paige, "Uncle Sam Gets Burned Out West," *Insight on the News*, June 19, 2000.
10. Available at http://www.gao.gov/archive/1998/rc98273t.pdf.
11. Perry Backus, "Former FS chiefs say fire costs eating budget," *The Missoulian*, May 5, 2007.
12. Cerro Grande Prescribed Fire Investigation Report, Delivered to the Secretary of Interior, Bruce Babbitt on May 18, 2000, available at http://www.nps.gov/cerrogrande/.
13. Paul Simons, "How California Reaped Its Firestorm: Nature Never Intended Us to Build Cities in Deserts," *Times*, October 26, 2007.
14. Ibid.
15. John Berlau, "The Environmentalist Fires," *The American Thinker*, October 29, 2007, http://www.americanthinker.com/2007/10/the_environmentalist_fires.html.
16. From the Greek, meaning "heat-loving."
17. The Edmonds Institute in Edmonds, Washington State; the International Center for Technology Assessment in Washington, D.C.; the Alliance for the Wild Rockies in Bozeman, Montana; and Yellowstone area guide Phil Knight. See Christopher Smith, "NGOs Gain Victory in Yellowstone Park Biopiracy Case: Yellowstone Bioprospecting Halted by Judge," *Salt Lake Tribune*, March 26, 1999.
18. For more examples, see Holly Fretwell, "Paying to Play: The Fee Demonstration Program," PERC Policy Series No. 17, Property & Environment Research Center, November 1999.
19. J. Bishop Grewell, "Decamping Politics From Public Lands," *Tacoma News Tribune*, July 4, 2004.
20. Genuinely so: his arguments in favor of abortion earned him criticism from the Right, while his arguments in favor of racial differences in intelligence earned him criticism from the Left.
21. Garrett Hardin, "The Tragedy of the Commons," *Science*, Vol. 162, No. 3859 (December 13, 1968), 1243-1248.
22. Aristotle (384 B.C.-322 B.C.), *Politics*, Book II, Chapter III, 1261b

23. Ludwig von Mises, Part IV, Chapter 10, Sec. VI, *Nationalökonomie: The-orie des Handelns und Wirtschaftens* (Geneva: Editions Union, 1940). The quote provided is that of Mises's expanded English translation, Chapter XXIII: "The Data of the Market," Sec. 6: "The Limits of Property Rights and the Problems of External Costs and External Economies," Human Action: A Treatise on Economics (New Haven: Yale University Press, 1949).
24. From a Natural Bridge of Virginia booklet, excerpted by Robert J. Smith in "Natural Bridge of Virginia," CEI Issue Analysis, June 1998, Competitive Enterprise Institute/Center for Private Conservation, Washington, D.C.
25. Because publicly owned bridges never collapse. No, sir.
26. Federal Reserve Bank of Richmond, Region Focus Weekly Update, May 2, 2007, "Nature for Sale," available at http://www.richmondfed.org/publications/economic_research/region_focus/weekly_update/archive/2007/20070502.cfm.
27. March 29, 1792, Papers 14:266-68.

Part III: The Best Laid Plans...

Introduction: **The Green Lobby**

1. Corey Hajim, "The Wizards of Ozone," *Fortune*, June 15, 2007.
2. Figures taken from the Capital Research Center's database and that of activistcash.com as of end-October 2007.
3. The U.S. branch is subsidiary to international organizations whose dealings are not as transparent.
4. Ian Shapira, "Fulfillment Elusive for Young Altruists In the Crowded Field of Public Interest," *Washington Post*, November 2, 2007.
5. Darragh Johnson, "Climate Change Scenarios Scare, and Motivate, Kids," *Washington Post*, April 16, 2007.

Chapter Five: **How Progressives Set the Cuyahoga River on Fire**

1. Carol M. Browner, Environmental Protection: Meeting the Challenges of the Twenty-First Century, 25 *Harvard Environmental Law Review* 329, 330-331 (2001).
2. Randy Newman, "Burn On," from *Sail Away* (Warner Bros. Records 1972).
3. Adler, "Fables of the Cuyahoga," *Fordham Environmental Law Review*, Vol XIV, Fall 2002, 92.
4. Joseph Schumpeter, *Capitalism, Socialism and Democracy* (New York: Routledge, 2006), 67.

5. Joseph A. D'Agostino, "Conservative Spotlight: R.J. Smith," *Human Events*, October 29, 2001.

6. Something often claimed to be a free market solution, when it is quite patently not.

7. Arthur Seldon, F. G. Pennance, Colin Robinson, *Everyman's Dictionary of Economics*, (London, UK: J.M. Dent & Sons, 1965); reprinted by Liberty Fund 2005.

8. Steve Hayward, *The Index of Leading Environmental Indicators 2007* (San Francisco: Pacific Research Institute, 2007).

9. The Nixon administration was responsible for many of the environmental laws you'll find criticized in this book. Lee Talbot of George Mason University said, "No president since or before, except maybe Teddy Roosevelt, has been willing to put as much political muscle into environment.... We could never have done it had the president not been willing to go along." (Quoted in Dave Hogan, "Nixon Legacy Includes a Long String of Environmental Laws," *Oregonian*, December 28, 1998.)

10. Http://www.sierraclub.org/cleanair/factsheets/benefits.asp.

11. Regulatory Studies Program, Public Interest Comment on The Office of Management and Budget's 2004 Draft Report to Congress on the Costs and Benefits of Regulation, available at: http://www.mercatus.org/repository/docLib/MC_RSP_PIC2004-04OMBBCReport_040511.pdf.

12. Personal communication with author.

13. Kenneth Chay, Carlos Dobkin and Michael Greenstone, "The Clean Air Act of 1970 and Adult Mortality," *Journal of Risk and Uncertainty*, 27(3), December 2003.

14. Michael Greenstone, "Did the Clean Air Act Cause the Remarkable Decline in Sulfur Dioxide Concentrations?" *Journal of Environmental Economics and Management*, May 2004.

15. Michael Greenstone, "The Impacts of Environmental Regulations on Industrial Activity: Evidence from the 1970 and 1977 Clean Air Act Amendments and the Census of Manufacturers," *Journal of Political Economy*, 110(6), December 2002.

16. See, e.g., "Did Federalization Halt the Race to the Bottom for Air Quality?" EM (*Environmental Manager*) (June 1998): 12-17, "The Environmental Transition to Air Quality." *Regulation* 24 (4: 1998): 36-46 and *Do We Need the Federal Government to Protect Air Quality?*, Policy Study 150, Center for the Study of American Business, Washington University, St. Louis, MO, December 1998.

17. "Environmental Kuznets Curves: A Review of Findings, Methods, and Policy Implications" by Bruce Yandle, Madhusudan Bhattarai, and Maya Vijayaraghavan, PERC 2004.

18. Adler, "Fables of the Cuyahoga," op. cit., 93-4.

19. Adler, "Fables of the Cuyahoga," op. cit., 96-7.
20. David D. Van Tassel ed., *The Encyclopedia of Cleveland History* (Bloomington, IN: Indiana University Press, 1996), 338.
21. Arnold W. Retize Jr., "Wastes, Water and Wishful Thinking," *Case Western Reserve Law Review*, Vol. 5, 1986, 8-10.
22. A. Myrick Freeman, "Water Pollution Policy in Paul Portney ed., *Public Policies for Environmental Protection* 114, Resources for the Future, 1990.
23. Adler, "Fables of the Cuyahoga," op. cit., 120.
24. Adler, "Fables of the Cuyahoga," op. cit., 113.
25. Adler, "Fables of the Cuyahoga," op. cit., 116.
26. Reitze, "Wastes, Water and Wishful Thinking," op. cit., 64
27. Roger Meiers and Bruce Yandle, "Common Law Environmentalism," *Public Choice* 94, 1998, 49-66.
28. Adler, "Fables of the Cuyahoga," op. cit., 126.
29. Adler, "Fables of the Cuyahoga," op. cit., 131.
30. Statement of Mayor Carl B. Stokes, National League of Cities, Atlanta, Georgia, December 10, 1970.
31. Adler, "Fables of the Cuyahoga," op. cit., 144-5.

Chapter Six: Endangered Species Act: Shoot, Shovel, and Shut Up

1. Ike Sugg, "Rats, Lies and the GAO: A Critique of the General Accounting Office Report on the Role of the Endangered Species Act in the California Fires of 1993," Competitive Enterprise Institute, 1994. Http://www.cei.org/pdf/4361.pdf.
2. Those letters are reproduced in the Ike Sugg study mentioned above.
3. Can you think of another popular, broadcast comedy that regularly shows the lead characters in Church?
4. Ike Sugg, "California Fires-Losing Houses, Saving Rats," *Wall Street Journal*, November 10, 1993.
5. Stephen J. Dubner and Steven D. Levitt, "Unintended Consequences," *New York Times Magazine*, January 20, 2008.
6. Sen. James Inhofe et al., "Big Government and Bad Science: Ten Case Studies in Regulatory Abuse," policy report no. 151 (Lewisville, Tex.: Institute for Policy Innovation, 1999); "Saving the Species," *Orange County Register*, September 29, 1995.
7. Jonathan Adler, "ESA's Dubious Track Record after 25 Years," *Washington Times*, December 28, 1998.
8. Http://www.sierraclub.org/wildlife/species/.
9. Http://www.nrdc.org/wildlife/habitat/esa/aboutesa.asp.
10. Http://www.environmentaldefense.org/article.cfm?contentid=1158.

11. Fish and Wildlife Service, Threatened and Endangered Species System database, as of November 13, 2006, http://www.fws.gov/Endangered/wildlife.html#Species.

12. Fish and Wildlife Service, "U.S. Fish and Wildlife Service Updates List of Candidates for Endangered Species Act Listing," Press Release, December 6, 2007.

13. Fish and Wildlife Service, "USFWS Threatened and Endangered Species System (TESS)," http://ecos.fws.gov/tess_public/DelistingReport.do.

14. According to the Fish and Wildlife Service's TESS database, Hoover's Woolly-star and the Eggert's Sunflower (both plants) are counted as recovered, but are also listed as having on original data error, which was recently discovered.

15. Http://agrigator.ifas.ufl.edu/gators/.

16. Randall O'Toole, "Analyzing the Endangered Species Act," *A Different Drummer* (Winter 1995), http://www.ti.org/Analysis.html.

17. Brian Seasholes, "The Bald Eagle, DDT and the Endangered Species Act," *Policy Brief* No. 63, Reason Foundation, June 2007, http://reason.org/pb63.pdf.

18. Ibid.

19. Roger Schlickheisen, "Don't Gut the Endangered Species Act," *Plain Dealer*, May 11, 1996, 11B. Seasholes has many other examples of such hyperbole.

20. Personal communication with author.

21. Charles Darwin, *The Origin of Species*, (New York: Signet Classic, 2003), 66.

22. See Sugg, "Reforming the Endangered Species Act: The Property Rights Perspective," Testimony Before the House Resources Committee, May 18, 1995, Appendix III, note 12, http://www.cei.org/pdf/4360.pdf; Randall O'Toole notes: "The Aleutian Canada goose was a victim of a fox that had been introduced for its furs by Alaska settlers. The Fish & Wildlife Service's animal damage control program wiped out the foxes, which led the goose population to quickly recover" see: O'Toole, "Analyzing the Endangered Species Act."

23. See Sugg, "Reforming the Endangered Species Act," Appendix III, note 11.

24. Ibid.

25. Ibid.

26. Ibid.

27. A recent delisting of the Robbins' cinquefoil, a rare plant that grows in the Service says only grows in the alpine zone of the White Mountain National Forest in New Hampshire. This may be an example of a case where the Service found a variation of a more common plant and dubbed it a separate species. In any case, according to the service it was endangered by hikers

who harvested and trampled it along trials in the park. The service and several private groups took efforts to ensure the plant has safe places to grow and for this, they claim credit for saving an endangered species. They may have helped a species, but this hardly represents a triumph of the ESA since these efforts were largely conducted by private organizations with the cooperation of the forest service. The service notes: "The White Mountain National Forest is committed to protecting this small plant's habitat, the Appalachian Mountain Club is committed to managing habitat and monitoring the population, and the New England Wild Flower Society is committed to successfully propagating plants for reintroduction. All were vital to Robbins' cinquefoil recovery." 27.

28. The Polar Bear is the only bear that stalks humans.
29. Gore, *An Inconvenient Truth*, 146.
30. Monnett, C., J.S. Gleason, and L.M. Rotterman. 2005. Potential effects of diminished sea ice on open-water swimming, mortality, and distribution of polar bears during fall in the Alaskan Beaufort Sea. Minerals Management Service, http://www.mms.gov/alaska/ess/Poster%20Presentations/Marine-MammalConference-Dec2005.pdf.
31. Marlo Lewis Jr, "Al Gore's Science Fiction: A Skeptic's Guide to An Inconvenient Truth," Congressional Working Paper, Competitive Enterprise Institute, 2007, 63.
32. "The bear necessities of climate change politics: A photo of two polar bears seemingly stranded on an ice floe has come to symbolise man's destruction of nature. But is it all that it seems?", March 16, 2007, http://www.spiked-online.com/index.php?/site/article/2969/.
33. Polyakov, I.V., R.V. Bekryaev, G.V. Alekseev, U.S. Bhatt, R.L. Colony, M.A. Johnson, A.P. Maskshtas, A.P. and D. Walsh. 2003. Variability and trends of air temperature and pressure in the maritime Arctic, 1875-2000. Journal of Climate 16: 2067-2077.
34. "NASA Examines Arctic Sea Ice Changes Leading to Record Low in 2007," NASA Press Release, October 1, 2007.
35. "Polar Bear Politics," *Wall Street Journal*, January 3, 2007.
36. David Jones, "Polar bears on the brink? Don't you believe it," *Daily Mail*, December 7, 2007.
37. Ibid.
38. "Ancient polar bear jawbone found," Jonathan Amos, Science reporter, BBC News, San Francisco, December 10, 2007, http://news.bbc.co.uk/2/low/science/nature/7132220.stm.
39. Salil Tripathi, "Tail of the Missing Tigers," *New Statesman*, August 22, 2005.
40. Http://web.worldbank.org/WBSITE/EXTERNAL/COUNTRIES/SOUTH ASIAEXT/0,,pagePK:158889~piPK:146815~theSitePK:223547,00.html.

41. "Rhinos: Conservation, Economics and Trade-Offs," Institute of Economic Affairs, London, April 1, 1995.

42. Barun Mitra, "Sell the Tiger to Save It," *New York Times*, August 15, 2006.

43. "Tiger Farming," *New Scientist*, December 16, 2007.

44. "Resolving the Tragedy of the Commons by Creating Private Property Rights in Wildlife," *Cato Journal*, 1981.

45. Michael De Alessi , "Private Conservation and Black Rhinos in Zimbabwe: The Savé Valley and Bubiana Conservancies," Competitive Enterprise Institute Issue Analysis, January 1, 2000.

46. "The Wood Duck," Private Conservation Case Study, Center for Private Conservation, June 1, 1997.

47. Pauly, D. and R. Sumaila. 2006. Catching more bait: A bottom-up re-estimation of global fisheries subsidies. University of British Columbia, Fisheries Centre Research Report. Vol. 14, No. 6 2nd Version.

Chapter Seven: Communism's Environmental Record: The Death of the Aral Sea

1. Peter Wilson, "The Lost Sea," *The Australian Magazine*, December 1, 2007.

2. Http://www.sairamtour.com/news/gems/35.html.

3. Quoted in Richard Hakluyt's *The Principal Navigations, Voyages, Traffiques and Discoveries of the English Nation*, 12 vols. (Glasgow, 1903-1905), vol. II, p. 463, available at: http://depts.washington.edu/silkroad/texts/jenkinson/bukhara.html.

4. All three quotations found in Tom Bissell, "Eternal Winter: Lessons of the Aral Sea Disaster," *Harper's*, April 2002, 41-56.

5. Http://www.craigmurray.org.uk/archives/2005/08/sanctions_again.html.

6. Fred Pearce, *When the Rivers Run Dry: Water—The Defining Crisis of the Twenty-First Century* (Boston: Beacon Press, 2007).

7. EJF, "White Gold: the True Cost of Cotton," Environmental Justice Foundation, London, UK. http://www.ejfoundation.org/pdf/white_gold_the_true_cost_of_cotton.pdf.

8. World Bank, "Water and Environment Management Project," 2001, Subcomponent A1. "National and Regional Water and Salt Management Plans," Regional Report No. 2, Phase III Report—Regional Needs and Constraints. Supporting Volume (November). Tashkent: World Bank.

9. Simon Jenkins, "Dull Echo," *The Huffington Post*, May 17 2005, http://www.huffingtonpost.com/simon-jenkins/dull-echo_b_1075.html.

10. Martin Fletcher, "The Return of the Sea," *Times*, June 23, 2007.

11. Philip Micklin, "The Aral Sea Disaster," *Annual Review of Earth Planetary Sciences*, 2007, 47-72.

12. Fred Pearce, "Draining life from Iraq's marshes: Saddam Hussein is using an old idea to force the Marsh Arabs from their home," *New Scientist*, April 17, 1993.

13. Camille Feanny and Kiesha Porter, "Scientists fight to save Iraq's marshes: Project seeks to restore wetlands Saddam drained," CNN, November 5, 2004.

14. Curtis J. Richardson and Najah A. Hussain, "Restoring the Garden of Eden: An Ecological Assessment of the Marshes of Iraq," *BioScience*, June 2006.

15. Christopher Reed, *Paradise Lost: What should—or can—be done about "the environmental crime of the century"?*, *Harvard Magazine*, January-February 2005.

16. *An Inconvenient Truth*, 117.

17. Center for the Study of Carbon Dioxide and Global Change, "20th-Century Drying of the Sahel and Southern Africa," review of Hoerling, M., J. Hurrell, J. Eischeid, and A. Phillips. 2006. Detection and attribution of twentieth-century northern and southern African rainfall change. *Journal of Climate* 19: 3989-4008, http://www.co2science.org/scripts/CO2ScienceB2C/articles/V10/N7/C2.jsp.

18. Hillary Mayell, "Shrinking African Lake Offers Lesson on Finite Resources," *National Geographic News*, April 26, 2001, http://news.nationalgeographic.com/news/2001/04/0426_lakechadshrinks.html.

19. Marlo Lewis Jr, "Al Gore's Science Fiction," Competitive Enterprise Institute, 2007, 53.

20. Ban Ki Moon, "A Climate Culprit in Darfur," *Washington Post*, June 16 2007.

21. Norwegian University of Science and Technology (2007, December 17). "No Connection Between Environmental Crises And Armed Conflict, New Study Argues," ScienceDaily. Retrieved December 31, 2007, from http://www.sciencedaily.com_/releases/2007/12/071216133126.htm.

Conclusion: The Promise of Stewardship

1. Edmund Burke, *Reflections on the Revolution in France,* (Dolphin ed., 1961) 110.

2. Ibid.

3. Quoted in Carl P. Russell, "Coordination of Conservation Programs," *Regional Review*, January-February 1941.

4. Quoted in Robert H. Nelson, *Public Lands and Private Rights: The Failure of Scientific Management* (Lanham, MD: Rowan & Littlefield, 1995), 48.

5. You may remember the Parable of the Talents.

6. Michael Copeland, "The New Resource Economics," in *The Yellowstone Primer*, J. Baden and D. Leal, eds. (San Francisco: Pacific Research Institute, 1990).
7. If a market researcher asks you how much you'll pay for a candy bar, you'll probably give him the right answer. When people are asked how much they value the environment, they tend to give answers based on exaggeration and guesswork.
8. Fred L. Smith, Jr., "The Market and Nature," *The Freeman* (September 1993), 352
9. Jonathan H. Adler, "Ecology, Liberty and Property: A Free-Market Environmental Reader," Competitive Enterprise Institute, 2000.
10. Fred L. Smith, Jr., "Conclusion: Environmental Policy at the Crossroads," in *Environmental Politics: Public Costs, Private Rewards* (New York: Praeger, 1992), p. 192.
11. Ryan Amacher, et al., "The Economics of Fatal Mistakes: Fiscal Mechanisms for Preserving Endangered Predators," in Wildlife in the Marketplace, Terry Anderson and P.J. Hill, eds. (Lanham, Maryland: Rowman and Littlefield, 1995).
12. Quoted on "Free Market Environmentalism's Bottom Line," National Public Radio Morning Edition, September 1, 1992.
13. Http://www.defenders.org/programs_and_policy/wildlife_conservation/solutions/wolf_compensation_trust/index.php.
14. Thomas Michael Power and Paul Rauber, "The Price is Everything," *Sierra* (November/December 1993), 94.
15. Ibid., 88.
16. Bob Franken, "Gingrich vs. Kerry: Shoot-out at the climate change corral," CNN, April 10, 2007. http://www.cnn.com/2007/POLITICS/04/10/gingrich.kerry/index.html.
17. Terry L. Anderson, "Free Market Environmentalism," PERC Reports, Vol.25, No. 1, March 2007.
18. Fred L. Smith, Jr., "Europe, Energy & the Environment: The Case Against Carbon Taxes" Competitive Enterprise Institute, 1992.
19. "Open Europe, Europe's Dirty Secret: Why the EU Emissions Trading Scheme Isn't Working," August 2007, http://www.openeurope.org.uk/research/etsp2.pdf.
20. Michael Shellenberger and Ted Nordhaus, "The Death of Environmentalism," The Breakthrough Institute, 2004, 8.
21. Ibid., 11.
22. Michael Shellenberger and Ted Nordhaus, *Break Through* (Boston: Houghton Mifflin, 2007), 17.
23. Ibid.,105-6.
24. Ibid., 130-1.

25. "2008 is set to be cooler globally than recent years say Met Office and University of East Anglia climate scientists," first line of press release entitled, "Global Temperature 2008: Another Top-Ten Year, UK Met Office, January 3 2008, http://www.metoffice.gov.uk/corporate/pressoffice/2008/pr20080103.html. January 2008 even recorded the biggest monthly temperature drop worldwide in recorded history, wiping out 30 years of warming.

26. You'll see this equation is mathematically unassailable by simplifying the right side. *Population X Per Capita Economic Output* clearly equals *Total Economic Output*. *Emissions Intensity* could be expressed as *Total Emissions/Total Economic Output*, and so multiplying *Total Economic Output X Emissions Intensity* yields *Total Emissions*.

Index

environmentalists
(cont'd): Endangered
Species Act and, 242;
endangered species and,
238–39; Kyoto Protocol
and, 89; liberal eco-
nomic thinking and,
1–2; malaria and,
31–52; stewardship and,
182; wealth vs. environ-
ment and, 13; Yellow-
stone National Park
and, 158–60, 167–73
environmental movement:
agenda of, 189–90;
basis of, x; DDT and,
40; forest management
and, 154–55; freedom
and environment and, x;
Gore, Al, Jr. and, 1;
"green", 1; green lobby
and, 190–201; hierarchy
of, 85–86; immigration
and, 113; large animals
and, 66–69; liberal
agenda and, 1; man's
interference with nature
and, 155; sacrifice and,
190, 199
Environmental Protection
Agency (EPA), 322; air
quality and, 213, 215;
Browner, Carol and,
203; Clean Air Act of
1970 and, 217–18, 219;
contraceptive pollution
and, 130–31; Cuyahoga
River Fire (1969) and,
228; DDT and, 36–37,
39; environmental indi-
cators and, 213
Environmental Working
Group, 191, 198
ethanol, 64–66; biodiver-
sity and, 66–69; Bush,
George W. and, 72–73;
cellulosic, 72–73; Clin-
ton, Hillary and, 79;
corn and, 54–55, 56,
58, 59–64, 71; environ-
mentalism and, 55;
gasoline vs., 56–57, 58,
75–76; Gore, Al, Jr.
and, 55; government
subsidies and, 58–59;

hunger and, 62–63;
land use and, 69–73;
liberals and, 55; oil hat-
ing and, 55–59; produc-
tion of, 58, 59–64;
sources of, 71–72; sugar
and, 73–75; taxation
and, 58–59; tortilla
prices and, 53–55. *See
also* biofuels
Euphrates River, 285,
286, 287
European Union (EU),
41, 68, 233; Common
Fisheries Program of,
270, 271; Emission
Trading Scheme of,
308; Kyoto Protocol
and, 89

"Fatal Conceit", 205,
207, 210, 274
Fire in Paradise (Morrison), 155–56
fish: feminization of,
118–21; intersexuality
of, 117–18
Fish and Wildlife Service,
U.S.: California wild-
fires and, 236; DDT
and, 37; Endangered
Species Act and, 244,
247, 254, 258; polar
bears and, 258
fisheries, collapse of,
269–72
Foley, Jonathan, 289–90
Food and Drug Adminis-
tration (FDA), 130
Food Quality Protection
Act, 130
forest management:
Endangered Species Act
and, 161; environmental
movement and, 154–55;
habitat preservation and,
164–67; "let it burn"
policies and, 157–58,
159; logging and, 154,
160–67; Native Ameri-
cans and, 153–54; "nat-
ural burn" policies and,
155; Yellowstone
National Park wildfires
(1988) and, 155–58

fossil fuels, 27; energy
use and, 314; global
warming and, 4
Foundation for Research
on Economics and Envi-
ronment, 302
Founding Fathers, 83,
178, 179, 185
Friends of the Earth, 67,
191, 198

Gaia, 85
Gaia Movement, 91–97
gasoline: cost of, 2;
ethanol vs., 75–76; lib-
erals and, 56
Genesis, 97–98, 100–101
George III, King, 180–81
George Washington Wet-
land Nature Reserve,
298
Glacier National Park,
171
global warming:
alarmism and, 3, 8, 19,
104, 255; American val-
ues and, 322–23;
anthropogenic, 8–9;
Aral Sea, disappearance
of and, 274, 278; car-
bon dioxide emissions
and, 3; Christianity and,
98; conservative solu-
tion to, 313–19; costs
of, 321–22; democracy
and, 13; Earth Mother
and, 85; energy use and,
14; fossil fuels and, 4;
Gore, Al, Jr. and, 2, 3,
4, 6–12, 314–15; green-
house gases and, 3, 4–5,
5fig, 12, 288, 315–19;
Hurricane Katrina and,
6, 10; *An Inconvenient
Truth* and, 6–12; Lake
Chad and, 287–91; lib-
eralism and, 3; Live
Earth concerts and,
19–25; malaria and,
321; as moral issue, 13,
290–91; Ocean Con-
veyor and, 9; population
growth and, 104–12;
scientific case for, 3–12;
Weather God and, 85